# In Necessity and Sorrow

# In Necessity and Sorrow

## Life and Death
## in an Abortion Hospital

### MAGDA DENES

*Basic Books, Inc., Publishers*

NEW YORK

## PERMISSIONS

The author gratefully acknowledges permission to quote excerpts from the following:

W. H. Auden, "Musee des Beaux Arts," in *Collected Shorter Poems 1927–1957*, Random House. Copyright © 1940, renewed 1968 by W.H. Auden.

John Lennon, Paul McCartney, "Eleanor Rigby," © 1966 Northern Songs Limited. All rights for the United States, Canada, Mexico and the Phillipines controlled by Mac Len Music, Inc. c/o ATV Music Group.

W.B. Yeats, "The Second Coming," in *The Collected Poems of W.B. Yeats*. M.B. Yeats, Miss Anne Yeats, The Macmillan Co. of London and Basingstoke, and the Macmillan Co. of New York.

Gerard Manley Hopkins, "My Own Heart Let Me More Have Pity On," in *The Poems of Gerard Manley Hopkins*, Oxford University Press.

e.e. cummings, "since feeling is first," in *Complete Poems 1913–1962*. Harcourt Brace Jovanovich, Inc.

T.S. Eliot, "Ash Wednesday" in *Collected Poems 1909–1962*. Harcourt Brace Jovanovich, Inc.

"The Medium," Gian Carlo Menotti. Copyright © 1947, 1967, G. Schirmer, Inc.

Library of Congress Cataloging in Publication Data

Denes, Magda, 1934–
   In necessity and sorrow.

   1. Abortion—Psychological aspects. 2. Abortion services—New York (City) I. Title. [DNLM: 1. Hospitals, Special—New York. 2. Abortion, Induced. 3. Abortion, Legal. WQ24 AN7 D3i]
RG734.D44   362.1'9'888097471  76–22188
ISBN: 0–465–03216–8

*I dedicate this book*

*to all wanted children,*

*including my own, Greg and Tim,*

*whose being in the world*

*is the heart of joy.*

About suffering they were never wrong,

The Old Masters: how well they understood

Its human position; how it takes place

While someone else is eating or opening a

window or just walking dully along. . . .

*W. H. Auden*

# Contents

ACKNOWLEDGMENTS xi

PROLOGUE xiii

INTRODUCTION xv

Chapter 1

*The Hospital* 3

Chapter 2

*Saline Floor: Staff* 43

Chapter 3

*Saline Floor: Patients and Parents* 91

Chapter 4

*D & C Floor: Staff* 128

Chapter 5

*D & C Floor: Patients, Parents, and Boyfriends* 161

ix

*Contents*

## Chapter 6

*Surgery*                                                        200

EPILOGUE                                                         242

# ACKNOWLEDGMENTS

My grateful thanks to all those who consented to be interviewed and whose generosity therefore made this book possible.

My apologies as well, to those with whom I spoke yet whose words do not appear here, due to limitations of space. My experience with them was not less important or less moving to me.

# Prologue

I am sitting on a hospital bed, barefoot, my legs dangling over the step stool. I am wearing a white regulation gown tied in the back at my neck and at my waist. On my head there is a green paper-like shower cap that encloses all my hair. The room is small. My husband, although he stands leaning against the wall opposite my bed, appears quite near. I can see the fillings in his teeth as his mouth opens and closes. He is yelling at me. As far as I know I am not weeping, although I can feel tears rolling down my face. I smell the scent of Norell, and a moment later my mother comes through the swinging doors. She looks well. She says, her face radiant, "Thank God it is over." In the course of the sentence she realizes her error and ends the statement in a question mark. "No, it is not over," my husband yells. "There is a stretcher waiting for her outside the door, she threw the nurse with the needle out of the room and she is now thinking." My mother says, "I don't know what you mean." My husband ignores her and takes a step toward me. "Of all the goddamn spoiled things you have ever done this beats them all. Twice in two weeks. What the hell are you thinking about—I want to know what has changed since yesterday or this morning." "Stop screaming at her," yells my mother. My husband yells back, "You stay out of it. I don't even know what you are doing here."

I have the overwhelming urge to laugh but the impulse ends in a sob. My mother says, "Don't cry." My husband says, "Cry, cry, but it won't get us anywhere."

In some ways I am an exceptionally privileged woman of thirty-seven. I am in the room of a private, legal abortion hospital, where a surgeon, a friend of many years, is waiting for me in the operating room. I am only five weeks pregnant. Last week I walked out of another hospital, unaborted, because I had suddenly changed my mind. I have a husband who cares for me. He yells because my indecisiveness makes him anxious, but basically he has permitted the final choice to rest in my hands: "It would be very tough, especially for you, and it is absolutely insane, but yes, we could have another baby." I have a mother who cares. I have two young sons, whose small faces are the most moving arguments I have against going through with this abortion. I have a doctorate in psychology, which, among other advantages, assures me of the professional courtesy of special passes in hospitals, passes that at this moment enable my husband and my mother to stand in my room at a nonvisiting hour and yell at each other over my head while I sob.

On this occasion I go home. But one week later I return again to the same hospital, and I am aborted.

It was this experience that eventually lead me to the questions put to people in this book. I wanted to know most urgently what lies behind the abortion myths. What happens to women who are not as privileged as I and who can not freely choose but are rather compelled by circumstance to renounce their child? Do they grieve less, or more? And what of those, who, endangering their lives, had to sneak to illegal back alleys, where butchers practiced—did that strengthen their resolution? Are there women free of sorrow at such a time? And again what of those who do the work? What forces move them? And how do they speak of their actions, which must in some way reflect their deepest attitudes toward their own existence?

What follows are the answers I have found.

# Introduction

As one more minor paradox of living, introductions are customarily written after a book is finished. Thus, for the writer, they represent an epilogue, a retrospective assessment of intent and outcome.

However disguised, they are an apology for the hubris of recording, as filtered through one's being, a portion of life. They also reflect a little hopeful pleasure at having temporarily overcome the vast muteness of most human speech.

With this in mind, I have several things to say.

First, on rereading it, my book appears to me boobytrapped. It seems a mined object ready to explode in utter destructiveness at the slightest corrupt or careless touch. For in fact I am for abortions. My rage throughout these pages is at the human predicament. At the finitude of our lives, at our nakedness, at the absurdity of our perpetual ambivalence toward the terror of life and toward the horror of death.

Abortions I think should be legal throughout the world. They should be at the mother's will, on demand, safe, dignified, provided free by the state, supported with mercy by the church.

And that, just exactly that, would make abortions more problematic than they have ever been before. For if we remove abortions from the realm of defiance to authority, remove them from the category of forbidden acts whose commission is the embodiment of risk and the embodiment of self assertion in the face of coercive forces, if we permit them to be acts of freedom as they should be, their meaning, private and collective, will inescapably emerge in the consciousness of every person.

I think it is a far, far lighter task to regard oneself as a martyr and to battle the world than to know the private sorrows of unique commitments and the heartache of self-chosen destiny.

I wish, therefore, to be taken for what I am. A proabortionist with a bad secular conscience.

Second, in another arena, I wish again to be taken for what I am, what any reporter is—a traitor. For to permanently fix any person at a point in time is always high treason. I have thus betrayed many trusts. And, although not regretful, I am full of remorse. And full of gratitude as well, toward all those who did, for whatever reasons, freely share with me the circumstances of their daily survival.

I have regarded my own contributions throughout this work as those of one more interviewee. One whose person I knew the best but whose reactions nevertheless must be weighed by the same measure as those of the others. Working on this book was for me a startling journey of many months on frozen lands of loveless need, where nevertheless I found, as I never have before, a knowledge of kinship and a certainty that being human is the worst and best of all possibilities.

Third, for the benefit of those who are interested in the mechanics of events, I should explain the procedure by which the book came to be written. Two weeks after my abortion I got in touch with the hospital again and obtained an appointment with its director. This was in July. I explained that I was a former patient, a university professor, a certified psychologist and that I wished to conduct in-depth interviews with all consenting patients, relatives, and staff. The idea appealed to him and to his then secretary, Rachel Stern.* They asked me for a letter of introduction from the chairman of the department at the university where I teach, and they told me to have my attorney contact the hospital's attorneys for legal permission and to draw up releases that those interviewed would

*All names used in this book are fictitious.

sign. The arrangements were well under way by August, at which time I left with my family on vacation.

Away from the city, from the continent in fact, the project began to seem doubtful to me. It appeared unrealistic to think that anyone would wish to answer my questions. Why should they? It appeared overambitious to fill a whole book with stories of abortions. In New York State they were legalized minor surgery. What else was there to know?

In some very special sense my doubts were justified. For this is only in part a book about abortions. It is also a book about the intransigent tragedies embedded in being human. A book about people in stress, their neediness and sorrow, their isolation and fellowship, their struggles, heroic and mean. In short about their beings, as I saw them unfold in the microcosm of one small abortion hospital at the center of a large cold city.

Above all, this is a document on the evasions, multifaceted, clever, and shameful, by which we all live and die.

# In Necessity and Sorrow

# Chapter 1

## The Hospital

Look at all the lonely people
Where do they all come from
Look at all the lonely people
Where do they all belong
John Lennon and Paul McCartney

The hospital is located in a good section of the city, on a quiet tree-lined street with relatively little traffic. The building is medium-sized, terracotta brick. It has two side doors and a central one that revolves. The glass on all the doors is smudged. Fronting the entrance stand two large brass flower-pots filled with assorted urban rubbish. Placed between them on the sidewalk is a big black rubber mat with the hospital's name stenciled on it in white.

Nothing in this ordinary exterior prepares a person for the impact produced by entering. Inside, the place is teeming with people. At first glance, it is difficult to distinguish individuals. The impression is of an ants' nest or a beehive or a swarm of locusts. There are bodies everywhere—sitting, standing, crouching, pacing, leaning. I think of wartime railway stations, of soup kitchens in famines, of first-aid dispensaries set up after earthquakes. None of that helps. The shock of this scene is supplied by a notion: "This crowd is here to abort." It is not a thought that I can comprehend or hold for any length of time.

I look around. The room is large and shabby. The carpets are worn, the walls look dirty, the lighting is poor. The atmo-

3

sphere is one of dense fog perpetually descending. Directly in front of me in a recessed wall space, framed by walnut panels of real wood, hangs a three-by-four-foot Renoir, purchased, unmistakably, at Woolworth's.

I scan the room for someone in charge. There is a small desk to my left in front of which the mob forms an unruly line. I join. It is a long wait. I shift from foot to foot, I smoke, I stare at the flaking ceiling. I notice here and there women weeping.

"And how far along are you, dear?" the lady in front of me asks, turning toward me and taking my measure. "Excuse me, what'd you say?" I say bewildered. "How far along are you? Jenny here," she says, pointing to a fat young girl in jeans, "she's my niece. She's only fifteen, which is why I come with her. She's six months, well nigh. We're from Kansas. I never did see this many ones with a mistake in their belly. How's about you?"

She's a wrinkled lady of about fifty, and she has rapiers for eyes. "Well, I am actually not. I mean not now. I mean I am a. . . ." Her gaze stops me. Clearly she thinks I am lying. To hell with it. "Eight weeks," I say, looking the lady straight in the face. "I am eight weeks." "Nothin' to be ashamed of, I say," she says. "I reckon you'll have an easier time, though, than Jenny here, who's six months." "I reckon too," I say, nodding vigorously, but it is not an expression I can carry off with any aplomb.

"Hi." I smile at Jenny who is blushing. She ignores me. "You got no cause tellin' everybody 'bout me, Auntie," she says to the lady. "Hush child," the lady says not unkindly. "Ain't nothin' to be ashamed of."

Perhaps I ought to go home, I think. Perhaps this ain't nothin' to be ashamed of, but maybe it ain't nothin' to mess with neither.

It is my turn at the desk. "Name," the girl behind it says. "Dr. Denes." "Not your doctor's name. Your name, please," she says, without looking up from the sheet of paper she is reading. She is speaking very loudly and in syllables; she assumes that I do not understand English and behaves as if that means that I am deaf as well. "Name, nombre, yours." I relent.

"Look, I am not a patient," I say. "I am Dr. Denes. I stood in line because I didn't know where else to go. I want to see Miss Stern. I have an appointment."

She gets angry. "This line is for patients, madam. You should have gone for information to the telephone operator. We are very busy here."

"Well, where is the telephone room?" "To your left," she says. "Name, please," she addresses the woman behind me.

I take a step to the left, but her directions are no good at all, because I get trapped in another swirling mob.

"Can you tell me, please, where the telephone room is?" I ask a woman standing next to me. "Oh, sure," she says, smiling broadly. "I am an old timer here. My daughter is a saline, but it didn't take, so I've been around here for three solid days. Just go straight ahead, then in about two yards, veer to the right. You can't miss it. You must be looking for Betty. Nicest person you'd ever want to meet." "Thank you," I say, bewildered again. Saline. Didn't take. Betty. I don't know what she is talking about. But anyway she steered me right, and I do get to the telephone room.

"Hi," I say to the fat-cheeked operator behind the sliding glass windows. "My name is Dr. Denes. I have an appointment with Miss Stern. How do I get there?" "I'll call her for you, Doctor. Please take a seat." She laughs. "I mean if you just wait a minute. There are no seats, of course. I can't get used to it, you see. All these people milling about. We used to have such a nice quiet hospital here. Oh, well. That's the way it goes." "Thank you."

While she is fiddling with the board I turn around and survey the room once more. My initial impression of total chaos has somewhat diminished by now. It seems that the receptionist at the desk has a list of names against which she checks the names of those in line. She then hands them some papers and with a gesturing arm directs them toward the elevators at the other end of the hall. I watch several women go through this process. I also watch a family. The pregnant one appears to be a young girl in a sweater and miniskirt. She is rather pretty, at least from this distance. Her father is a

5

serviceman. Her mother wears a kerchief on her head. As the girl behind the desk points toward the elevators, the mother throws her arms around her daughter. She hugs her tightly, and although I can not make out her tears, I think she is crying. The father purses his lips, shakes his head, separates the two by thrusting a gentle hand between them. He then leans over, lifts and hands a brown battered suitcase to the daughter. She takes it. He says something. The daughter nods. The father takes the mother by the shoulders. The mother says something. The girl turns and starts to walk away. The couple head for the exit. Naturally, they could be her aunt and uncle. Or friends. The man might be the girl's aged lover and the woman a kindly neighbor. There is no way to tell.

Actions hint at truth, they do not reveal it. Neither do words, if it comes to that. Reality is a matter of courtesy. A matter of agreement not to rock the tempest-torn boat.

I notice Miss Stern approaching me. She wears a name-tag clipped onto a chain around her neck. It reads "Rachel Stern, Acting Director." We have met only once before. Otherwise we have conducted our transactions through the mail.

The acting director is a tall, slim redhead with hair down below her shoulders, long red fingernails, freckles, glasses, red lips, excellent teeth, and a nervous manner. She makes me ill at ease. It is a condition I am unable to overcome throughout my work at the hospital, even though I feel overwhelming gratitude toward her for permitting me to pursue my research.

"Well, dear, hello! I am sorry, but this just won't do. I mean I apologize profusely, because I know I told you to come today and at this hour, but you just cannot imagine how busy I am. You would not believe if I told you what goes on here. I sometimes wonder what would happen if I fell too ill to come in. I, of course, come in just the same when I am sick, but I mean if I fell really ill. The incompetents here or maybe they just don't care. Well, anyway, that's neither here nor there. The thing is, there is nothing I can do for you today. I have an appointment right now with somebody else. A referral source. I have a luncheon date. Strictly business. Then I have a meeting. Meanwhile I am behind in my phone calls. Any-

way, how are you?" "Fine. Fine, Miss Stern." "No, please
don't call me that. You may call me Rachel, of course, I hope
you do. But I think 'miss' is a little outmoded. I mean I think
'ms.' is really where it's at. Don't you?" "I guess so." "Look,
I know you must be very busy yourself, being an analyst and
all, and I feel bad about this, and I will introduce you to
everybody very soon. I mean I am very interested in your
project, I think much more of that is needed, but it cannot be
today. I also don't want you to waste your time, so I'll just call
the key people and tell them you are in the building and that
it's okay. And then maybe you can walk around on your own.
That might even be better, don't you think? I could get you
a tag and a doctor's coat. I am really taking more time here
than I should." "I am sorry. And thanks, but I don't want a
doctor's coat." I am no bloody doctor in a hospital where
people can get physically ill. "Just being able to walk around
would be fine." "Very well, then, it's settled. I will call everybody, but I must run now. Good luck. Come back tomorrow
at ten, please. Goodbye, Dr. Denes." "Yeah." I am mute and
paralyzed. She is halfway across the room before I recover
enough to shout after her, "Magda. Call me Magda, please." I
am at once the center of at least sixty pairs of curious eyes.
Rachel, unheeding, continues on her path.

Next morning at ten Rachel and I meet in her office. "From
the waiting room they come up here to the second floor," she
says. "This is where they get admitted. First the lab tests are
done, then they get examined, then the counselor speaks to
them. If there are no special problems they proceed to the
appropriate unit. You want to come and see?" "Yes, please.
But first tell me, what might be a special problem?"

"Oh, there are many. The girl may be underaged and not
have a letter of consent from a parent or a guardian. If that
happens she has to go home, we can't do her. Or someone may
be clearly over the twenty-four week limit. We can not do that
one either. Or if they appear mentally very disturbed, we call
a psychiatric consult, and proceed only if we get an okay.
Sometimes they are physically ill. One kid for example, fourteen years old, had had open heart surgery two months before

7

she came here. Dr. Berkowitz, he is one of our anesthesiologists, refused to do her. We sent her to a clinic where they do spinals. The most frequent problems are those just on the border. If the doctor can't tell whether they are at twenty-four weeks or just below or just above we have to refer them for a sonogram. We don't like letting them go alone. I mean a counselor or one of the social workers will go along. Sometimes when everybody is busy I have had to do it myself." "What's a sonogram?" "Oh, you don't know. That's funny. Being a doctor I would have thought you would know. Although I didn't know it either before I came here. It's a new thing. Kind of like a ship's sonar. They scan the abdomen with an ultrasonic probe. It is sound waves that vibrate the belly so that different tissues send back different echoes. That way they can tell a baby from a tumor. And it's not harmful like X-rays. If you wanted to keep the baby, the sonogram would still be safe. It also tells the exact size of the fetus, through which they calculate time of gestation. That's why we use it. It's really very fascinating. They know, for example, that at twenty-four weeks of gestation the diameter of a fetal head, from ear to ear, is 6.0 centimeters. So if the measure is that or smaller we can do them. If it's bigger we send them away." "Fascinating." "Okay. Let me show you this floor." "Great. Thank you."

I gather my handbag, tape recorder, briefcase, and follow Rachel into the corridor. We turn left. Directly in front of us there is a small desk behind which two women are seated. Both look to be in their early twenties. They are counselors. The hospital employs seven of them, I was told. Their backgrounds vary, but none is a professional mental health worker. They have received on-the-job training. They admit patients, explain the procedures to them, collect money, calm fears, and refer those who appear to be problem cases to a doctor or a social worker. In time I get to know most of them rather well. They all like their work. All of them report that it gives them a sense of purpose and accomplishment. Not a single one among them has ever seen a D & C (dilation and curettage) performed nor watched the expulsion of a saline fetus.

"Good morning, ladies," Rachel says as we reach the desk.

"This is Dr. Denes. She is a psychologist. She will be with us for a while doing research. I ask for your cooperation. This is Edith," Rachel says, pointing to the girl on the left side of the desk. "And this is Joan," she says, pointing to the right.

"Hi," Joan says. "Sure thing," says Edith. They don't sound very friendly. "Hi. My name is Magda." The girls grin.

"Well then," says Rachel, "come and meet the lab technician. This is a satellite lab for immediate work. The main one is on the eighth floor."

We walk around the desk and enter a small room. There is a black woman inside in a white coat. "Good morning, Ms. Stern," she says. "Good morning. This is Dr. Denes, Minnie. She'll be doing research here." Minnie takes my breath away. She is a pretty woman, with lively eyes and a full growth of beard. The sight is uncanny.

"What is done here?" I ask, turning toward a small table laid out with the paraphernalia of taking blood. I simply have to find something other than Minnie to look at. "Oh, we do regular CBC's (complete blood counts) here, and we type for Rh factor." "I see." "We also do urine tests for pregnancy. They give the sample in the bathroom there. By the time they get to the doctor we have all that information ready." "I see." "Dr. Denes may want to have a chat with you sometime, if you don't mind," Rachel says to Minnie. "I love to gab, Doc," Minnie replies, turning to me. "What kind of a doc are you?" "Well, sort of a harmless shrink." "I known them," Minnie says, frowning. "I have known a bunch." I seem to have goofed. "Well, I am just me here. Just looking around. You know, doing a job."

"Okay, but don't do it on me, Doc," Minnie says, breaking up at her joke. "If you know what I mean." "Yep. I know what you mean. I won't do it. So long." I open the door and step back into the corridor. Rachel follows me.

"See all those girls, I mean women, sitting in that row down the hall? They are waiting to be seen by a physician. A counselor has spoken to them, their lab tests are done, they need to be examined. Then they'll go upstairs to the unit where they belong. D & C or Saline. That's all there is to it. The admis-

9

sions are done here, the procedures are done upstairs. That room," she says indicating a door next to the satellite lab, "is the place where the patients wait before the counselors have a chance to talk to them." "You mean those two girls at the desk?" "Please don't call them girls, they are women." "Right." "Not them. They simply check names, take initial data, and assign the patients to other counselors in private rooms at the western end of the floor. They have a rotation. Nobody likes this desk, it is too hectic. So we make each of them work here for a couple of hours, then they change places. They feel in the private rooms they really get to do important work." "Right."

"I am really sorry, but I am very busy. I must go now. You know how it is. If I don't do my work no one will do it for me." "Sure. I understand. Thanks very much. You've been very helpful. I really appreciate it." The truth is, I really do.

I wander into the waiting room. I sit down on one of the molded plastic chairs with metal legs, of which there are about eighteen or twenty in the room placed in a circle. I feel drained. It is as if I had spent the past two days in a state of negative enchantment, trapped in a castle of black, black magic.

There are several women in the room, but I am too weary to look at them. Instead I focus on the round coffee table in front of the blinded windows. The table has four square wooden legs and a black glass surface. On it there are three issues of *Time* magazine, also a yellow metal urn filled with a large bouquet of dirty plastic flowers in the replica of pink and white wild hawthorns and green thistles. There is music in the air. WPAT, 93.1 on your FM dial.

On the right wall hangs a large hand-lettered sign in blue and purple ink:

> We're sorry 'bout
> the LONG waiting
> periods. . . . please
> BEAR with us!
>                   Thank you.

I gaze at it for a while in amazement, for the evidently unconscious, macabre humor of its wording.

A nurse appears at the door. "Amy and Mrs. Stone," she shouts. Two women get up. One young, one older. They are both blond and plump. They are both dressed in sweaters and dungarees. They could be twins with a time lag. The older one, who is obviously the Mrs., wears a large photograph button of Nixon, below her left breast.

"This way, please," the nurse says. They follow, and I trot in their wake. "Take a seat in this row, please," the nurse says, pointing to one empty chair in the long corridor. "Hold on to this number. The doctor will call you soon."

"Thank you, nurse" Mrs. Stone says as she sits down and takes the slip of paper handed to her. Amy says nothing. She stands facing her mother, legs apart, torso bent, head downward, poised for whispered secrets.

The doctor on duty is Dr. Jesus. I have seen him walking around earlier, while Rachel was introducing me to the other staff members. He is a short, stocky man, of swarthy complexion and a foreign accent. He has clouded eyes and a distracted manner.

As he steps into the corridor from one of the three examining rooms, I approach him. "Hello. I am Dr. Denes. I do research here. Could I join you in your office?" He is glazed and hesitant. "As a matter of professional courtesy," I add. He visibly wavers. "We have not met, but Ms. Stern told me about you and authorized this request." "Okay," he says, "okay of me, but I be very busy." "I will be no trouble at all," I say. "Okay."

"Number fourteen, next please," he shouts. Amy turns, and Mrs. Stone jumps up. "That's us," she answers in the tone of one who has just hit the jackpot. "Both you?" Dr. Jesus asks, startled. "At once? Meaning, together?" "Yeah we're together," says Mrs. Stone. "Sisters pregnant?" "No, no." Mrs. Stone melts. "She ain't my sister, she's my little baby." "Yeah, yeah, but you want rid of baby, right?" Dr. Jesus is obviously offended by what he considers Mrs. Stone's inappropriate sentiments. "No, no, Doctor, I love my baby. She done wrong, but I love her." Mrs. Stone is about to burst into tears. "I confused," Dr. Jesus concedes. "Who are you? Are you number fourteen? Which you are number fourteen?" "This is Amy. I am her mother. She's twelve weeks we were told at home." "I see, I see," says Dr. Jesus. "Why you no say so in first place? You sit. Amy come in please." He turns on his heels and leads the way. Midway he flicks himself half around. "You come too," he orders in my direction, pointing at me a nicotine stained forefinger. "Right. I am coming."

The examining room is small and sparse. It contains a gynecological table, an instrument stand, a wash basin, a desk and chair, and a slotted wooden screen behind which the patients undress. "In there," says Jesus to Amy. "Everything off. Put on the white gown. When ready, exit." Amy, wordless, slinks behind the screen. "Okay, Doctor," Jesus says to me. "We first fill out this form." The title on the printed sheet he shows me says "Admission Record." The items on it range from name, address, city, zone, date admitted, diagnosis, insurance plan, etc., etc., all the way to the last line above the physician's signature, which is "Cause of Death." "No worry," Jesus grins, placing his pencil on the printed sentence. "That one never get filled here, hardly." "Great," I say. "Great. What else?" "Oh, let's see. You in there, you over twenty-one, dear?" "Yes, sir," Amy replies. She has a thin small voice. "I am twenty-two." "Okay. No parent consent necessary, but we must do a Papanicolaou." "A what?" I say. "A Pap smear, Doc, a Pap smear. I knew I fool you." Jesus shakes with his joke. "Right. Very funny." "Law require Pap smear for everybody over twenty-five. In this hospital we do for all over twenty-one. Unless they sign 'No.' Amy, you want Pap smear or sign?" "Whatever is right," Amy says, walking out from behind the screen. She looks pale and even more subdued than when she entered. "Pap smear is right," Jesus says. "On the table, please."

Amy scrambles up, lies down, spreads her thighs, and hooks her feet into the stirrups. Obviously it is not the first time she has been so examined. "Good girl," Jesus says as he pulls on a transparent plastic glove. He puts Vaseline on his thumb and two fingers and enters Amy. Amy says, "Ouch. You hurt." "Breathe deep, push down," Jesus instructs.

"Doctor," he says to me, "do you want to examine her?" I have moved to the other end of the room. I am not prepared to watch these proceedings. His offer gets me angry. Suppose I felt like it. Could I just stick my hands up this girl, on the basis of a generic title? These are awful conventions, unfair courtesies. "I am not that kind of doctor," I say. "I am an analyst. Here I do research." "I better not talk to you," Jesus says. "Anyway, she all right. About fourteen weeks. No complications. Two weeks over the home doctor's diagnosis. Maybe just time pass. Now I do the Pap. It won't hurt either." He sticks a small probe up her, withdraws it, and smears a slide. "Okay, dear. You be okay. Get dressed."

Amy disappears behind the screen, and I thank Jesus. "A minute," he says. "Could I ask you. My wife is not so well. She sometimes thinks people are against her. Should she have help?" "I can't say. But probably, since you ask. You are her husband, and if you ask she should probably have help for one thing or the other." "Thanks." "It was not much. I thank you."

The next station of the patient's journey is the counselors' private office. I lose Amy to a misplaced suitcase, in search of which both she and her mother leave the floor. Instead I get to watch Edith Bernstein counsel Lyuba Yanov, nine weeks pregnant, born in Yugoslavia, naturalized at the age of seven twelve years ago.

Lyuba and Edith sit across from each other, separated by a narrow battered desk, marred with butt burns. Edith is twenty-one, slim, haughty, and Manhattan-efficient. Lyuba is shy and terrified. It is the first time she is in a big city, the first time she is pregnant, the first time she is alone (she comes from a family of six siblings), the first time that she has to examine her thoughts and give account of herself to a stranger. She does pretty damned well considering, or even not considering.

"It is not what I would want. It is what I must," she says, nervously turning a band on the ring finger of her left hand.

"Are you married?" Edith asks. Lyuba blushes. "Because of

the ring? No. I just thought it would look better coming in here and all. I bought it myself, at home." She pauses. "I wish this would be over," she adds with a sigh. "Okay then. Let me tell you the procedures." Edith replies crisply. I think she has misunderstood Lyuba and thinks that the girl is getting impatient with their conversation. "First of all I need to see proof of your age. Do you have any document that tells how old you are?" "I have a driver's license." "That will do fine." Lyuba rummages in her pocketbook and produces the license. She hands it over. Edith notes down its serial number and returns it. "I also need some signatures from you. One for 'Consent For Diagnostic Procedures,' one for 'Authorization For Release of Information,' one for 'Agreement For Administration Of Blood And/Or Blood Derivatives,' one for 'Specific Permit For Operation,' and finally one for not holding the hospital responsible for your valuables." As she speaks, Edith hands Lyuba a pen and places a printed sheet in front of her. At the mention of each category she points to a different section of the sheet, where Lyuba duly signs.

"That's fine" Edith says. "Now one more, which says in case of emergency we may notify your parents. Is that okay with you?" Lyuba nods and signs. "Good. Put your left arm forward please." Lyuba does as instructed. Edith snaps an identity band on her wrist. "You must wear this at all times while you occupy the premises. It is a safety precaution."

As I sit watching these two young women, I am overwhelmed by the bureaucratic banality of suffering. Obscure chatter, legal forms, repeated signatures, waiting, these are the structured anesthetic necessities that oil the machinery of institutions.

At this hospital, downstairs they wait, in this unit they bear witness, further up they are delivered. In between they endure the purgatory of routine and fear, of lab-tests and regrets and reaffirmations of purpose. Until it is over. Until the crisis recedes, and the dull comfort of monotony asserts itself once more. Well-being is also banal.

I become aware that my musings have made me miss a large chunk of the dialogue. "So that's the D & C procedure," I hear

14

Edith saying. "Do you have any questions about that?" Lyuba shakes her head. "Fine," Edith says. "Two more things remain. Here are your post-op instructions, and I want to tell you about the various birth control methods." She hands Lyuba a Xeroxed sheet, on the upper right-hand corner of which there is a stylized emblem of the Medical Arts.

"Have you read one of these, Doctor?" Edith asks, turning toward me. "No. I would like to, thank you."

"Here you are." There are a few minutes of quiet, while Lyuba and I both read:

## POST OPERATIVE INSTRUCTIONS

1. The amount of bleeding after this operation varies from patient to patient, but does not normally exceed 7–14 days, and would probably be less than your normal period.
2. You should rest for at least 24 hours after the operation, then you may resume normal activities except strenuous physical activities, dancing, etc.
3. You should not lie in a bath or swim until all post operative bleeding has ceased, and in any case not for at least 7 days from the operation—external cleaning only. Douching is not advisable. Showering is O.K.
4. To avoid risk of infection after the operation:
   a. Internal sanitary wear should not be used until the next period.
   b. Intercourse should not take place for 2–4 weeks.
5. The next period will occur within 4–6 weeks of the operation and bleeding may be more than usual.
6. Contact the Hospital or your physician in the event of:
   a. Profuse bleeding.
   b. Persistent abdominal pain.
   c. Offensive vaginal discharge.
   d. Temperature and chills.
7. See your own physician for a checkup within 3 weeks.

As with any operation, certain minor complications may occur. These most commonly are excessive bleeding, fever or cramps. If you have concerns about your condition, feel free to call us at the Hospital for advice at any time. However, if you seek outside medical advice without consulting with us, we cannot be responsible for the decisions made by outside physicians.

"Okay," Edith interrupts the silence. "If there are no questions, let's talk about birth control." "No," says Lyuba. Edith looks astonished. "What do you mean?" "I don't want to talk about it," Lyuba says with total finality. "I don't want to hear." "What do you mean?" Edith says again. "Don't you want to protect yourself? I mean look what has happened." "No," says Lyuba. "No. I will not talk of that. It is a sin." Edith gasps. Her mouth opens and closes independently of the rest of her face. To her great credit, she recovers almost at once. "Okay. Here is your chart," she says. "I will escort you to the elevators. Go to the fourth floor. I will phone up and a nurse will be expecting you." "Thank you," says Lyuba. "You are most kind."

We all get up, exit, and go to the elevators. As one passes without stopping, Edith shouts, "Up, please." "Down please," I yell. All three of us laugh. "I think I'll walk," I say. "Goodbye. Thank you." I nod toward Edith. "Good luck." I smile at Lyuba. Both wave.

———

About six months pass before I conduct the interviews that follow. At first I am irresistibly drawn to the upstairs units where the patients are and where I believe the vital action takes place. I come to understand only gradually that the downstairs staff, who speak here, are like cornerstones in a building, without which the structure would collapse. They are like a Greek chorus, indispensable witnesses to a drama that excludes them, yet which without them could not occur.

They are also like most of the workers in this hospital—dedicated and full of doubt, committed but uneasy.

## Miss Minnie Brown, Age 36

*Laboratory Technician*

"Well, personally I had quite a bad reaction to these abortions. Quite a few people had to talk to me because I couldn't see having an abortion after three months, where it becomes a saline. It bothered me in the fact that I have a personal reason. Because I've always wanted children and I haven't been able to get pregnant. And here you know the girls are so young to start off with that are getting pregnant left and right. I found after a period of three months that we had from eight to ten that were coming back a second time or three and four times, and it gave me the impression that the abortion law being passed just gave the girls the opportunity to really become loose or do whatever they want to, because with the law they had no more problems. They could just keep on enjoying sexual things. Then my supervisor talked to me. He used the phrase of the fact that I had to realize I was a technologist, this was a job and I had to accept it as a job and not a personal thing. It's a problem where I had to condition myself. I had to be the one to do the turnover. I resented it more than anything else plus the fact with me being Catholic. And with me having nursing training. I am an RN. And I know the time when life begins. . . .

"I used to say to a lot of people that I talked to, that I wouldn't have an abortion. Because my mother had twenty-seven kids."

DR. D.: How many?

MB: Twenty-seven, and so I've always been brought up around a lot of kids. Many of them were twins. A lot died in childbirth. My mother was in the cotton fields, and they were what you call blue babies. All she knew was they changed color and died. . . .

"I just can't make myself believe that salines are fair. It disturbs me when I see them. A full-term baby that, let's say if the salt hadn't been introduced into the uterus, would have

18

lived. When you could see features and toenails and everything. Ugh.

"I had to decide really which way was I going to go because my supervisor just about had it with me. I didn't get rude or nasty with the girls, but it was a form of hostility that could be sensed. I would have an attitude. You find a lot of girls that come in say sixteen, seventeen, and they'd be sliding in the chair and say 'Do you have to do it.' And I would get so annoyed with them. I had told one girl 'This little needle won't hurt as bad as what you got.' I meant when she had her man I know that hurt because of her age—she was fifteen—I mean how big could she be? All this made me have a new look on life really.

"I was forever crying. I would have a lot of older women that felt embarrassed to be with so many young girls and they would want me to talk to them. In the beginning I would just take their blood, send them to the bathroom, then shove them out the door and tell them where to go for the examination. But then I began to talk to them and ease their problems. For some reason, I just felt better myself. . . .


"I have never had a black boyfriend. I have never had black friends. For some reason I always find myself with other races. I am treated more as a person or I am accepted for what I am, more by white men. I keep myself on a pedestal. I try to stand very high.

"Black men haven't learned to appreciate black women, such as women. To them a woman is to work or to take care of them.

"Another thing, I never go out like uptown. It has always been downtown here and when I'm taken out it's always to the better places. They'll take me to places that mean something. The National History Museum [sic], the Guggenheim Museum. With colored fellows their interest is drinking, drugs, or numbers, or running around to see who has the most women, or getting money. It's a horrible thing to have to say because

I do know that there are some nice guys, but let's put it this way, I haven't been able to find them or they haven't found me. . . .

"I love sex. All kinds. It's just beautiful to me. There's nothing like it. Nothing can beat it.

"I'd love to get pregnant even though I am not married. I'd love to have a child. This is why it hit me so hard in the beginning when these abortions started. Because I have tried. I've tried every kind of way. Sixty-nine, in the tub, in the chair, upside down, on the floor. Some tell you 'don't jump up and take a douche.' Well I layed there all night long in this messy stuff and nothing happened yet. And then I found out about two months ago that I have a fibroid and this is what was stopping me from getting pregnant.

"Also I always had this hormone trouble, so that has a lot to do with it too. I have more male than female hormones. I didn't get a chance this morning but I usually shave. They tried to treat it but the medicine made my clitoris grow. I told him I don't want to be a boy so I had to stop taking that stuff. It's hard to explain."

*Minnie is the Queen of Wigs at the hospital. She must have two dozen of them, each very fancy and very beautiful. Everyday another one sits on her head in regal splendor.*

*As she walks in the corridors the women compliment her. She nods her thanks with the largess of a monarch.*

## Mrs. Betty Heller, Age 58

*Telephone Operator*

*Betty Heller aims to please. She is sweet-faced, gentle, and chubby.*

*Seated at her switchboard she chirps into the wires and into the more immediate world. "Nice to see you, Doctor. Isn't there a terrible wind today? It nearly knocked me over. I hope you were all right.* *"It is meaningless talk, yet her voice and manner are such that on her days off the waiting room seems a worse place to me.*

*Still, fluffy, tender, aging Betty, unbeknownst to her conscious mind, believes that she would have been better off unborn.*

"I went to night school to learn the switchboard and typing. I love it. I love people. You have to have a love affair with people to get along with them, especially patients. That's what I've done all my life, be with patients. I was a practical nurse for thirty years, until I got sick and couldn't do it anymore.

"My daughter is twenty-six. I was with my husband for fifteen years and then we separated, and I took care of my daughter ever since myself. She's a lab technologist. I'd love to see her get married.

"I love my daughter very much and she loves me and we understand each other and that's rare with girls today. I wanted a boy but I'm glad I got Sue and I have an adopted daughter, Eve.

"Eve's mother used to take care of Sue when I went to school at night, and then when I worked. And then Eve was about fifteen when her mother died and I adopted her. I figured she's living with us so why shouldn't I adopt her? So I did.

"Eve lives in New Jersey. She's married to a statistician. He works for the government. We speak on the phone every Saturday. Sue lives with me. . . .

"Sex, I think, is where all the trouble started in my marriage. I don't talk about it much, but I was cold. I just wasn't interested. I still am not.

"He drank a lot and he ran around and he went out with other women.

"I think that's what got me cold toward him, and he was very demanding on sex. I think that's what started it off. I was

21

brought up in an orphanage. I was straitlaced. Before I got married I wouldn't let no one touch me. . . .

"I feel sorry for the mothers that come in here. Not the girls because they knew what they were doing. I feel sorry for the mothers for one reason, they're embarrassed. You can see that. And they come in and several of them start to cry. I say, 'You must remember it's a bad experience for the child too, as well as for you.' I say, 'Don't be harsh to them. We all make mistakes.' . . .

"I used to work in the New York Foundling. I used to give one day a week there. I volunteered. I saw all those babies never smiling. Those things come up in my mind here, and I say to myself, I know I'm a Catholic but it is good that these babies aren't brought up in the world because it would be like me in the home. I was brought up in a home. These kids in the Foundling, you should see some of them, they were never happy. They'd be in the crib and you try to play with them, you sing to them, you cuddle them, all they wanted was love. If these kids here were born a lot of them wouldn't have that. Does that sound plausible? Some of these mothers beat these kids up, so why should they be brought up to tolerate all that?

"They're sinning, I know it, they know it, but it's none of my business. I feel that way because I spoke to the priest when they started the abortions here. He told me as long as you're not participating in the actual service it's okay. A lot of nurses quit though. Because of abortions. They said it was a sin to work here. I said it is not. The priest said that I wasn't sinning and I shouldn't feel guilty and I don't. Not one girl will tell you or their mothers that I was ever nasty to them, because I have compassion for them. What I was is upset because I wanted more children. Damn it, I used to say, look at them coming in and I can't have any and they're getting rid of them, and I went and I talked to the priest about that too. . . .

"My mother and father had thirteen children. I was the last one and they put me in a home. I don't know why. At the orphanage the mother superior said, 'If you don't want to have your feelings hurt and if you'd want to live miserably don't find out anything,' and I never did. . . .

"I was resentful, very resentful, and even when I was sixteen I was still at the orphanage and I used to go to work. I used to live in Newport, Rhode Island, and the twelve-mile drive had all the rich people, the aristocrats in the summer. I used to work for them to earn the money to go to nursing school. I trained there and then I came to New York and I never went back. . . .

"The women here are lucky for what they're having done, because if they brought that child up it might be like me. Do you know what I mean, they would have only nuns to take care of them, and I had a very hard life. There's a lot of things in my memory, like I can't stand closed ceilings. I have claustrophobia very badly. I used to have a persecution complex that was awful. Not anymore because I'm getting older. I realize that it wasn't their fault probably. They must have had a reason.

"When I used to be a naughty girl they used to put me in the potato cellar. There was no windows and I used to hear the rats in there, and I got such a fear that I still have it."

———

## The Hospital

The staff eats in the cafeteria at mealtimes and in between. The cafeteria is in the basement, windowless and air-conditioned, sharply lit. The coffee is fair and always available.

At around four every afternoon the clerical staff arrives for tea. They are a cackle of huge overweight, formidable women who always sit together and with no one else. They eat large portions of pie. Their fat hands daintily hold forks that seem too small for them. They do not so much sit as seem planted on their chairs, legs slightly apart to accommodate the spreading flesh of their thighs. Their heads, hair set and glistening with spray in the fluorescent light, bob up and down, biting and talking, chewing and talking, swallowing and talking. Their vivid collective excluding presence transforms their table into an island and removes it from its surroundings. There is no more cafeteria, no more hospital, no more feeling world. Only this devastation of noisy fat remains, emanating an air of inexplicable hostility. They could be in a space capsule lost in the stratosphere, perversely preserved forever exactly as they are: self-righteous, alien, ugly, unrelated, unaware.

Sometime soon, I think, I will try to speak with them.

Months pass before I do.

Each, alone, proves to be helpful, eager to talk, cooperative, mostly honest. I speak with several of them, and I am very pleased with our newly established relations. Some days later I see them again in the cafeteria. They sit, disconnected, hostile, chewing on pies, chatting privately. All of them ignore my greeting.

24

# Mrs. Margaret Briggs, Age 37

*Bookkeeper*

"I don't hide it, but I don't advertise it, the fact that I work here. I say I'm a bookkeeper. However, I'm very much for abortions to a certain extent.

"I'm not completely and wholly for it. We've had several patients in here who came three times in two years. Girls in their twenties, some of them married. Abortion is not to be used for a birth control method. It's ridiculous.

"Everyone talks about that abortions are not bad as long as they're before the twelfth week. A lot of people feel the fetus is not alive yet. I agree with that to a certain extent, but they also believe that all the salines should be stopped. And I can see why they believe this, because the baby is more completely formed. But if they stop that, the only people they hurt are the young girls—I mean, from the ages of twelve on up to eighteen. Because they don't know what they're doing and they become pregnant. They won't tell their parents if they're afraid, or they don't know. These are the ones that are always caught too late to go for a twelve-week abortion. You'll hurt the ones who need it the most."

DR. D.: I understand you have a daughter who came in here for a saline. How did that happen?

MB: Well—let's put it this way, who knows. She's always fluctuated weightwise since she was about fourteen—got chubby. I'm not a real straitlaced person myself. I believe in a certain amount of freedom. And, of course, you always hope that if anything happens, they will come to you—which she eventually did. She was eighteen. . . .

"I knew the boy but I didn't personally care for him. But, I believe that they will find out more themselves than by me saying, 'I don't want you going with this boy because he is not of your race, or nationality, or of your church.'

"He was a Puerto Rican boy, but very nervous, very jumpy.

25

Anyone that she goes out with I've always allowed to come to my house. I feel that if a child can bring their friends home, you don't have half of the problems. My husband, of course, was saying, 'I don't want my daughter going out with a Puerto Rican,' and what not.

"She finally came and told me. But I had asked her a couple of times because, to me, she was thickening out too much. She never really got that big or anything, but, to me, that's what it reminded me of. And I asked, and I asked, and she said, 'No, no, don't be silly, and I couldn't be.' But in the meantime, she had stopped going out with him. She got frightened, you know.

"He never knew she was pregnant and my husband doesn't know either. My husband is very narrow-minded. She would have been ruined in his eyes. He is the type that will throw things up in later years, or pass remarks. I just felt it would be much better for her and him if he didn't know.

"No matter what people say, and this is a liberal civilization, and everybody is very open-minded now, a lot of it is baloney. You know it and I know it. If people say free love is nice, and you can have babies, you don't have to be married—to the majority of the population it's still frowned upon. You're shunned. You may be ostracized. I told my daughter that.


"I'd say the first five or six years that I was married, sex to me was a very big disappointment. I expected so much and it was sort of a letdown. I wouldn't say that it was bad. It just wasn't everything I had heard about. But I've found that in the last five or ten years I've come to enjoy sex more. I don't know if it's just that women mature later, or myself in particular, or what."

DR. D.: Did you ever have an abortion?

MB: No. I have always had the other problem. I think this may be why when I see married women come in here and have two and three abortions in two and three years, I would like to take my fist and hit them. Because I only had one child. I went to a clinic ten, twelve years, trying to become pregnant.

And tests showed nothing. One tube was open. I ovulated. My husband was tested first. Because I think one child has a very lonely life. But, then again, I do not believe in large families either. I'm out of a very large family.

"When you get into your teens—and you have four brothers, smaller than you and every week another one needs a new pair of shoes, and yet you can go months and be lucky if you ever got a skirt or a blouse. I was never bitter about it, because I knew that whatever my mother or father was able to do, it was done. But I also feel that you can give much more to a child if you don't have that many, unless you can afford them.

"With the saline fetuses you do have a resemblance of a baby. I mean, there is a shape—it may be only this big, but, you know, you feel a little bit of sorrow. But then again, you could never make me believe in a million years that God ever wanted a twelve-year-old child to give birth to a baby. And that's just the way I feel."

DR. D.: Are you Catholic?

MB: Yes, I am.

DR. D.: Let me ask you something else. You know how the grapevine is in a hospital. I was told that you were asked to sign a petition in favor of abortions, before this recent ruling, and that you refused. Is that true?

MB: True. Yes, it is. They had a petition that they were taking upstate to register directly against the Right to Life platform. When they had this big rally just before they tried to get the repeal. I would not. I may believe in a certain number of things, but I also love my husband. I mean, I know what he is. I may know that he is narrow-minded, but I still love my husband. And it could have been a very, very embarrassing thing for him. Say my name was singled out. And I would rather not embarrass him, because he has been a very good provider, he has been very good in many ways. I accept him for what he is. And I know that I won't change him. As people grow older, they become milder in some things and more crotchety in others. But he enjoys his Christian work.

He volunteers innumerable times at a foundling hospital, and a retarded children's program, which I believe in very heartily. It's just that I do not believe in a repeal of the abortion law. People will get abortions anyway, they're butchered, people's lives are ruined. It's something that goes on anyway.

"A couple of people passed remarks, 'Hmph, of all people, I'd think you'd sign for it.' I said, 'This is my business. You sign what you wish, I will sign what I wish.' And this is just how I feel about it."

*I think that the quality that I that most prize in people is valor, especially the sort that is un-self-conscious.*

*Here we have Margaret Briggs, thirty-seven, looking fifty. She is acne-scarred and missing many teeth; those she has hang loose. From the texture of her skin and the redness of her eyes I deduce that she drinks too much. But what does it matter?*

*The important fact is her gallantry, whereby to protect her husband's feelings, she has, among her peers, passed herself off as a hypocrite—and offered no extenuating explanations.*

*A stubborn mule, some would say, might do the equivalent. Perhaps. But I admire those blessed with a brave mule's heart.*

## Mrs. Nancy Stein, Age 48

*Controller*

"Before the abortions started here, I was a one-girl office. I did the payroll, the accounts payable, the accounts receivable, the general ledger, all alone with one biller. Now I have nine girls who are inside. We went from a small, private, not too important hospital—in that we didn't do major surgery—to a hospital that had a tremendous influx of patients. From 4,500 patients a year, we went to 22,000 patients the following year. Ninety-eight percent abortion cases. . . .

"They were very generous with money. They gave everybody a raise at the very onset, and then as time went on, the work got even more tremendous and there were additional increases. It was very lucrative after a while. . . .

"I felt that a woman should not have to have a child that she doesn't want. I have reservations about that statement. I think that it became a little too easy to have an abortion. I know, personally, I would have had an abortion now, at this point, whereas probably before the law I might not have had one, and that might have been the best child that I had of my children. That's the thing that I think—for a young girl, or people who couldn't afford to have children, it was a great thing. But for the middle-class, middle-aged women, married, with two children, to be able to have an abortion because they didn't want another child, I felt that they were depriving themselves of something which might have been great.

"For the young it was a good thing. What they're doing, they're doing anyhow, and to be saddled with a child for most of them would have been terrible."

DR. D.: Have you seen any of the procedures?

NS: No. I am chicken. I stay as far away from that area as I can. I don't think I could watch a procedure. I'm really squeamish. I've never seen anybody in labor or being induced.

"I went up to the lab one day and on the pathologist's table was what I thought was a little rubber doll until I realized it was a fetus. I got sick. I got really shook up and upset and I couldn't believe it. It had all its fingers and toes, you know, hands and feet, and I really didn't know what a fetus was going to look like. I never thought it would look—so real. I didn't like it. . . .

"I don't think abortion is good for all of the people. I think it's being a little too promiscuous—a lot of them are just taking abortions as the way out. And I think—as I say, I know friends

29

of mine who have had a late baby, so to speak, and it's made their whole life new, all over again.

"I feel it's very sad. You never know which is going to be the one that's going to be best to you, or for you, or the most considerate. . . .

"I've been married twenty-nine years. I am happy with my husband. We enjoy sex together. It's something we look forward to, and it's not on a once-in-a-while basis—it's pretty regularly, about two times a week. Sometimes more, sometimes less. It used to be more. But we're getting a little older, I guess a little tireder. If he really wants to have sex, I will never turn him down or say, 'No, I'm too tired.' I don't think I've ever done that. But he realizes when I'm exhausted. And there are days when he's exhausted. . . .

"My daughter is twenty-eight. She is married. She has a little boy two years old and a girl five. If she became pregnant again I don't think I would be happy with her deciding to have an abortion now. She's too young, really. And there is no reason for it, financially. As long as she's strong enough and she has help, she should have it. I think two children are plenty, by the way. I think that if you have a son and a daughter, it's a nice family. But if she becomes pregnant, I don't think she should have an abortion, if she's healthy enough."

DR. D: Your son is not married?

NS: No.

DR. D.: What if he got someone pregnant?

NS: I would want her to have an abortion. Especially if they weren't ready to be married. I've mentioned that to him. He said there would be no doubt in his mind that he would want her to have an abortion, and I have no doubt that I would want her to have one. I can't see her being saddled with a child she may not want, or if they never become more seriously involved than they are now. It would be foolish for her to have a child. . . .

"The only time I'm upset with the girls that come in are the girls that I feel are financially taking advantage of us. Those girls I resent. They come in, they don't have the full amount of money that they know they have to pay. They promise. And then we have to dun them for months and months, turn it over to collection agencies, and we get letters from them saying, 'Go to hell.' That type of thing. I have a letter right on my desk like that. And those girls I resent very badly. That burns me no end because I think we do a good job. Here it is by the way. I have been dying—this letter has been sitting on my desk. It really gets to me. We don't even know who it is because when we send the letter asking for money, we put their account number up here on the envelope and she blacked it out so we couldn't read who she was. Those are the girls who make it bad for the rest of the girls.

"I mean, you could just write a book from the letters we get explaining why they haven't paid, or why they can't pay, or when they will pay, or why they won't pay. But this was the classic. Here, you can read it."

She hands me a torn white sheet on which, in a childish, halting scrawl, is written: "Please stop writin. I'm not going to pay. I got what I wantin. Now you get your. Sucker."

*Mrs. Stein's views appear to me like the refrain of a song in the top ten of a hit parade—daughters ought not to have abortions; son's girl friends should. Late children are fine; mostly for others. The procedures are awful, not to be seen; but the strange young, who are foolish, need them available—within limits, undefined.*

———

*The Hospital*

The counselors comprise a very special group. All of them are single, young, exposed and extremely vulnerable themselves to the pitfalls that have brought the majority of patients to this hospital. It is as if by some powerful sorcery these young women have been permitted to observe the darkest, most mossy underside of their lives, enacted and endured by other souls.

The effect is staggering and uniform. They become devoted, guilty, erratically pious, self-searching, and explosively grateful to the blind fates that have chosen to spare them—that, in their arbitrary wisdom, have made them into aids and not victims. As is the case with many who survive catastrophes, nearly all the counselors change while working here.

# Miss Joan Martin, Age 23

*Counselor*

*Joan is a pale presence. Her voice whispers, her eyes hide. She carries her body as if she would rather be a shadow. Entrapped in all that, there lives a lively girl of convictions and compassion and tentative courage.*

"Well I'm definitely for abortion but I'm a little bit hesitant now as to how far it should go. I think six months is a little bit too much. I think as far as safety goes, and I think as far as the experience for the patient, it's a very difficult thing. The idea that they abort in bed, the idea that they're free to look at the fetus if they want to can be a pretty traumatic experience. Unless the nurse is right there and insists that the patient doesn't look, my impression is that the patient can look down and see what is there. I don't know for sure. I have never been with a patient when she's aborted. . . .

"I haven't had an abortion myself, but I've had a procedure —something to do with gynecology—and so I know basically what they go through, with having people examine you, and having pain, and bleeding and hemorrhaging and things like that.

"During the actual labor they get extremely emotional, and once it's over they either block it out of their minds or they just keep a clear face until they get out of here. Then I don't know what happens to them after that. But during labor you hear them yelling and they're in pain and they just want to go home and they want their mother and it's much more than a D & C because they are aware of it all. . . .

"I think of the patient more than I think of the fetus. I don't think a woman should have to have a child if she doesn't want it, because I can't forget that the fetus will eventually become

33

a human being and grow up and all the stigma is placed on it if it's not wanted. I guess I've gotten that from my sociology. I can't have very much sympathy for the fetus because I keep thinking more in the terms of the people who are living with the experience, themselves.

"When a child is wanted and it's born dead, or dies soon after birth, that to me is much more upsetting. Not this. I think it's better not to be born than to be put in an institution or a foster home. . . .

"I've gotten girls that were sixteen and seventeen who were very confident and knew what they were doing and felt very secure about it. Then I'll get a woman of twenty-six who will tell me that it wasn't her fault.

"I explain the procedure to them, but I don't get too graphic. As far as a saline patient goes I like to emphasize to them that they can take the pain killer. I also try to emphasize that they're not going to be alone. There are other people there and nurses. The pains are real but being in the hospital makes it a lot more traumatic than it would be otherwise. Especially if they are left alone. I try to go up there as much as I can. It's sort of discouraged because we are needed down here but sometimes I do it on my lunch hour or after I have punched out in the evening. The trouble is after a while, because there are so many women and the interaction is so brief, I'll walk into a room and I won't remember which patient I admitted. I don't like that but I just can't remember everybody and everybody's story. . . .

"I have had several affairs. I started when I was about twenty. I started late and I can't say that I am sorry about that.

"He left and had twins with another girl, without getting married. But I am over it by now.

"I use a diaphragm. I don't know if I would feel comfortable on the pill. To be very honest it probably has a lot to do with some of my sexual hangups. You see, I am slightly guilty about what I'm doing, and so I feel that the pill would be too much declaring my freedom in a way which I'm not quite ready to do yet. The diaphragm sort of says to me, 'You don't sleep around,' whereas the pill might say, 'You're on the prowl.' Then again, the diaphragm is a nuisance to put in and take out, but the pill I don't trust physically to be good for me. . . .

"Ninety-nine percent of the time I will not start off a relationship with somebody and immediately go to bed with him and then never see him again. I have to feel something. I'm not asking for commitments or promises, but for my own enjoyment and for my own state of mind there has to be a mental hookup. It doesn't have to be a total involvement but it has to be something."

DR. D.: Earlier you said you feel guilty.

JM: Because of my parents. My parents don't know about my personal life. I imagine they have had their suspicions at times, but my mother is adamant about sexual experience before marriage. It would destroy her if she knew about me, I think.

"My parents have never been physically very demonstrative toward me.

"As a matter of fact, since I moved out I've been a lot closer to them, I mean for the first time I feel honestly that I love them very much, which I did not feel very confident about saying when I lived with them. And I feel that they were the same way. They did not appreciate me as much. They didn't understand me.

"I think it's because of them that I used to be very frightened of people being physically demonstrative towards me. If people kissed me I got terrified. When I was about fifteen or sixteen whenever I went out on a date one of my biggest problems was worrying about a goodnight kiss before I came home. Not so much the 'Would he or wouldn't he,' but, you know, where should I stand, what do I say to the boy, and I was so bogged down with that that it would totally ruin the evening and for a while it was like that with intercourse."

## Miss Berta Meyer, Age 32

*Counselor*

*Berta Meyer is a very nice woman. She is composed and involved. She is liberal and empathetic. She also thanks her stars, a little complacently, a hundred times a day in confessed silence and out loud, for her luck at not being in the shoes of any of the patients.*

"I started here on a part-time basis and I felt so very rewarded that I am now full-time. I feel a tremendous sense of accomplishment at the end of the day. I feel that I have helped people and as a result I'm going to school at night. I'm going to be a speech pathologist. It's not related but it is helping people and that is important to me. . . .

"I know that if I did become pregnant I would have an abortion. I'm not married so I feel that I would do that. I would want to plan the time that I would want to have a family. Take each step at a time. I wouldn't want more than two children.

"I would try my best not to have a saline. You have a lot of time before you're sixteen weeks to find out whether you're pregnant or not. So I think I would be very careful about that.

"I have my own apartment and the landlord owns me and it's lovely. It's a lovely life living in the city.

"I see one fellow. I don't have a tremendous social life. I did when I was much younger. It seems that I am more selective now. My taste has changed considerably. It's kind of difficult right now. I guess my age has a lot to do with it. Being that there are very few single men in my age group. You come up against a lot of juicy situations. . . .

"I worked on passenger liners for four years and I've traveled and I've experienced a lot of things and now I feel that I would just like to settle down, but it is very difficult.

"I worked on three American ships and two Greek ships and I've met people from cooks to countesses and it was fascinating and I learned a lot—and I saw a lot.

"When I started on the ships my father hung up on the telephone when I broke the news. Both my parents and I are on totally different wavelengths. They thought Jewish girls don't do things like that. They get married and have their husbands take them across the ocean. They're very unhappy that I'm not married and taken care of. Really, they look at marriage as being taken care of, and I can take care of myself well I feel.

"I've observed the younger generation much more closely. I'm in more contact with them and they do have some very deep guilt feelings about abortion. They come in here with the preconceived notion that their life is in danger. Abortion still has some very old-fashioned connotations.

"Once I make it clear that their life is not in danger, they seem to relax a little bit. And their attitudes toward abortion is very good in respect that the kids who are going back to college, they got to get back to school. There's no question about it. They're not engaged, their boyfriend does not accompany them. They've got things to do in their life and a child doesn't have its place right now in their life and so there is really no qualms about that.

"I feel, though, that some of these girls are acting out certain problems. Their friends were here last month, they're here now and they're smiling about it. I feel that a lot of them are competing with each other. But it's very destructive. . . .

"Medically I think this hospital has a very good record. From what I can observe they are very very good. And I say an abortion doctor is a good doctor. He's a good person. Thank God there are doctors that can do these things.

"I guess my primary concern is the person that is living that is enjoying her life, but at this particular time is very troubled and cannot really have a child. And to go through a pregnancy, I even thought about this myself. Could I carry through a full term, have the child and then give it away. I don't think that is something that I could cope with well. I think that would hurt tremendously. More than the abortion.

"Of course all of it is very sad. You can't turn off those feelings if you're going through it. It's very sad and that's why I feel for these girls."

## Miss Teresa Etienne, Age 22

*Counselor*

"I went to an agency and I found this position. When they said 'hospital' I was ecstatic. I said, 'I'll learn something.' And I have. Some terminology and about people. I want to go into nursing now. I have applied to a few schools. I want to see if I can manage working and studies.

"I didn't know it was an abortion hospital. When I started working here I said, 'Gee, there are an awful lot of females here.' You know, I thought it was a women's hospital. They said, 'This is for abortions you know.' Well, I had heard that it was legal but when I saw it in full scale, I was really happy that now people could do something about unwanted pregnancies. Because I remember one of the girls in school threw herself out of the window because she was pregnant and the guy didn't want to marry her and everything. She didn't die, she just broke a whole bunch of bones. It wasn't anyone I knew really well. . . .

38

"I believe in God but I don't go to church because I don't believe in a lot of things that they have. I think it's all a bunch of malarkey, when they do one thing and say another. I just don't go, not even on Christmas.

"The only time I thought about abortions in terms of religion was when I saw fetuses and one was born alive. I saw one of them, in fact, I even felt the heart beat. I touched it. It looked like a baby, but it was very tiny. It was real cute. Very quiet. In fact, it was starting to die. The heart beat was getting very low. It was going to Bellevue Hospital and the guy was saying 'Oh, I don't see why we have to take it over there, because it's going to die anyway. Why go through all the trouble?' And the nurse, who was the supervisor that day, got really angry. She said, 'Well it still has life. You shouldn't take that attitude. There's a chance it could live.' She was all upset. She used to get very upset about them. It died by the time it got to Bellevue. One lasted two days. I think that was the most."


DR. D.: Did that upset you?

TE: No, because I've known people who have been adopted, and they really have crummy, messed up lives. They feel like killing themselves sometimes. Or, something like that. Also I used to know a girl, she was from a family of twelve, and like she always wore hand-me-downs. Like having a real miserable existence. And maybe they can do something for themselves when they grow up or maybe they can't. So why bring somebody into the world who is going to be so miserable. What you don't know doesn't hurt you.

"My parents were divorced when I was nine. My grandmother had me since I was four. My mother had a first husband who divorced her. Then about a year later, he died. But she was already living with my father. Then my father married my mother, after I was born, because they wouldn't, now dig this, baptize me in the church, because my parents weren't married. Which was another stupid thing I thought about the church.

"They got married and they figured, 'Well, for the kid, we'll stay together.' But they got divorced anyway. . . .

"I was married too. I married at eighteen and busted up at twenty. No soap. He wouldn't look for a job once he got back from Vietnam.

"Now I just see different people. At first I used to think, hmm, I wonder what's in all this sin business. But then I said, 'Oh, hell.' 'You believe in what's right for you,' the nuns said at school. So I guess it's right for me what I do. I love it. In fact, I had a termination here in '71, a few months after I started working here. Dr. Holtzman did it. I was six weeks pregnant. . . .

*After a while, talking with Teresa feels like traveling downward on a narrow, serpentine mountain road, built on the side of a precipice, in a conveyance whose brakes have failed. There is no way to tell what lies ahead.*

"I used to belong to a swingers' club, but I got sick and tired of it. Some people are interesting and some people are not. Sometimes there are four couples, sometimes twenty. It depends on the size of the house. Right now the one I left, it was a definite. Like about five couples that we all liked each other and we always went to the same house."

DR. D.: What do swingers do?

TE: They switch. All do it in the same room. Or in a different room if you wanted to be by yourself.

DR. D.: So how many men might you have intercourse with in one night?

TE: I can only take eleven.

DR. D.: Are you putting me on?

TE: No, honest. I've done that. But now I am sick of it.

"You know, it's weird. It turns some of the guys on to see

girls swinging together. But if one of the guys starts getting friendly with another guy, word spreads around like fire and they never invite him anywhere again."

DR. D.: Are any of the other counselors swingers?

TE: Not that I know of. But I am not that quick at spotting a swinger. Not like the regular old-timers can. It's weird.

———

Anticipated danger has a smell of its own. It is produced by sweat glands and tear ducts, and gas expelled in terror.

Here, on this second floor, it is compounded further. Here, each day a hundred urine samples, duly leaked into plastic containers and labeled with name and assigned number, go slowly stale on shelves and emanate gruesome fumes reminiscent of the helplessness of childhood. Each day the sweet and sticky smell of fresh blood lingers in the air as, at least one hundred times, syringes are emptied into vials for necessary reasons. From time to time, gripped by unmanageable and otherwise inexpressible revolt, someone vomits in the corridor on one of the yellow plastic chairs or in the middle of the vinyl-covered floor. Intermingled with this is the odor of cigarettes, of coffee, of wax-coating eroded by coffee, of a variety of colognes, perfumes, hair sprays, and deodorants, of unwashed private parts, and of excreta-coated gynecological gloves thrown into wastebaskets.

Lysol periodically sprayed into the air mixes with all this and also with the odor of surgical soap, of adhesive bandages, of toilet disinfectant, of roach killer, rat poison, and pea soup. The last drifts into the unit from the elevators that stop here, coming directly from the cafeteria.

Under these circumstances of stink, it is difficult to acknowledge the importance of abstract notions. I cannot think of abortion as right or wrong, good or evil, moral or murderous. Judging by the smell, it is merely a symptom of a painful and terminal disease, which is human consciousness.

# Chapter 2

## Saline Floor: Staff

> The ceremony of innocence is drowned. . . .
>
> W. B. Yeats

Stepping off the elevator on the seventh floor, I find myself in the saline unit. The fact that this is where I start my research appears to me purely accidental, although later I realize that it is not.

Earlier, in Rachel Stern's office, I am introduced to one of the social workers. The three of us discuss my project. I am excited, uneasy, and still intent on selling myself. I very much need the cooperation of both these women, and there is no obvious reason on earth why they should cooperate with me, except their free good will. As a consequence I feel a little awkward and off balance. I am having trouble knowing how much space my body should occupy.

As we speak, Rachel gives us somehow to understand that she and I are on a par while the social worker is "one down." I do not yet grasp the full meaning of this message, but it does make me uncomfortable, and I feel compelled under its weight to pretend that I am absent. I lapse into silence. Rachel talks. The social worker fidgets. Phones keep ringing, Rachel answers them between breaths in her lecture to us. She used to be assistant to the director, but he was removed and she is now acting head. She is reorganizing the hospital, building morale, eliminating the chaff, weeding out the unfit, making people wear their name tags, showing who is boss, returning this world of women to the hands of women at last. "Barry, you know [he is the past director], is like a child and very incompetent." I begin to suspect that she believes this of all men and most women, but I say nothing. I also wonder how many female doctors they have on staff, but I do not ask.

I watch the still fidgeting social worker instead, whom I will name Dora. She is a small, dark girl, mostly round black eyes and the rest of her is the circles under her eyes. She reminds me of various vaguely identified people in my childhood whom I think I liked.

At last the audience with Rachel is over. "Ladies," she says, "you must excuse me now." We are dismissed.

I collect my stuff and follow Dora into the corridor. She asks me where I am headed, and I explain that I don't have the vaguest notion how to start this first day of actually talking with patients. Although for the past week Rachel has been introducing me to the key nurses on every floor, and I have hung around and met many of the doctors and other personnel, I have not yet been on my own at all, nor have I spoken with patients.

I feel myself enormously shy at the prospect of walking into a patient's room and asking her intimate questions. Dora says, "But you are a psychoanalyst." And that is true, of course, and it is part of the problem. As an analyst I do not approach patients, they approach me. I do not talk with them for my benefit, but for theirs. I do not just listen; I listen and become anchor and catalyst. In that context I am not a reporter, I am a doctor. I do not simply observe, I also participate. I ask intimate questions of my patients to enable me to contribute to their welfare. What will I contribute to these women?

All this feels too obscure and complicated to share with Dora, so I say instead, "Yes, that is true," and I ask her where she is going. "To the saline floor," she says. "Any particular reason?" "Not really. Both Suzy and I find—that's the other social worker—that if we don't have anyone specific to see, we just naturally go to the saline floor. There is always someone who needs us there. Also it's the floor where everything happens. I mean, you never know what will happen. And Szenes is up there too." "Who is that?" "Oh, he is one of the saline doctors. He is Hungarian. Wait till you get a load of him." "What do you mean?" "You'll see." "Can I go with you, then?" "Sure, come along."

We take the elevator, but by the time we reach the seventh floor, Dora has had a small change of heart. In the confines of this world, I am the novice, a bit disoriented, a little tongue-tied still. Beyond this world, I might be Dora's teacher or supervisor. She might pay to attend one of my lectures or write me for a reprint of one of my articles. She must have become aware of this during the ascent of the elevator, because as we get out she says, "Come to think of it, I do have to see someone in 702. Why don't I just meet you back here at the nurses' station in half an hour." She evidently does not want me to see her work. I can understand that very well. It hasn't been that many years ago that I would have hated a supervisor-type to sit in on one of my sessions. I say "Okay," and I am on my own.

The building has three adjacent elevators, and consequently each floor has three adjacent elevator doors. I am standing with my back to them, in front of the middle door, which has a little printed plastic sign stuck into the ledge of its glass and wiremesh window, bearing the legend "Stretchers and Staff Only." The sign is superfluous, no one observes its rule.

Directly in front of me the corridor opens through a doorless archway into the nurses' station. It is a small room about nine feet by five, with a little window that overlooks the housetops of New York. Two metal desks, pushed together to make one, run the length of the left-hand side of the room. Above these desks there are some bulletin boards with pamphlets and instructions stuck on them. In front of the desks stand two swivel chairs, on which the doctors and nurses sit to make notes in the charts and do other clerical business. In

45

front of the window there is a patients' chart stand. On the wall opposite the desks (on the right-hand side of the room and behind the chairs) there is a large blackboard. Long, white-chalk lines divide the board lengthwise into nine sections. On top of each section there is brown tape on which the title of each section is written. I suppose they write them on tape so that when the rest of the board is erased, the titles will remain.

I move closer to the archway so that I can read the board, but a nurse intercepts me. She is not someone I have met.

"Can I help you?" she asks. "What is your room number?" She does not sound helpful at all. In fact, beneath the words, the question is a slap. It means, "What the hell are you doing here—how dare you wander about—get out of my sight—salute when you see me," and the Lord knows what else.

I get angry. It is true that I am new here, but I am not new to nurses. I draw myself up to my full height, which still makes me half a head shorter than she is, and say in my most reproving tone: "No, thank you, nurse. I am just looking at the board. I am Dr. Denes." As I say this, I put the words "nurse" and "doctor" in italics. It works, of course. She becomes apologetic and anxious to accommodate. She does not check me out at all. The title of "doctor" works its magic by itself. I feel a kind of childish glee, followed by remorse. Floor nurses are the drill sergeants of hospital life. They are like mistreated older children who, for injuries received from cruel parents, vent their rage on younger siblings, of whom they have been put in charge.

Now unimpeded, I examine the board. The headings read:

| ROOM | PT'S NAME | AGE | SIZE WKS. | INDUCTION I. A. |
|------|-----------|-----|-----------|-----------------|

| OXYTOCIN | LABOR | DELIVERY FETUS | PLACENTA | REMARKS: |
|----------|-------|----------------|----------|----------|

Entries are made in white chalk except for the markings under "Oxytocin" and "Remarks," which are written, for quick visibility, in yellow. Also, I learn later, whatever pertains to blood is always written in red. This applies to both hemorrhages and transfusions. Today, there is one entry under "Oxytocin," next to the name of a fifteen-year-old, twenty-three weeks pregnant, who, as I see from the date written under "Induction," has been here for three days. Oxytocin is a drug that speeds up uterine contractions. Under "Remarks" there are three yellow entries: "Allergic Penicillin," for a seventeen-year-old; "Rhogam," for a twenty-five-year-old; and "Refused Rhogam," for the oldest patient on the board, a woman of thirty-two. Rhogam is administered to patients with Rh-negative problems to prevent possible complications in future pregnancies. There is an extra charge for it. Nothing on the board is red.

Altogether there are eighteen patients listed. Full house for the floor. Three are fifteen years old; one, sixteen; seven, seventeen; two, eighteen; one, twenty-one; one, twenty-five; two, twenty-seven; and one, thirty-two. Their periods of gestation range from sixteen to twenty-three weeks. As I noticed earlier, the one twenty-three weeks pregnant is fifteen years old.

I know that this is a shocking piece of information, but I have difficulty making sense of it. Fifteen, that's being a freshman in high school, I guess. I used to invent stories of having been kissed. But I was a fat foreigner with no opportunities. And twenty-three weeks, what does that mean? I think both my boys were kicking by then. The first time Gregory kicked I was in session, sitting across from a woman patient a few years older than I, unmarried, childless, envious of me. Professionalism be damned, it was my love for her that kept me from jumping up and shouting for joy: "It's alive, it's alive. It knows Morse." When the session ended, I telephoned my husband and everybody else who might care. Was that at twenty-three weeks? I begin to have the uneasy feeling that perhaps this research will require something of me I have not yet anticipated.

Leaving the nurses' station, I sit down at a desk placed in the corridor, just outside the station's archway, about four feet across from the elevator doors. I am waiting for Dora. The desk at which I sit is small and made of metal. On top of it there is an old beaten-up *Physician's Desk Reference*, a box of tissues, and a life-size, hard plastic model of a uterus and vagina, manufactured by a pharmaceutical company for the purpose of advertising its product. The vaginal part of the model is transparent plastic, the uterus is pink. When I pick the model up to take a closer look, I notice that inserted between the uterus and the vagina there is a real rubber diaphragm. I take it out and put it back a couple of times. It works. Just above the desk there hang two stethoscopes, and to the left of the desk, toward the center of the corridor, somewhat underfoot, stands a machine to measure blood pressure. As patients get admitted to the floor, this is where they stop first, to have their blood pressures and temperatures taken.

The thermometers in this hospital are fantastic. I saw one several days ago in the hands of a nurse. Watching it work, I kept laughing, and the nurse, a large, black, bespectacled older woman, with many fine wrinkles, laughed with me, despite herself. She said I was wacky. She said most psych-doctors are wacky. The thermometer consists of a disposable mouthpiece attached through an electric cord to a little box, the size of a small portable radio. On the box there is a window behind which tiny lights run around shaping different numbers. The lights are very fast, and they look like luminous children playing tag. Suddenly they stop, and there it is: "Your fever, madam," presented in lights on a miniature Broadway marquee. The incongruity between the function of this machine and its toy-like appearance cheers me enormously. After all, paradox is still the best reminder that we are human.

I am tired of waiting. I gather my paraphernalia—bag, briefcase, and tape recorder—and start down toward the north end of the corridor. On my way I notice a service kitchen with the door ajar and a sign on it that says "Staff." There are several nurses sitting inside drinking coffee and smoking cigarettes. They watch me pass.

Straight ahead of me, about six feet away, I see the television room. The regular door is open, but the slatted, swinging half-doors, common to old hospital rooms and Western saloon entrances, are closed. Below the doors I can see a pair of bare legs in pink fur-like booties; another pair of bare legs in green wedgies; and farthest from the door, the bottom part of a wine-colored paisley robe. As I come closer the legs disappear from view and I can hear the television going. The seventh floor is the only one that has a television room. They need it here, because it is in this room that the girls wait, together, to be ushered by the nurse, one by one, into the treatment room for induction.

I knock and enter without waiting for an answer. Four faces look up at me. I had missed a pair of propped up legs. "Hi," I say. "I am Doctor Denes, I am here to. . . ." I am stuck. These are very pregnant children. My shock is unclassifiable. It is not moral indignation, not compassion, not identification, not horror, not anything I can name. It is an organismic response of paralysis. As if by a blow in the solar plexus, the wind has been knocked out of me. Abortions in my mind happen to grown-ups who are unwillingly pregnant but don't look it. These are little girls far gone with child. "I am here to. . . ." Quick, Denes, quick! ". . . to sit down for a while." "Oh," one of them says. "Okay," says another, and they all turn their heads back toward the set which stands in front of the window. I sit down and force myself to look around. It is a small shabby room made shabbier, and at the same time more friendly, by the strong Indian-summer sun streaming in. As the rays hit the gently peeling wall, they form a golden avenue in the air, connecting at a slant wall and window. Within the avenue, gleaming dust particles shimmer in motion and collide with each other from time to time. I am filled with immense sadness at the familiar sight of this illusory celestial road. Times long past, of stuffy schoolrooms, solitary games, narrow hiding places,

come to mind, and the desolate yearning for one lost friend.
I look on.

The furniture in this room consists primarily of chairs.
They are of molded plastic with metal legs. There are two
green armchairs and eight yellow armless ones. They stand,
wedged tightly against one another, in a semicircle, around the
television set. In one corner, outside the circle, there is a metal
filing cabinet with a broken padlock on it. In the center of the
circle stands an ashtray filled to the brim with butts. Scotch-
taped to the wall and lit by the sun, there is a large map of New
York City and Counties of.

I gradually shift my eyes to the girl sitting nearest to me. She
is the one with pink fur-like booties. She must be one of the
fifteen-year-olds, although she appears much younger. She sits
totally absorbed in the show, the title of which is "Hospital."
Her lips are slightly parted, and in the left corner of her mouth
there is a small bubble of saliva. Her hands, folded, rest on her
large belly, in the age-old posture of pregnant women. From
close up, her legs are thin, vulnerable, little-girl legs, covered
with long blond transparent hair.

Suddenly I have had enough. I don't want to talk to anybody, or see anybody, or stay around here anymore. I gather
myself together, say goodbye, and rush to the nurses' station.
My adversary sits inside. She smiles. I tell her that I want to
leave a message for Dora, but it turns out that she has left one
for me. It is a short note, saying that she is sorry she missed
me but she had to take a patient for a sonogram. Just as well,
because I am going to my office, where I know what to think
of what problem. In my haste I neglect even my ritual clock-
out from Rachel.

The following day I am back on the saline floor. I stay for
many weeks, day after day, to the exclusion of other floors
and other patients. I am drawn to the unit, irresistibly,
by my reactions of disbelief, sorrow, horror, compassion,
guilt. The place depresses me, yet I hang around after working hours. When I leave, I behave outside with the expan-
siveness of one who has just escaped a disaster. I have bad
dreams. My sense of complicity in something nameless grows

and festers. I consider giving up the research, but it is unthinkable to not return to the saline floor without knowing more.

One time I describe my feelings to Suzy and Dora over lunch. The cafeteria is filled with the steady hum of casual voices and the stink of institutional fish. It is Friday. I see on the food line Mr. Smith, the chief operating room nurse. He is in his scrub-clothes. He waves. His black arm looks moist against the green of his gown. The scene is too ordinary for what I am saying. I become uncomfortable.

Dora says, "As time goes on you will feel worse. I am a little surprised that you feel this bad so soon." I look at her quickly to see if she is making fun of me, but she appears completely serious. Suzy, who has a slow drawl and whose voice is a melodious instrument with a crack in it (I like very much to listen to her when I am not in a hurry, as I am not, now), says, "I am having difficulty with my feelings about late abortions also. More and more, I don't even know anymore if I believe in it. There is just so much pain." She has worked here for two years.

After lunch, we run into Rachel at the elevators. She tells me that Dr. Szenes has returned from vacation and I must come along to meet him. As we enter the elevator there are three nurses inside. Rachel glares at one woman's chest a little to the left and above the region of her heart. "I see a little something missing from there, dear," she says to her. The nurse's left hand shoots up to the area, and without looking she fumbles like a blind woman to locate her name tag through touch. "Sorry Ms. Stern. I guess I forgot it this morning." "I don't know how you can forget a thing like that. Please, ladies, I said so in my memo, you must wear your tags." "Yes Ms. Stern." The nurses are black. All three have that disconcerting black talent of emanating cold rage without moving a muscle or altering a breath. I frantically search for some gesture of fellowship that they might accept from me, but it is hopeless. There is no way I can declare myself on their side without being taken for a condescending, patronizing fool. They get out on

51

the fourth floor and Rachel calls after them, "Have a good day, and don't forget the tags."

We hear Suzy being paged. The elevator man drops back to the fourth floor to let her out. Dora says, "Eight please." That's where the social workers' office is located. It is a tiny cubicle where linen used to be kept before the hospital became converted for abortions only. I do my interviews with relatives in that room whenever I can. The eighth floor stands as an oasis of laboratories, housekeeping, house physician's room, and social worker's office, between the saline unit below and surgery above. I think Dora is going there to recover from the elevator ride. Rachel and I get out on seven.

Things are evidently in progress here. I can hear loud talk from the television room—many voices, high and thin with anxiety. A girl is having her blood pressure measured, sitting on the chair in front of the desk in the corridor. Another girl, who looks ill and who is for some reason barefoot, is being escorted by a nurse down the hall toward her room. The loudspeaker calls for Ms. Stern. Rachel dashes off to the nurses' station to answer the call, and I proceed toward the treatment room. As I turn the corner Betsy intercepts me. "Hi," she says. "Come on, come on, meet Szenes."

Betsy works in research. She is tall, blond, shy, wasp, and very bright. She appears to be suspended permanently from the slackened strings of a puppeteer. Each time I meet her I am surprised to find her at this hospital. Her best friend here is Edie, also in research. Edie is short, dark, cute, Jewish, and talkative. I see her standing outside the treatment room talking with a waiting patient. As we reach them, Rachel catches up with us. We all exchange greetings. Edie is trying to buck up the frightened waiting girl. "It only hurts for a little while," she says. Rachel glares at her. The rest of us laugh, including the patient.

Szenes emerges from the treatment room. He is a young man of medium height in a white doctor's coat, with a well-groomed, moderate-sized Afro. Pretty tricky hairdo for a Hungarian. Rachel says, "Dr. Denes, Dr. Szenes." We shake hands. Szenes says, "You must be Hungarian." I smile. Rachel, Betsy, and Edie watch us; the girl, half dead with fear, watches only Szenes. Rachel launches into her usual introduction of me: "Dr. Denes is here to do research. She will interview blah, blah. . . ." Szenes says, "An excellent idea." I realize something is expected of me, but I am not at all clear what it is. Rachel becomes kittenish, so do Betsy and Edie. They fawn on Szenes, who loves it and encourages it by pretending to be indifferent. "Shall I bring you coffee, John?" "You weren't at the meeting, John, naughty, naughty." "I bet you lost at bridge again." The women all talk at once while Szenes remains silent.

It dawns on me why "meet Szenes" has been such an item. This is an ongoing competition among the women, with winner take naught. I decide to win. I ask him in Hungarian, "Where did you go to school? To high school, I mean." Szenes smiles. I have exchanged the playing board for one where the starter always wins. Unless one wants to kick the whole table over, which he has no reason to do. It is an old émigré game, and he obviously recognizes it. The next question will be "On what street did you live?" and then, "What did your father do?" The object of the game is to fix the other in the context of the past. The quality of the pedigree one can produce is, by and large, irrelevant. What matters is that one has to once again justify one's life in terms of dead history. The rules do not permit immediate counter questions, thus providing one hundred extra points for whoever moves first. Szenes is clearly uncomfortable and enjoys it hugely. In this, he is very Hungarian.

I look at our audience and chalk one up for being multilingual. In mock petulance Edie mutters to Betsy, "There must be something to this business of being Hungarian." Szenes and I laugh, ridiculously pleased. Still speaking to me, he says in English, "I have to get back to work, do you want to watch?" "Very much, thank you." "Stand here, then," he says, opening the swinging door and pointing me to a strategic corner where

I can see but will not be in his way. To the girl he says, "Come in, young lady, I am Dr. Szenes. This is Dr. Denes, she'll be with us for the duration. Okay?" The girl nods, yes. He guides her to the treatment table and hands her over to the nurse who has been silently waiting. The nurse helps the girl onto the table and makes her lie down. She lifts the girl's white hospital gown to her waist and covers her thighs and genitals with a sterile disposable towelette, leaving her round protruding belly exposed. With a small gauze pad she washes the area with alcohol. Meanwhile, Dr. Szenes scrubs his hands at a tiny sink in the corner opposite to mine. "What is your name, young lady?" he asks. "Flo. Florence Sullivan." "Sullivan. Irish, eh? And how old are you?" "Well, my father was Irish. Sixteen and a half." "That's pretty young, to be going through this. When was your last period?" "June or July." "Which?" "June, I guess." "That makes you twenty-two weeks pregnant. Right?" "That's what I was told." The conversation goes on, partly to gather information, partly I suppose to reassure the girl, who looks terrified.

When he is through scrubbing, Szenes stands in front of the nurse, who holds open first a left, then a right sterile rubber glove so that the doctor can slip his hands into them. "Now this whole thing should not hurt you," he says, again addressing the girl. "It will be uncomfortable, but it should not hurt." The nurse hands Dr. Szenes a syringe. He expels a little liquid into the air, then injects Flo, near her belly button, just under the skin, holding the syringe parallel to the girl's abdomen. About two seconds later without removing the needle he jerks the syringe upward to make the needle plunge straight down into the abdominal cavity. At this point the needle is invisible and the syringe is completely vertical in the doctor's hands. The injected liquid is 5 cc's of Novocain. Flo winces and her eyes well up, but she remains silent. Szenes smiles at her. "That was the worst part, the rest is apple pie."

The nurse sprays the area with iodine solution, tinting Flo's skin the color of brown mustard. She takes the syringe from the doctor and hands him a needle. It looks enormous. He holds it up to show me. "It is an eighteen-gauge, three-and-a-half-inch long spinal needle. We use this to tap the fetal sac. It works very well." Turning back to the patient he places the needle on the exact spot of the injection and pushes it in to the hilt in one firm fluid motion resembling the choreographed movement of a dancer. Now that the horsing around is over, Szenes's first-rate professional competence is unmistakable. There is no reaction from Florence. The needle ends in a pink hub about half an inch long. Holding on to it, Szenes removes the stylet to permit the free flow of amniotic fluid. As he lifts the stylet, I see a little squirt of yellowish liquid shoot up through the pink hub. Szenes says: "That's good. We're doing very well." The nurse hands him a short, thin rubber tube, one end of which he attaches to the needle hub. To the other end of the tube he connects a large syringe. Holding it steady, he slowly pulls the plunger outward, filling the syringe with a thin liquid the color and consistency of urine. He is suctioning out the amniotic fluid. When the syringe is filled he disconnects it from the rubber tube and squirts the liquid into the corner sink. The process is repeated three times—amounting altogether to one hundred and fifty cc's of amniotic fluid removed from Flo's belly.

"How do you feel, young lady?" "Fine." Flo's voice is barely audible. Her hands are clutched on her chest, and she is very pale. "Excellent, because we are almost finished. I am going to hook you up now to the saline to replace the fluid we took out. While that's going on, you'll have to tell me whether you feel anything unusual. Like if your face gets flushed or if you suddenly feel numb or very thirsty. Things like that, okay?" Flo nods. "Talking doesn't interfere with this process, you know." The intent is to console, the result is disaster. Flo breaks into racking, body-shaking sobs. Her belly heaves up and down causing the rubber tube to flop about. "Stop it," says Szenes, his voice rising. "Stop it at once, you will dislodge the needle." The nurse, who until now has not uttered a sound, puts her hand on

Flo's forehead and says, "Come on, dear, it is almost over." Flo grabs a corner of her folded-up white gown, stuffs it into her mouth and bites down on it. She looks like a broken-hearted three-year-old. For the first time since I have entered the room the context of the scene reasserts itself in my mind. Riveted, I have been watching on the level of pure performance something I have not seen before. Szenes, the nurse, even Flo, have been actors in a dramatic medical procedure, for me to observe and learn first hand. But the sobbing? The hand on the forehead? The rising inflection laden with concern of potential danger? This is no instructional demonstration, and the withdrawn liquid is no urine. It is fluid essential to the life of the child whose heart is beating in the belly of this other child. This other child who lies here, terrified, heartbroken, tormented, sucking on her shirt.

Next to the treatment table there is an intravenous stand about ten feet tall with an inverted bottle hanging from each side of its crossbar. One of the bottles has a long rubber tube attached to it. Szenes removes the short tubing from the hub of the needle in Flo's belly and connects it to the long tube leading from the bottle. The bottle contains hypertonic saline solution. He checks that the flow is steady by lowering and raising the bottle a couple of times, before replacing it on the crossbar of the stand. "I want about two thousand," he says to the nurse. It is evidently her duty now to keep an eye on the amount and the evenness of the flow.

Szenes sits down at a small desk in my corner to make notes in the charts. "Look here," he says to me, pointing to a number that exceeds nine thousand. "What is it?" "The patient's number." "You mean you have done this many?" "Well, not I, the five of us. Four, really, because Dr. Marcus joined us only a couple of hundred ago. I'd say it's about two thousand apiece, give or take a few."

The words of a pamphlet I had picked up weeks ago come back: "As a result of the concentrated solution of saline in the uterus the fetus will not survive more than a few hours after

56

the injection." There is no way then to assert, except by pretense, that what is being salinated in its mother's womb is not alive or not human. There is no way to say that this is not a type of murder. And yet, there is no way to say that it would not be just as surely murder, more cold and vengeful, to force little Flo to give birth to her bastard.

This is no floor for self-assurance. No floor to feel good about anything.

"Okay," says Dr. Szenes, getting up and checking the bottle. "I think we can remove this now." He disconnects the bottle, retracts the needle, and the nurse puts an adhesive strip on the tiny puncture site. "Do you feel all right?" Flo nods. "You can go back to your room now. Lie down for a half-hour. Then drink two glasses of water. After that, you can walk around. Watch TV. Make phone calls, whatever you want to do. When dinner comes you must eat it all whether you like it or not. All of it. After dinner you are to stay in bed. The house doctor will come to your room and put an intravenous needle in your arm. Once that's done you may not move at all, nor eat or drink anything. The IV contains glucose to nourish you and a medicine called Pitocin to stimulate labor. If the cramps get bad you can ask the nurse for some Demerol, a pain killer. You must ask for it if you want it, because the nurses can't tell when your pains get really bad. Don't believe anyone who says it retards labor. It does nothing of the sort. With any luck, you should be all done twenty-four hours after the IV is inserted. Any questions?" Flo has climbed off the table and is adjusting her gown in the back, where it is open, in preparation for leaving. She says, "No." "Fine. Good day, young lady." Flo leaves, and Szenes sticks his head out the door: "Next please."

I look at my watch. Fifteen minutes have passed since I entered the room. I am drenched in sweat. I have a bellyache. I gather my stuff together. "Oh, you are leaving?" "Yes. I think so. Thank you very much. And I'd like to come back later if I may." "Any time, a pleasure." I walk out as I hear him begin to explain the procedure to the new girl in the room, who is black, whose name is Joan, and whose age is thirteen.

I do not get to see Flo deliver. In fact, I do not see anyone deliver for a very long time.

Once the IV is inserted the patients are confined to bed, and they deliver there, anywhere from twenty-four to thirty-six hours later. The precise moment is unpredictable. The process is exactly like giving birth to a child: cramps, water-break, fetus, placenta, end. Although I frequently hear screams from this room and that, I am somehow never in the right room at the right time. "Did your water break?" "Yes." "Then you'll deliver very soon." "Within the hour, I was told." "Oh, my God, it's ten to four, I have to be in my office at four o'clock. Goodbye. Good luck." I never invent my excuses, they just come up. Repeatedly.

I decide to put an end to my stalling and spend an uninterrupted afternoon on the floor. Nothing happens, not even screaming. Toward evening I turn in desperation to one of the nurses. "Isn't anybody going to give birth today?" Before she can open her mouth, her face tells me that I have spat in the soup. "Doctor, that is not what happens here." "I am sorry, I mean deliver a baby, I mean fetus. To hell with it, nurse, I am going home. Good night."

The next afternoon I return determined, regardless of where I am at the time of delivery, to look inside the buckets.

Two doors down from the nurses' station there is a little room with several large garbage cans, each neatly marked for different types of garbage, and a medium-sized table on top of which stand paper buckets—the type in which one buys fried chicken from take-home stores. The buckets are covered with their paper lids. Attached to each lid there is a white cardboard label bearing—printed in ink—the mother's name, the doctor's name, the time of delivery, the sex of the item, the time of gestation. Inside each bucket, I have been told, there is a fetus and its placenta stored in formaldehyde. At the end of the day the buckets are transferred to the laboratory where the contents are examined for abnormalities. That done, they are collected in a large plastic bag, and a special messenger takes them to a sister hospital in possession of an incinerator. There they are burned.

I ask the nurse on duty for some rubber gloves. "What size?" she asks. I am unaware that they come in sizes. Somehow I always thought that they were one-size-fits-all stretch. I hold up my left hand to show her its size. She misunderstands the gesture and says astonished: "You want size five gloves?" "No, I mean six," I answer, faking it. "I have only six and a halves." "That's fine, thank you." I have learned that with nurses I must disguise my ignorance of medical matters, otherwise they become suspicious of my right to do whatever I am doing and they put obstacles in my way.

I go into the little room, place my stuff on the floor next to the garbage cans, and pull on the gloves. Their fit is remarkable. My hands feel completely protected without any noticeable loss of agility. I enjoy very much having them on. I touch several objects at random—my pencil, the curving outside of a bucket, the edge of the table, the handle of my briefcase, my nose—and I am delighted with the experience of false contact. My hands can gather accurate information without being in the slightest way exposed. I can touch anything, I think, and feel what it is, and yet it can not touch me. A paradise of one-sidedness. I have a vague sense that there is some kind of parable hidden in the experience, but I cannot arrive at it in words. Besides, I am also a little ashamed that I can stand in this garbage-can-filled graveyard, playing with gloves.

Planting myself in front of the table, balanced, legs slightly apart, I remove with one hand the lid of a bucket. The sharp fumes of formaldehyde instantly hurt the insides of my nose and throat. The smell also brings with it the long-forgotten memory of fetal pigs. The association strikes me as unseemly; nevertheless I remember, with unwanted total recall, the misery of my sophomore year in college, when in Bio. 1., every Wednesday from three to five, for six months, we dissected the fetal pig. On the first day of class the instructor brought in a huge container filled with formaldehyde and floating pigs. He fished out one pig for each student, tagged with the student's last name, giving the impression that the pig was a lost, finally returned relative, in regrettable shape. My English at the time was very poor so that it took me weeks to catch on why the pigs were so small. I thought "fetal" was a brand name like "Jersey" for cows. When I did catch on, I cut classes for a month. That entire semester I would at odd and inconvenient moments think that I could smell the burning odor of mildly decomposed flesh stored in acid.

I look inside the bucket in front of me. There is a small naked person in there floating in a bloody liquid—plainly the tragic victim of a drowning accident. But then perhaps this was no accident, because the body is purple with bruises and the face has the agonized tautness of one forced to die too soon. Death overtakes me in a rush of madness. Oh yes, I have seen this before. The face of a Russian soldier lying on a frozen snow-covered hill, stiff with death and cold—on one hand an erect, bloody stump, where someone has cut off his ring finger to get at his wedding band. Oh yes, I have seen this face before, on humans and on a castrated horse, left lying in its blood across some uprooted streetcar tracks by someone demented with hunger who thought he had found food. Oh yes, I am no stranger here—I have seen brains spilled on sidewalks and hearts crushed forever with one blow. Who says you can't go home again? A death factory is the same anywhere, and the agony of early death is the same anywhere.

I take the lid off all the buckets. All of them. I reach up to the shelf above this bucket graveyard tabletop and take down a pair of forceps. With them I pull aside in each bucket the placenta, which looks like a cancerous mushroom shrouding the fetus. With the forceps I lift the fetuses, one by one. I lift them by an arm or a leg, leaving, as I return them again, an additional bruise on their purple, wrinkled, acid-soaked flesh. I have evidently gone mad. I carry on the examination, whose sole purpose by now is to increase the unbearable anguish in my heart. Finally, I lift a very large fetus whose position is such that, rather than its face, I first see its swollen testicles and abnormally large stiff penis. I look at the label. Mother's name: Catherine Atkins; doctor's name: Saul Marcus; sex of item: male; time of gestation: twenty-four weeks. I remember Catherine. She is seventeen, a very pretty blond girl. Not very bright. This is Master Atkins —to be burned tomorrow—who died like a hero to save his mother's life. Might he have become someday the only one to truly love her? The only one to mourn her death?

"Nurse, nurse," I shout, taking off my fancy gloves. "Cover them up."

———

# Charles Bender, M.D., Age 37

*I meet Dr. Bender for the first time on the OR (operating room) floor in the director's office, where the doctors hang around to drink coffee and smoke cigarettes, while they wait for the patients to be brought onto the floor for surgery. The meeting happens early in my work when I am still being introduced to everyone by Rachel. There are three men in the room as we enter. Dr. Bender, Mr. Smith, the chief operating room nurse, and Dr. Davis, one of the anesthesiologists. Rachel starts right in: "This is Dr. Denes, who. . . ." I shake hands with each of them. We discuss my project. Everyone thinks it's a good idea until Davis notices the tape recorder hanging from my shoulder. "I will not talk into that," he says. He is a bald, roly-poly man with an air of total absence. It's as if he were a body with no one inside. "It's not on," I say, "and of course participation is purely voluntary." "I will not talk into that," he says again. I wish he would shut up or drop dead, because I know that this kind of fear is contagious, and I am worried about the others. Dr. Bender rescues me. "Well, I will," he says. "You can interview me anytime you catch me free." I do not know it yet, but I have just met the essence of Charlie Bender.*

*He is a dark, slight, young-looking man with tremendous intensity, who would be quite handsome if he were at all sexual, which he very definitely is not. Charlie is earnest. He is serious. He is passionately committed to being nice, and it costs him his manhood.*

"There was very little personal choice in my becoming a physician. My father was a physician in the very classic sense of the word. He recently died. Someone not long ago in a lecture defined the classic physician as a man who has attained Christ-like posture. My father was Christ. And it is not easy being the son of Christ. I think it was a matter of upbringing where I was always expected to become a physician. Actually, I don't enjoy being put in the role of the savior. I enjoy the patient that I can relate to as a human being. . . .

"I have very specific feelings about medicine. I mean the definition of medicine in most classic terms is the art and science of diagnosing, of dealing with, and alleviating and curing disease,' and I find that neither to be an art nor a science. I think in the true practice of medicine we are not scientists. A scientist is in a laboratory somewhere. The practice of medicine is a very technical craft, and it's not an art either. The art of medicine, to me, is dealing with a human being who may happen to have a disease. Or a sick organ. But this is within a human being, and that's the way I practice medicine. . . .

"I guess we started the unit about two years ago, in February of '71. Sam and I had been working at the other hospital doing suctions, and salines were not being done. It was a question of what happens to patients above the size when people could do suctions on them. We suggested a saline unit. And the owners of the hospital agreed against the feelings of the people doing D & C's. We've had antagonism from them ever since. It becomes rampant at times. Because we are doing something that they can't, number one, and we are making more money than they are, number two. . . .

"Initially, there were two kinds of patients that I aborted. The patients I had always had in practice who needed an abortion and I was unable to do it prior to the abortion law. Although I knew there were physicians doing abortions in New York. Bringing patients into the hospitals with phony histories of bleeding and so on and so forth. As a resident I was well aware of who was doing quote, illegal abortions. It was not something that I would do, but I would go through all of the heartache with my own private patients, how we were going to refer them to Cuba originally, to England, and to Miami, when the Cuban abortionists came from Cuba.

"So that when the abortion law was passed it was those

patients that I felt relieved that now I could extend my medical care to. To complete what I had always felt was an unnecessary restriction.

"That was a very gratifying thing and a very easy thing for me, to extend my medical care that I had been providing prior to that. Okay, then with the availability of the abortion law initially what happened was the many friends that I had, practicing medicine throughout the United States, began to contact me. Some people with very big gynecologic and obstetric practices in Florida, in Detroit, in Chicago, and so on. To refer patients to me for an abortion. Their patients. I then ran into psychological difficulties of my own. Okay, here was a patient who didn't know me, I was not extending my medical care, I wasn't their physician, they didn't have a relationship with me. All they knew, in my mind, was that the patient was coming to New York to an abortionist. Vis-à-vis them I was an abortionist. That bothered me."

DR. D.: And what's an abortionist?

DR. B: Well, I guess an abortionist is somebody who ends a pregnancy, who does something that I must have some very basic feelings about. *(Laugh.)*

"My feelings about doing abortions were very significant and it was a long period of time for me to work it out. I dare say any thinking sensitive individual can't not realize that he is ending life or potential life, you know. I certainly don't enjoy that. I have no conscious conflict over killing a fetus. There's certainly nothing enjoyable in the act, except providing a necessary something to a person to make their life or burden happier, or easier, or whatever. But there's got to be more to it. I don't enjoy, that's a bad word, I don't relish *(long pause)* delivering the fetus. Now I think the nurses have a harder job than we have. They are the ones who see the fetus. I don't see a fetus—maybe once a week, one—so that there's a separation of the final product and what I do. When it comes out, I don't want to cry, and I don't feel great remorse over this lack of life. It's not pleasant to me by any means. But I don't know if it is to anybody. . . .

64

"In my marriage we have some problems which we're conscious of but we are working at it. But I basically think yes, it's a good marriage. She's an interior designer and does freelance work.

"I've never had an extramarital relation. I've had temptations and I've had opportunities, and on one or two occasions I have toyed with the idea, but I have elected not to. I mean not even a casual sexual relationship. There were two occasions that I remember well, that I could have and thought of it, and it would not have been any long-term thing. I'm not looking for another definitive relationship. If I was, I would terminate my pregnancy *(big laugh)*—I mean marriage, and proceed. It would only have been a sexual relationship. I think one of the significant reasons for not doing it would be that my wife then would also have the right to do that, and I really would not want her to. I'm not secure enough to feel that my wife has the right to have an extramarital relationship. . . .

"I've had this come up in my practice and I've spoken to girls, I mean women, about it, and I don't feel that any girl goes into Maxwell's Plum just because she wants to have sexual relations. She's going in there because she's seeking a relationship. We are not that liberated. The relationship is being sought, I feel, sadly, through a sexual contact. I think this has to reduce one's self-image, one's self-respect. It takes, I feel, a significant and meaningful aspect of one's life out of context. I think we're certainly living in a time of decreased human respect, of decreased human relationships, and of decreased sensitivity to killing off things.

*The preceeding sentence is uttered by Charlie without a trace of self-consciousness and without the least awareness of its intrapsychic implications. "Decreased sensitivity to killing off things," he says, referring to other people and to the spirit of the times. Not referring at all, as far as he knows, to his earlier statement: "I have no conscious conflict over killing a fetus."*

65

"If you lose that importance or significance in sex, you just in another way erode another means of humanistic response and we've lost enough."

## John Szenes, M.D., Age 36

*Dr. John Szenes has Hungarian charm. He is the sexpot of the saline floor and his accent seems to enthrall all the ladies.*

"I think abortion should be integrated into one's obstetric or gynecological work more closely. I agree that abortion patients should be segregated from patients having babies, as far as the physical facilities are concerned, but it doesn't have to be twenty blocks away. It can be one floor versus the other in the same institution. That would be considered ideal by me. This totally separate institution is, I think, overdoing it. But these are the realities of New York practice. That you have to separate it, because most of the large hospitals still don't consider abortion as something that has to be integrated into their programs. Most figures, European and even evolving figures in municipal-type hospitals in this country, seem to suggest that it will probably level off someplace at one abortion for each term delivery. This has been so for a number of years in Europe. And it's getting so even here. Now I don't know any first-class institution where the ratio is anywhere near that. The term-live births far outweigh the abortions performed, I mean by an unrealistic ratio. This is why clinics and specialized hospitals like this have to be in existence. . . .

"I think that every woman should be given the right to determine whether she wants to be pregnant or not. And if she doesn't want to be, and it's not two days before term, but at a reasonable time before the fetus becomes viable, she should be able to go to any gynecologist, whom she would go to for a Pap smear, or for a discharge, or whatever, and that gynecologist should *not* sit back and say 'Now let's see what are your reasons for having this abortion.' I don't think that should be *our* decision.

"With somebody who wants to have a child, you should do your utmost to help bring that direction. And with the one who doesn't want it, you should do your utmost to help her out of that situation.

"You have to become a bit schizophrenic. In one room you encourage the patient that the slight irregularity of the fetal heart is not important, everything is going well, she is going to have a nice baby, and then you shut the door and go into the next room and assure another patient on whom you just did a saline abortion, that it's fine if the heart is already irregular, she has nothing to worry about, she is *not* going to have a live baby. I mean you definitely have to make a 180 degree turn, but somehow it evolved in my own mind gradually, and I have no trouble now making the switch. . . .

"The volume is a significant factor, but since this procedure is so well defined as a two-stage procedure, and you really have to concentrate at every point while you are doing it, how to do it and what exactly to do, and there's so many pitfalls that constantly sort of churn in your mind, that 'this is okay so far' and what the next step is, that you really are not concentrating on anything else, except the technical aspects of it.

"Of course, that took a couple of hundred cases before one gets like that. You should see when people are starting at first. The residents, their hands are shaking, and every move is jerky because they are so concerned."

DR. D.: What's the real danger?

DR. S: That you go through the placenta and you pierce the cavity, which even now happens now and then. But the main danger is depositing the salt in the wrong compartment. Not in the uterine cavity, but either in the maternal circulation or in the outside of the uterus or in the uterine wall. Those would be disastrous.

DR. D: Fatal?

DR. S: Oh, yeah. Patients have died of complications like that. But this is where it's very important that experts, with experience, in other words not just a surgeon but an obstetrician who is more trained, somebody who has experience with saline induction per se, do it. This is how this whole unit was designed. I had the chance of selecting people and restricting it to that group. So somebody who may be excellent in doing D & C's elsewhere was denied access to this unit because I wanted to work only with people who have already had vast experience with saline. . . .

"It was a gradual change, because at the beginning we were doing abortions on fetuses that were not quite as large. And the kicking and the fetal heartbeat did not manifest itself quite as obviously as it does now, in the larger cases. So I can imagine, if I had started doing twenty-four-weekers right off the bat, I would have had much greater conflict in my own mind whether this is tantamount to murder. But since we started gradually, with fifteen-, sixteen-weekers, where the overwhelming interest of the mother was so obvious, the fetus just never got consideration. It just did not enter the picture. Then, as one gained experience, the whole range of cases that we had to take care of started to become larger. All of a sudden one noticed that at the time of the saline infusion there was a lot of activity in the uterus. That's not fluid currents. That's obviously the fetus being distressed by swallowing the concentrated salt solution and kicking violently and that's, to all intents and purposes, the death trauma. You can either face the method or you can turn the other way and claim it's uterine contractions. That, however, would be essentially repressing, since as a doctor you obviously understand that it is not. Now, whether you admit this to the patient, that's a different matter.

"The whole technique of saline abortions has come in so gradually, that there was no outstanding dramatic event which would have signaled, 'Now here is an issue that I have

68

to face whether I do it, or I don't.' It never happened like that. The patient's distress by unwanted pregnancy is to me the primary consideration and I am willing to put that ahead of the possible considerations for the fetus. We'll just have to face it, that somebody has to do it. And, unfortunately, we are the executioners in this instance.

"In my view it would be unfair to say 'Well, I enjoy taking out fibroids but I just abhor doing abortions.' That's not fair. Whether this is a rationalization on my part or not, I'm not sure. But I think I have no conflict in my own mind of representing the patient's interests all the way. . . .

"To me individual rights are very important. I think it probably has to do with my Hungarian background. I got out of a country which has blatantly abused the individual, and I wouldn't have risked my life getting out of it, and at that time when I decided to get out, it did amount to risking your life, if it wasn't very important.

"And I came to the country where I thought that individual rights had a better chance than anywhere else. Since then I have had doubts in my mind, but anyway I think it still has a better chance here than in most places.

"Now I think a decision of this sort is very well within the individual's rights. Same way as somebody who wants to die. I don't believe in medical stunts in keeping people alive when they're hopeless. I am not prepared to defend euthanasia outright, because it has too many pitfalls, but I think that there are certain situations when at least the physician shouldn't stand on his head to save somebody with terminal cancer, for example. Even though it's unpleasant to turn off that last switch, by having gotten to the point where your authority may include that, you have to do it. There has to be a person where the buck stops. This joint responsibility is a lot of nonsense. I mean you didn't become the leading member of a health team by virtue of training and what-not if you cannot assume responsibility. And being an obstetrician *does* propose just this sort of decision. Since you have the tools, you have the

69

training of doing it right, and the woman has no other person to turn to. Aren't you withholding something that she's entitled to by refusing her? And I think somebody before going into obstetrics and gynecology should decide in his own mind is he capable of doing that. And if he's not, then, I mean if the heat is too much in the kitchen, get the hell out.

"If medicine or certain specialities were not a monopoly, which they are, then it would be easy to say 'I don't do this, I don't do that, I only do certain things, the more pleasant aspects of it and somebody should do the garbage.' That's fine, but it's not so. This is part of our profession, and I think we should face up to it."


# X, M.D., Age 39


*Dr. X is the only woman physician on staff. She has that crisp, matter-of-fact manner one so frequently finds among Indian professional women. Her attitude is not quite aggressive, it merely lacks the grace with which Western women learn to yield.*

*Slim, wiry, her black hair gathered at the nape of her neck into an efficient bun, she is permanently rushed, perpetually busy, attending three or four floors at the same time.*

*In sharp contrast to her lack of openness, her physical presence is astonishingly vivid. I am also surprised to discover that during our interview, to which she readily consents, she retains her style, and answers even my most intimate questions with energetic specificity and dispatch. I am nevertheless left with the impression that we have not yet had a conversation.*

*About a month after the interview I drop in at the hospital to ask her to supply me with an Indian pseudonym, to use in my notes instead of her real name. As I get off the elevator on the saline floor I see her on the corridor chatting with Edie and Betsy. Uncharacteristically she is wearing makeup. Also high boots and a miniskirt under her open white doctor's coat. When I am near enough to be noticed, Betsy calls to me by way of greeting: "Guess what? Dr. X*

*is taking off the afternoon to take her daughter to the movies."
"Great," I say. "Yes, and I better go right now," says Dr. X. "One
second please," I say. "I need to ask you for an Indian name other
than your own, to use in the book, but one that correctly reflects your
status." "What do you mean?" she asks. I repeat myself. She panics.
"I do not want to be named. You should use numbers or letters. No
names." For a moment I am not sure whether she is kidding me or
not. Then I remember that she never jokes. "But I told you about
it, before," I say lamely. In fact, I did. She pulls herself together and
sets her jaw: "Letters or numbers." "Okay," I say, "Okay, I will
use a letter."*

"I think as far as my country is concerned to be a woman
gynecologist is no different from a male gynecologist in general. In India, too, normally men think themselves to be clev-
erer or superior, and tend to sort of put down women. In any
country, that stands. But professional level, employmentwise,
woman gynecologist just as good as a man gynecologist. But
I find it in this country woman gynecologist it's a very difficult
situation. One thing, they're never given an opportunity to
show their skill or ability. They are sort of taken for granted,
a woman gynecologist is second best, or second choice. In any
job opportunities, as soon as they know you're female gynecologist, you are given a job only if they can't get any other help.

"As far as I'm concerned I tried for a job, partnership, or
something for one solid year, and there were offers to me
immediately, so long as they don't know my sex. As soon as
they know your sex everything is closed. Some excuse or the
other. Secondly, when you're married still you are a little bit
less opportunity. And if you've a child opportunities are mini-
mum. I'm married and have a child too. Six years old. She was
born here. I have been in New York exactly six years. I
finished university training in India and England.

"I know one friend of mine, Indian gynecologist, and he had
a very good time. He got a good job and a residency in Ohio
and got a partnership in the very first week. They would also
love the other male gynecologists, non-Indians, who applied
with me and which had much less qualifications and I should

say, without being modest, less skilled, but they were offered the job which I was turned down. And it is because I am female. I have absolutely no doubt about it. . . .

"When I was in training, and when we used to do some therapeutic abortions for German measles and some psychiatric reasons, I never used to like it. When I started reading more about legal abortion, and woman's privilege, and all, I think I agree with it, that up to a certain stage like twelve or fourteen weeks it's nothing. The woman has a right to decide. I don't know my opinion as far as after eighteen or up to twenty-four weeks, I still don't know.

"When you are delivering a twenty-four-weeks fetus, which looks almost like a little baby or when you hear the fetal heart tone, I don't have any feeling of it like murderer, or like other people tell, that it is murder. Those feelings I don't have it. But somehow or other, I just feel that a woman at this stage is always involved with the baby. You know it has already been kicking for some weeks. And how can she dare give this thing up. Because it's part of you. What we don't realize is that these very women go home and in a quiet moment they must be thinking about it.

"I feel sad, but as I told you, I don't have a guilt feeling like murder, and I hear men talking "Abortion is murder.' I still give it, it's a woman who is going to be mother, she is the one who decides. This is my primary feeling. I'm not a Catholic, and I'm not an antiabortionist who has a strong opinion about it as a murder. I come from an overpopulated country, and I see the great need of controlling the population. I see the load of feeding kids and also the problems of it, so I do believe that if they want it, it's better off this way, than leaving them on the street, to the peddlers and the pushers. So I'm very scientific and very practical. It's only inner sadness comes when I think of a baby of twenty weeks or twenty-four weeks when I see it. So I just think that this very baby, if it can move me so much, has to be moving the person who has carried it so long. . . .

72

"I've been married twelve years. The day my husband got his Ph.D. I got pregnant. Maybe it's just coincidence or maybe it isn't. Maybe I was too worried that something would happen and I didn't want to get stuck in this country with half education. I wanted to bring up a child when I could enjoy the child, you know, not blame for our failures the poor child. I'm willing to say that my marriage is a very good one. At least I'm very happy.

"I always think sex is more important for a man than a woman. Because a woman, if she did not get sex, it does not start reacting to other things, but a man, if he did not get the sex, his reaction will come in the day-to-day behavior of husband and wife. In the relationship, you know, anger, frustration, dissatisfaction and like that.

"There is plenty extramarital affairs all around India and particularly in the rich class and very low class. Only the middle class which is caught in so-called moralities and lack of space, and lack of opportunities and everything. But the lower class does not care two hoots where they do, they go to the fields and here and there, and the upper class has plenty of opportunity, because they have motels and hotels, and they have an extra apartment. It's only the middle class which has been struggling hard to preserve the value, rightly or wrongly, because they just don't have an opportunity.

"We are very happy married, that's why it's not possible. And we are living in this country, too, and there are not that many Indians around to get an extramarital affair. I just think I give my body to one person and that belongs to him only."

DR. D: What's your reaction then to these thirteen- and fourteen-year-olds who come in here?

DR. X: I don't consider this my place to become judge or a jury. As an intelligent discussion I can discuss it. I don't think it is right for these girls for many things. One thing, as I told you, for the sex. And secondly I think the dangers of VD, third thing pregnancy, fourthly carcinoma of the cervix. Epidemiologists study say that earlier the coitus, is more chances of cancer of the cervix, which was direct relation to the age when coitus was started. But I would never be judge and a jury, basically because I'm a gynecologist.

## Dora Greenwald, M.S.W., Age 28

*Dora Greenwald is the very first person in the hospital whom I interview. She is friendly, cooperative, accommodating, and enormously helpful. We do not develop into friends. We are stopped by her ability to see the delivery of a fetus as a pictorially pleasing event.*

"Most of what we do is with the saline patients on the floor. When we get to see them is really a matter of chance. Because our priorities are set by need rather than what we feel might be best. I mean, we have to meet the needs when they come up. So one of us most likely will see the patient before she gets her shots. We try to see them before we go home, to make sure that they know exactly what to expect, we try to calm them down.

"We don't give them written material when they're here about the procedures, only about postoperative instructions. So on the floor, if there is a patient who's in a difficult labor, who is very scared, we could spend time with her. Hopefully we would be there at the time of delivery, but that's so unexpected you never know when it is going to be. Luckily sometimes we're in the room, and unfortunately sometimes we're not. But that was one of our big priorities when we started to work here. . . .

"At first I was very upset by the deliveries. I'm not one to see blood and mess and things like that. But I have since gotten so excited about it that I've thought about going back to nursing school. When you think about it on a certain level, it's a really interesting thing that is happening. It's fascinating, when you can think about it clinically and not get involved in the people, or the babies. What happened when I was first working here was that I just thought about the baby and that was very upsetting. I'm very proabortion. I think that if women want it, and need it, they should definitely have the opportunity to get it. So I had to try to make myself keep thinking of that and the fact that these people need it. And when you hear their stories and get involved in them as people, it's much easier to take.

"I think I must have overcompensated, you know, over-reacted and tried to look, and like really get into it, and not shy away from it. And several times I saw really beautiful things happen, I mean it's physically beautiful. . . .

"Sometimes you can see the vagina opening up and the entire thing coming out at once. Most of the times the water will break, and then the fetus will come out and then the afterbirth. You know, in sequence. But sometimes this all comes out at once, like a balloon with the fetus inside and the afterbirth just sitting on top. It's a really interesting thing, and it got me very excited.

"Also, the fact that these patients are so grateful for whatever comfort and support you give them. It's the first time that I've been in any kind of social work where people say 'Thank you.' You know most of the time in therapy they are working along with you, or whatever, but there's not the same response. Here they don't expect to have the comfort and the support, and they are so grateful when they get it. They feel so helpless."

*At this point in the interview the telephone rings. Dora picks it up. "Hi, this is Dora," she says. "Okay, yes. Where is she? What's her name? Where does she live? How far along is she? Okay, thank you."*

*"Do you have to go?" I whisper.*

*She shakes her head. Covering the receiver with her hand, she says, "No, I can see her later. She's a sixteen-year-old girl who got raped by her step-father. She's a saline patient. She's twenty-one weeks."*

*Turning back to the telephone she says, "Hello. Yes. Fio. Okay.*

*Okay. Does she have a parent here with her? The father who got her pregnant? Oh, she's here with her real father. Oh, my God. Has anybody been in touch with the mother? I mean does the mother know? Oh, Jesus! Okay, thank you. Right.*(Laughs.) *Bye."*

She hangs up and turns to me again. "Her real father is here. She ran away from home, and she went to her real father. He suspected something was wrong."

*"Does the mother know?"*

*"That's what I just asked. She doesn't know."*

We continue talking.

"There is a lot of work to be done afterwards too. The patients, I think, do feel some sense of loss or just a tremendous relief. There's such a long waiting period from the time they found out that they are pregnant until the time that it's completed. I think that that's really what affects them. And now it's over and it's like some people just don't know what to do with that feeling. I think that many patients experience a kind of high. Many girls giggle afterwards. Like this excited nervous reaction. Then there's a period after that which I think some girls go through almost like a postpartum depression. When a patient comes in who's very troubled in the beginning, not knowing what kind of choice she should make, whether she should have the abortion or keep the baby, we find that there is more of an immediate feeling sorry right afterwards. . . ."

"A lot of people say they're killing their baby. You get a lot of that. Some people afterwards get very upset and say 'I killed my baby.' Or even before, they say 'My circumstances are such that I can't keep it, but I'm killing my baby.' They wouldn't rather have the baby, and give it up for adoption either. If you go into that with them they will say that they could never do that because if they carry it to term they'd want to keep it. And yet they still consider it killing the baby."

DR. D.: How about you? What's your position?

DG: Well, they are killing a baby. I mean, they are killing

76

something that would develop into maturity, but under the circumstances that's necessary, and probably better for the baby. You have to realize that these children would be unwanted and a lot of times uncared for, so it's much better that they are not brought into the world. . . .

"The fetus actually looks like a baby, only it doesn't have any fat. We've noticed that very young patients are more apt to ask the sex, and be curious about what it looks like. We discourage it. And, we're supposed to have a policy that we're not going to tell the sex although it can be seen if you're looking. They have to contort themselves into almost a somersault position to see, but some mothers will. Then their reaction is real shock. . . .

"Sometimes people will look like they are going to cry but when you start talking with them they start operating on another level which usually stops the tears. My basic reaction though to somebody who is crying is to let them cry. Suzy and I are in constant conflict with the nurses who go in and tell them to stop crying, 'Be in control of yourself' and 'Be a big person.' We go in and say 'Cry.' 'When you cry then you can talk about it and get it off your chest.' So we do try to encourage people who are teary to let it out. . . .

"I guess sometimes I get jealous that here are all these women who are pregnant and they want to give it up and I'd like to get pregnant. I have a little girl. She's two. She's very cute *(laughs)*, but I'm not the kind of person who can stay home all the time and I also don't want to be away all the time. Also, the population doesn't remain, so it doesn't matter that I'm here part-time. I very rarely have the feeling that I'm sorry I'm not here the next day. Sometimes there's a patient that I work with a great deal when she comes in, and I go through the shots with her, and I see her before I leave, and then I wonder how she does the next day, and I'm a little sorry that it has to be Susan that follows through. I've also met some fascinating people, like a pecan picker who comes from a family of about fifteen children."

## Susan Lindstrom, M.S.W., Age 27

*Suzy Lindstrom is a tall young woman with auburn hair and violet eyes. She is devoted to her work, and the concerns of her day settle on her face as worry lines, lightly etched, deeply felt.*

"I am having a lot of difficulty with my feelings about late abortions. All the pain that seems to be there so much of the time after the baby is moving and everything. And I saw this movie of a live birth recently and it just was so terrifically painful to me, to see and feel the difference between what a live birth is and what a saline abortion is. You could just feel all the joy and excitement of seeing this live baby come out. A whole different color, like white and light and alive and moving, crying, and doing all these things, and you know, having seen a considerable number of fetuses being all dark and red and blue and dead.

"I'll never forget the first fetus because it was the very first week I was here. This little bitty girl from, I think, Wisconsin, a black girl, very, very scared. And she was just in incredible pain, and screaming and calling to God and all kinds of things and I was holding on to her and Dr. Szenes came in and broke her water and helped her deliver right there, and it splattered all over the whole room. . . .

"And then to see, to be with somebody while they're having the injection when they're twenty-three, twenty-four weeks, and you see the baby, moving around, kicking around, as this needle is going down into the stomach, you know, oh, I forgot, shit! I forgot to speak to John because he said something he never should have said to this one girl that I'm talking about because she had just a lot of feelings about it. 'It's a baby,' 'It's a person,' 'I'm killing it' kind of feelings which she had talked to me about. And at the induction he was having trouble, because the baby was moving around and blocking up the needle, and so he gets angry and he just makes the comment that the baby was putting his finger up against the needle. You know, just personalized it. . . .

"I really feel that about several of the doctors. That there's really pathological things in their involvement with abortion. Like Dr. Rodrigo. He is very sarcastic and he really, you know, like goes after people. Recently he had a horrendous fight with Rachel. It was absolutely, totally disgraceful. It happened right at the nursing station. He flew at her. Cursing, screaming out loud, yelling, you could hear it all over the whole floor. It was incredible, I mean, imagine the kind of feeling that gives the patients on the floor. He was just out after her and it had to do with her being a woman, in her position, kind of. . . .

"There was one week when there were two live births in the same week. And just, you know, there's this baby crying on this floor while all these women are in the process of trying to deal with their feelings about aborting their babies. One survived for a while."

DR. D.: How did the mothers react who gave birth to the live babies?

SL: Well. This *one*, she didn't talk much. The mother delivered when there was no one there and there was some period when the mother was holding the baby. And it was grabbing on to her. That's what the little nurse said. She was extremely upset by this whole thing.

"There's such conflict because there's so much pain in the mothers. Mixed emotional pains, conflict of what to do. And being concerned about killing something. They don't want to kill something. . . .

"I didn't go out looking for a job in the abortion field when I came here in the first place. I don't know, I feel emotionally beaten up. And when I leave here every day, I have a hard time turning it off, and turning on the next thing, because I start my second day's work at five-thirty. And I think it wouldn't be so bad if my work were not this kind of painful and draining as it is to me, here. I think mostly I've gotten more sensitive to what abortion is about and more in touch with my own feelings. I'm a very good blocker, generally, and I used to handle everything by just not feeling anything. So I could pick up and go right on to the next thing because I hadn't been there in the first place.

"The drain is from what the system is like, in addition to whatever the procedure is like. And the emotional built-in thing, because it's abortion. A lot of the drain is from the way people don't work, or tell lies to each other all the time. It's a horrible environment to work in."

———

Dora and Suzy each spend two and a half days at the hospital. Because of the overload of their cases, they have time only for the unending crises of the saline floors.

Dora works Mondays, Wednesdays, and Friday mornings. Suzy works Tuesdays, Thursdays, and Friday afternoons. The one time they meet is Fridays at lunch, as a kind of changing of the guard. Otherwise they communicate through short notes, alerting each other to patients most in need. The notes mirror and summarize the atmosphere of the unit. Their common theme is terror. The subplots vary. Madness, incest and rape mingle with more ordinary contingencies like disease, cruelty, desertion, and pervasive neglect.

*11/19*

Dora—

*It was a bad day. I walked around the streets for 1/2 hour keeping a girl from walking out into the traffic—also the street blew up at 3 A.M. and broke several windows last night.*

*Martha Andrews, 15—psychological consult. and epilepsy. Dr. Schwarz recommended her mother spend as much time as possible with her. She'll have a med. consultation later today or tomorrow so won't get saline induction until tomorrow. She'll need support with all the waiting. Very anxious and doesn't talk much.*

*Margot Parker—rejected because of medical reasons (ask Dr. X, re medical history) I referred them to Family Planning Info. Service. Other possibility is Kings Co. Hospital. Will do to 24 weeks (she'll probably need hysterotomy). J. Sz. suggested calling Dr. in charge of saline there. Wasn't in.*

*I hardly made it to the floors at all so I don't know how things are.*

Suzy

*11/25*

Suzy.

*I had to leave early, my sister & her newborn baby are in danger and I'm too distressed to stay.*

81

*Saline Floor: Staff*

See my note re J. Schecter. She doesn't know about my conversation w/mother, just that I called to say everything's OK—perhaps you can see her, to help her open up & maybe motivate her to get help. Valerie Mattson—7th floor. Mother given your name, go see first thing in AM no saline induction & no plans yet.

See you,
Dora

12/8

Dora

707—Mrs. Marchant still here. Re-saline induced today. Feeling very depressed—though worried re husband's anger at her for being gone so long.
703—Lynn Barron, 19, very scared. Shaking. Bender tried saline induction. No fluid. Will pitocin her & try SI again tomorrow. Alone in city.
709—Amy seemed pretty calm, anxious—wanting to get home.
710—Interesting lady. Only female auto mechanic & car dealer in the west—handles all aspects of the business. Worried re pain, but no conflict re abortion.

Suzy

P.S.—Magda asked me a while ago if she could have some of the notes we write each other. It seemed okay to me, so I've been saving our notes in a folder in top drawer.

3/19

Suzy

Please see: 701A—crying when I left because a nurse yelled at her for spilling water on the sheets, is now scared to call for help, asked her to get the nurse's name.
701B—Denise been here since Saturday, being saline induced again, boyfriend John in lobby.
704—Heidi 15 yrs. old, no roommate for the night & scared shit!
705B—Patricia 13, rape victim—spoke a little w/mother Mrs. Winter, Midtown Hotel. Mother also experiences Patty as very with-

*drawn, was hoping we could help—I didn't get anywhere—good luck!*
*706—Michele—elle parle Français seulement.*
*707—Mary Booth had to have surgery, her womb had a tear—husband will be calling you.*
*Otherwise things are pretty calm—saline inductions were late again today.*

*See you Friday*
*Dora*

*4/3*

Dora

*Should we file sonogram rejects separately from other cases? Might as well keep it altogether for the time being—we have code at top!*
*701—Jean nothing happening, still cries if I try to talk w/her. Father visited during day & talked with Dr. X.*
*704—Madeleine—no cramps yet, is waiting also for Sherry in 605 to go home together—they'll want your help.*
*707—Louise parents have no idea where she is, never told them she wasn't coming home tonight! Swears she's going to walk out of here tomorrow.*
*708B—Grace, methadone, very frightened.*
*Had a lot of action. People changing their minds, etc. . . .*
*Talk with RS when you get in, re NEWS.*

*Suzy*

*4/8*

Suzy

*Hope your conference was fun, missed you! Be sure to see RS NEWS! FINALLY!*
*709—Angela—RS can tell you about her, she'll probably be very excitable.*
*701A—Suzanne, will also be upset. I anticipate a screamer—see yellow sheet.*
*702A—Julie Parks—parents are very upset, second saline induction for Julie—see yellow sheet.*

**83**

*Saline Floor: Staff*

*703B—Janet has to go for sonogram, please be up on that, she'll need a lot of support.*

*707—Melissa here with fiance and his mother and psychiatrist—she's scared shit and has no pain tolerance.*

*708A—Toni is only 12 and very stoic, her aunt will be in touch with you. Her aunt's husband raped Toni.*

*Sorry I didn't write up sheets for anyone, but Julie and Suzanne. See you Friday for our BIG MEETING.*

*Dora*

——

# Andre Winston, Age 20

## *Messenger*

*The messenger is a lanky young man, in T-shirt and jeans, with many pimples on his forehead and chin. Some days he does not shave, and he sings to himself quietly as he goes about his business. Occasionally I say "Hi," but there is no response. I hear other people call to him also, "Hello, Andre, how's tricks?" but even to those whom he knows, he answers only sporadically and at random. Some years ago he was in a car accident that left him in a coma for three months. He suffers from epilepsy.*

*One noon, at lunch, I walk over to him and as he is about to take his tray of food I say, "Hi, I am Dr. Denes. You have probably seen me around the hospital." He looks me fully in the face. "No. Never. I never seen you." For a moment there is total silence. I am unaccustomed to this degree of matter-of-factness. "Well, anyway, I have seen you. I am interviewing people here, and I would like to talk to you too, if it's okay." The silence descends again. I am not sure if he understood me or what the next step is to be. His eyes are blank, and his stubbly face is without clues. I am about to start in again when he unexpectedly says "It's okay. But I am going to eat my lunch now." After some haggling we agree to meet in the lobby at three o'clock. Unavoidably I arrive five minutes late, but Andre has waited for me. We go to the eighth floor, to the social workers' office. The messenger changes. He is clear-eyed, present, a willing talker. It is obvious that he has decided to accommodate me as a personal favor, and to abandon for a time the safety of his withdrawal. In my grateful surprise I forget to ask him many of the questions I had prepared.*

DR. D.: What's your job, Andre. What do you have to do?
AW: Messenger.
DR. D.: What kinds of things does that mean?
AW: I go around to the city delivering papers. I deliver drugs to floors. Take the fetus over to the other hospital.
DR. D.: How does that work, who packs them up?
AW: The doctor. He wraps them up and puts them in a box.

A regular cardboard box. But first they put them in plastic bags. You know, bunched together. And, well, I have to tie it up.

DR. D.: How do you take it?

AW: Taxi.

DR. D.: And you've been doing this all through the year. Even when there were many, many of them.

AW: Yes.

DR. D.: How do you feel about that, doing that work?

AW: It's work. The only thing bad about it is that it stinks, the smell. That's really the bad thing about it.

DR. D.: Has any cab driver asked you what you're carrying in that?

AW: Yea, but I made excuses.

DR. D.: What do you say?

AW: I say, oh towels or something. Twice only they smelt so bad he could smell it. I just say experiments for the other hospital, that's all.

DR. D.: What happens in the other hospital?

AW: Oh, I take them downstairs, and they burn them.

DR. D.: Have you ever seen them burn them?

AW: Yes. They have a furnace, they put 'em in and burn them. At first it upset me 'cause I didn't know what I was takin' over there.

DR. D.: Didn't they tell you?

AW: No, they thought I knew, but I didn't. That only happened after the first day.

DR. D.: Tell me about that first day.

AW: The other messenger who was here was showing me what to do, and it just came that at eleven-thirty I go over to this place. We came up here to the lab, picked up these boxes, took them over there and took them to the burner, and that was it. But then a fellow that works over at the other hospital came to pick me up, and he asked me if I know what was in the boxes and I told him no. He told me and after that I realized what I was doing.

DR. D.: What was your reaction when he told you?

AW: I was kind of shocked. I really didn't know. I wish I

would have knew from the start, I wouldn't have felt so bad.

DR. D.: Does it bug you now?

AW: No, only when it stink 'cause it might be hard to get a taxi. If I have a bunch of 'em and it's hard to get a taxi. Then they don't want to put it in the trunk, they charge you more. They just give you a certain amount for you to go over and get back with.

DR. D.: How do you come back?

AW: By bus.

"I felt bad about it, then it was the people's business to get an abortion. I couldn't say anything or do anything about it. I mean I could say something, but I just let it go. You don't feel bad when you see these really small containers like no egg or whatever is formed. But in the ones where you could see the babies with the hands and the feet and the heads and everything, and you can tell what sex, a boy or girl. Really sometimes it gets nasty. They are so big sometimes. Some are small and still have hands. It's just too bad the baby had to go that far and then end up here. . . ."

DR. D.: What do you like to do when you're off work?

AW: Relax, sit home and rest.

DR. D.: Do you have any hobbies, anything you especially like to do?

AW: Well, I like music. Music from the stereo.

DR. D.: What kind?

AW: Soul music.

DR. D.: Do you have a girl friend?

AW: Oh yes. *(Laughs.)*

DR. D.: What if she got pregnant?

AW: I'd marry her. Seeing what I've seen and everything—and I've worked around here and seen these dead fetuses. I wouldn't want to have to come here, or have my girlfriend come here, and have an abortion, and I end up seeing the kid that was almost mine, look where it ended up at. I wouldn't like that. . . .

DR. D.: What are your plans for the future? What do you want to do?

AW: I don't want to be in no hospitals. I would like to go back to school. Even though I've been two and a half years out, I'd like to go back.

DR. D.: And study what?

AW: Just keep on.

DR. D.: To do what in the future?

AW: I have no idea. See I would like to better myself, not what I'm doing here but like, say, going back to school. So when I come out I'll be qualified. Ready to get married and then I'll really have a job. The kind of job that will promote me.

———

The saline floor is a difficult place for lasting clarity and durable convictions. One day I speak with Debbie, twelve years old, six months pregnant by her uncle, who, through the convoluted miseries of Debbie's short life, also happens to have been her stepfather for the past ten years. "He has been messing with me for two years, but I only got my first period eight months ago," she reports, her brown eyes full of tears behind gold-rimmed glasses. "What hurts, Debbie?" "I don't want him to be in jail, where they put him. I love my uncle. He was like a father to me. We played games." By now she is sobbing, bitterly mourning a vanished parent as any child will. "But, Debbie, what he did with you, what about that?" "It was wrong, but I miss my uncle," she says, her shoulders shaking with grief.

The baby in Debbie's belly does move. But who cares? Certainly no one on this floor, where for the first time in many months, there is a spirit of solidarity bordering on joy. Debbie's bright, sad face has banished for the moment all doubts; the stated purpose of the unit is reaffirmed in Debbie's need. The groped-for, seldom-found certainty that the work done here is truly in the service of humankind is manifest again in the swollen-bellied body of little Debbie, whose spirit everyone in concerted effort wants to spare and to comfort.

The attendants give her candy. Dr. X, in departure from usual procedure, orders no IV for her to avoid confining her to bed while she waits to deliver. The nurses call her "little Debbie" and keep asking her how she feels.

There is a live child on this floor whose future people are hard at work to save.

And yet, quantity has a way of radically altering the essence of quality. When, under one roof, the number of dead fetuses mounts into the thousands, the simple fact of death gradually overshadows the significance of individual histories. It seems that none who work here can witness the extinction of a segment of the future generation without guilt and fear. The word "murder" surfaces again and again, and it sticks on the tongue like a searing coal of fire that one knows will do further damage whether it is swallowed or spat.

A struggle evolves between reason and conscience, between pragmatic morality and one's own commitment to all human seed. With the struggle there also evolves a shamefaced solution: "I do not decide for these women, I just do my job"; "I give them what they want"; "I only help out." As if disclaiming responsibility could make one free of it.

# Chapter 3

# Saline Floor:
# Patients and Parents

My own heart let me more have pity on; let
Me live to my sad self hereafter kind,
Charitable; not live this tormented mind
With this tormented mind tormenting yet.
                              Gerard Manley Hopkins

Tragedy sharpens human features and unnaturally enlarges the eyes. The faces here are topographical testimonies to critical times and accumulated sorrows. Each is a map to serially sustained and survived savageries, all of which in retrospect always seem less devastating than the torment about to begin. Eyes here are liquid prayers of remorse and accusation that this too, in addition to all else, must be suffered. That the daily injuries, the hidden humiliations are not enough. Now this too, and probably for some well-deserved reason.

It hardly matters into which eyes I look, which face becomes focal. Only the content of calvary differs; the stations of the cross remain the same: bewilderment, guilt, helplessness, recurrence, blame, astonishment, shame, and grieving, grieving, grieving.

Male, female, old, young, patient, parent, possibly even fetus—the lesson on this floor is in the sameness of heartache, in the frightful uniformity of the structure of pain.

What else does it mean to be human but the absolute and incontrovertible certainty that each and all of us sometime, somewhere, is susceptible to the same visceral blow, to the same turbulent uncontrollable tremor within the gut?

So with these people. I see faces that cling and some that strut. Faces that pretend, faces that are laid bare. Shut and open faces, faces shining with sweat, faces dry with the horror of things to come. Faces in the accusative, faces in the declarative, mute faces. All of them bleeding under the skin. And eyes, deep eyes, unbearably wounded.

———

# Mrs. Ann Miller, Age 36, Separated

## *Twenty Weeks Pregnant*

*Mrs. Miller is a large black woman. She sits on the bed as we talk, with her feet dangling over the side. She is dressed in a hospital gown, stretched to its limit by her bulk. Her exposed, pink-nailed, dark, plump toes, in their misshapen nakedness typify her inarticulate sorrow and helpless resignation.*

*These used toes, those worn feet, customarily hidden from inspection, ordinarily protected from public view, are now suspended in midair as exhibit A in the assessment of meaning in human existence, as represented by one Ann Miller, daughter of sharecroppers, mother of five, subject of prejudice, agent of sin, in search of God. She is both symbol and reality.*

*Her life is what it is, but it is also more, although she does not know that. She does not understand that the steady stream of tears that traverse her prematurely lined face, and which she, from time to time with a darting motion of her tongue, takes into her mouth and swallows, are her tears and yet not. They are also common property, a universal resource, on which cosmologies are built and through which, by some other name, the God for whom she searches lives.*

*"I say it is a sin," she says, burdened by what appears to her strictly private remorse. Referring, in her view, to the one event of which she speaks. She fails to note (does not even know that the matter requires attention) that each of us alone represents the species, and, again alone, each must from nothing, from sand, construct those imperatives by which the value of all being is judged.*

"Me and my husband are not living together, but we still sometimes see each other. The baby is his. He wanted the abortion. He is paying for it.

"I was on the pills but they started to swell me up, and the doctor had to stop me from taking it. Then I weren't having any relationship for a long time, then we were going to try to start back living together and that's when I began to feel sick and everything."

93

DR. D.: Why did you and your husband separate?

AM: Mostly people today, I don't know. If you can't get along with somebody there's always no peace, no this, and no that. Like you can't explain it, because you really never know. Who knows maybe we just got on each other's nerves.

"Everything has changed, today nothing is like it use to be. Today I figure the way people are like they really don't care about each other any more. It seems everybody cares about themselves, that's why you feel so bad about this, this abortion, like people stopped caring about their own selves. Like when you have an abortion you just destroying a part of yourself, that's the way I feel anyhow. I just feel bad inside, that's all. I didn't really want to do it. It's a sin. I know that it is. I'm studying with the Witnesses. I'm studying for another religion, and I know that it's wrong. It's a sin.

"My husband is older, and sometimes I don't feel so good, and the kids are getting very bad, you never can tell what's going to happen. He said it might be better to do it. And I'd be better off to maybe pray and be forgiven.

"Of course five kids is a lot of kids. And it hasn't been easy, but my kids never gave me a whole lot of trouble. But this friend of mine, her kid left home, she don't even know where he is. Too many things is happening. I don't know. My husband had some pretty good arguments, it made a lot of sense. He said the world is getting so terrible with these kids, you hate to go through it again. . . .

"We had a big family, my mother had thirteen kids. We always got along okay. We was brought up on a farm, you raise all your foods, you always have plenty, you don't know whether your mother and father is having a hard time or not. We was the farmers that you called "thirds." My father had all his own equipment, so he rented a farm and then he like run it and give the owner a third of what was made on it, because he used his own everything. . . .

"I went up to eleventh grade and I got married in high school. The schools weren't integrated in our town until about ten years ago. To me it was okay, because in South

Carolina the people are not that bad. I'd say I would get along with the white people that we grew up with better than the people here. The man that my father rented his farm from, we and his daughters was like friends, we played together and we're still friends today. Like if I go home they come to see me. There you have a feeling that, like the people don't really care if you are black or white, but here most of the people pretend like they don't care, and then when something come up they do care."

## Miss Marsha Read, Age 22, Single

*Twenty Weeks Pregnant*

"I was referred to this hospital through Planned Parenthood. It's a pretty rough decision to make, but I felt like actually the child would be better off this way, then to bring it up without a father. And too, my parents are both still living, but they're old and I think they have had enough misery in their lifetime without me adding to it.

"I just didn't want to get married. I felt that it would be a trap for both of us. We've been dating almost three years. He himself was brought up without a father and he just couldn't stand the thought of my having the child.

"I wanted to keep it but then I really got to thinking about it and I just decided I didn't want to raise a child. I didn't want to bring one up 'cause things don't seem to be getting any better. You don't know if they would marry in their own race. Maybe by the time they grew up he wouldn't know any better than just to marry a Negro. That's coming to pass in this day and time. It's just disgusting to me to think that a white girl would do that, or even a Negro would want to marry a white girl, but it's happening. The biggest majority of people don't care about themselves. I mean the things they do. I think that if God meant us all to be one color He'd have made us that way and He would not have made any black or white."

DR. D.: What do you think he had in mind in making us many colors?

MR: I don't know what He had in mind, other than just what it used to be years back, you know, the Negro being a slave to the white. I know around my territory the Negroes would all like to see whites as their slaves.

*The venom of her outburst is staggering. The gentle, lyric rhythm of her Southern speech coupled with her hatred confuses me. My experiences of murderous diatribes derive from the crackle of Teutonic "ch" 's.*

*And yet I also note her intermittent screams of labor, her desperation, and her need to find something, somebody, anything, anyone, lower than she thinks herself to be.*

"It's always the woman's fault. I mean people don't realize that it took two, and the woman always pays for it. She's the one that's the trash and the man gets out without nothing.

"Well it was kind of sudden. At first I was really amazed. It hurt. But, I don't know it just kind of gives you a warm feeling. I mean, I don't know if I could enjoy sex with anybody else like I do with Dwight, but I know that we enjoy each other as much as any two people could. I think that marriage takes something out of two people. I believe that you enjoy it a lot more than if you were tied to somebody. . . .

"That's always been my dream ever since I been big enough to know what fixing hair was. I've always wanted to be a beautician. There's one other beside me in my town. It's a small town where I live. Both of us have plenty of work to do. . . ."

DR. D.: Before this, what did you used to think of abortions?

MR: Well, I don't know, I guess I was against them like everybody else. You really just think of people being not decent when they do things like that. But you don't ever really think about it until it comes home to you. And then, you have to go through with it, and it's not an easy thing to accept, and I know it couldn't be easy for any of those girls in here either. I mean, I made up my mind to do it and like I could let it drive me crazy, any woman could, but you can't, because you've got to live with it and there's really no sense in letting it drive you right off the edge. Of course, I guess a lot of people sometimes really consider killing themselves. Getting out of it completely. It passed my mind, I don't deny it, but I wouldn't have the courage to do it. Some people do, but I don't.

## Mr. Ronald Powers, Age 41

*Father*

*Mr. Powers is a big man with a soft mouth. He agrees readily to be interviewed but reveals little. He is not angry, sad, curious, or comfortable. His one opinion is that children ought to finish high school. He regrets nothing and desires nothing. Throughout his life he has known only one woman—his wife—and her only because she insisted. When asked about his work he upgrades himself a little without embarrassment or pride. He looks in his late fifties.*

"Well, what I've been able to get from her she kind of felt left out. She's got an older sister that's married with a boy a year old. They seem very happy. Then her older brother just had a baby boy. Well, that's about all that I could get out of her, that she didn't have any excuse. She was going with the boy for quite a number of years and, well, she told me that she thought that he really loved her. Well, they broke up shortly after this happened, I guess.

"There again is something that I can't understand. His parents, well, he didn't have too good of a home life really. His parents weren't bad, but I mean they didn't have the money, and they had a fairly large family, and they moved out of our school district when he was in high school two years. So he stayed with us his last two years in high school, which were no problem. You see he's been out of school over a year now. He lived with us during the school years. He called my wife 'mother' and he called me 'father' and, I mean, he was considered more or less just one of the family. Well, I don't know, I really can't dislike him. I mean you can't blame it all on him. But as my wife would say, it's a poor way of saying thank you.

"He's been to the house a couple of times to talk since we found out. We just discussed what, you know, what they were going to do. They broke up in the middle of summer, and he's been going with another girl. I don't know what they said to each other separately, but as far as when we were all together there is no hard feelings showing. I can't blame him really much more than I can blame her. I blame them both really because, the oldest girl had to get married, I mean, she'd finished school, but I mean, she was carrying the baby when she got married. And my daughter's also seen this happen to one of her aunts. . . .

"One reason we waited so long before my wife called down here, is because she thought she was too far along anyway. And then they went to see the doctor and he said he didn't know sure whether it was or not, so we decided to see if we could, because, well, it would be better for her schooling for one thing. I mean it's the main thing actually. . . .

"My wife wouldn't drive down here. I didn't really relish it too much, but I had been in cities before some, so it didn't bother me as much. And I, oh, I felt it was no more right that my wife should come than myself. Well, I mean she's our daughter and if one's to blame well then the other's to blame too. . . .

"My wife was pregnant when we got married, but I won't say she left me no alternative. She was one month or something like that. I won't say we had to get married because when she told me about it, she said that, you know, she didn't want to force it, because she didn't feel it would last if she did. But I don't know, maybe that made me like her more because she was like that. But no, in all, I've never been sorry. I mean I didn't start it back in high school. There's never been anybody else and I mean, I won't say we haven't talked about it when we were out with the fellows but really deep down, no I don't feel that I've missed anything."

*Children often pay the piper of parental fantasies. "She kind of felt left out" is the first and fateful statement that Mr. Powers utters in the interview. It contains levels of truth inaccessible to Mr. Powers' ken. For indeed, Patricia, unbeknownst to her, or to any other immediate witness, through her pregnancy and painful fruitless labor, merely enacts the rites of passage that this family holds necessary for entrance into adulthood and into, what then comes to pass for them, a committed life.*

## Miss Patricia Powers, Age 16, Single

### Twenty-two Weeks Pregnant

"Well, it was my nineteen-year-old brother's best friend. He wanted to finish out school, so he came and lived with us and paid my mother ten dollars a week for groceries and stuff like that. The first year he couldn't stand me and thought I was a little brat, and I'd always liked him, so I more or less forced myself on him.

"I used to talk to him all the time and we got to be really good friends and things just went from there. He wanted sex all the time and I didn't. It just didn't throw me as much as it did him. I don't know. Not everyday or everytime I saw him, because I kept telling myself it's because I'm insecure and it made me feel that was the only reason he kept going out with me. To me it's something special, it should be treasured, or something like that, you know, but with Bill it was just a necessity. It wasn't a necessity to me and so I just said no and he got mad. I've read about them, orgasms, but I've never even come close to one. I suppose maybe that's why I didn't enjoy it so much but I never told him I didn't. For him it was like whenever the opportunity came up and for me it was something I'd rather plan for and look forward to rather than everyday. Not like brushing your teeth, and I don't get a thrill out of brushing my teeth either. All the guys that I go out with, it looks like they're only after sex. There's only one thing that they go out with you for and they don't care about you, or anything else, and that doesn't thrill me too much. You say no and somebody else is going to say yes. . . .

"I still have a crush on him so that makes things worse, and he's going with a nice-looking Mexican blond from Florida. I feel defeated and the only thing that keeps me going now is that nobody else has to know. . . . Why should he come and see me, well he should of, but, I mean he's not going with me anymore so there's really not any need for him to come. I broke up with him before I had any idea that I was pregnant. My mother more or less blames him rather than me, because I'm her daughter, but it was my fault too. I don't know. What gets me is we were talking and he said, 'We could keep the baby,' and nothing else was ever said about it and he started going with Christine. . . .

DR. D.: When did you realize that you were pregnant?

PP: The end of June. I figured it. I mean, I've never missed my period before and then I did.

DR. D.: Did you tell anyone?

PP: Bill. He wasn't too thrilled, concerned, whatever. He didn't really care anymore, so. . . .

*From June to October both Pat and Bill ignore the pregnancy. They go about their business as usual and nothing is said. At one point Bill speaks of it to Mike, Patricia's nineteen-year-old brother, but he too fails to respond. In Pat's words: "He's too old. He doesn't care about his little bratty sister, so. . . ."*

Finally in October: "My mother asked me when they were going to kick me out of school, and I knew right off what she was talking about. It greatly upset my mother really, more than I thought it would. It upset my father because it upset my mother so much, I mean more on top of what it already had upset him. Another reason my mother wasn't too happy was because my sister decided she wanted to be a lab technician, but she got pregnant and got married. My brother talked about studying oceanography, and he had to get married because his girlfriend got pregnant. So I'm definitely determined to study secretarial science because Liz and Mike never made it. . . .

"Nobody ever offered me information about nothing. My best friend and I talked about it a lot. And we both decided that when we had kids we were going to talk to them. She read a story, it was called 'Born Knowing.' Well, the mother in it had a little girl, and she used to sit in a rocking chair when the kid was going asleep and used to tell her how she was conceived and born and everything. I wonder sometimes, like nobody ever told me anything. Everything was from kids at school. I just want to make everything available to her so she'll know. I'd tell them that's not the most wonderful thing to get involved in, but everybody does, so you might as well have something to protect yourself. . . ."

DR. D.: Do you regret it at all, not having the baby?

PP: No. It's selfish. Well, I don't think of it as being selfish except when I talk to somebody else about it. My life comes first. I've got my plans before this happened. They've already been made and I want to keep them, so I'm going to. I wouldn't have kept the baby anyway, so it doesn't really matter.


# Mrs. Jean Douglas, Age 33, Married

*Eighteen Weeks Pregnant*

*Mrs. Douglas is an exceptionally good-looking woman. As we talk, her fine eyes fill with tears again and again, but she does not permit herself actually to weep.*

*She speaks of a possible divorce and her fear of it. She speaks of the pity and the bewildered rage she feels toward her husband. All that she says sounds honest and straightforward. It is only when she refers to the abortion that she lies, not so much to me as to herself. Past eighteen weeks pregnant, she says: "I have not felt life. If I had I don't think I could go through with it."*

101

"My husband drinks. I believe he is alcoholic, but he won't admit it. He knows he drinks to an excess, but he doesn't think it's a problem. He thinks he can quit any time. He gets chills, and he usually sits in the car and sleeps the rest of it off and then may not eat for a couple of days after a really bad weekend. He can't even look an egg in the face anymore. He does funny little things like hiding his empty beer cans instead of throwing them in the garbage, which is silly because I find them. I don't look for him to keep his job much longer. . . .

"I had been on the pills for about eight years and I was silly for taking them off. Well, with him drinking the way he does, there are times when we've tried to have sex and he just is not able, and I've tried to help and it just didn't seem to work. One night it did I guess, and this is the result."

DR. D.: How does he react not being able to make it sexually?

JD: He gets upset, and I know sometimes he sits on the bed and cries and says, 'I'm sorry,' and I say, 'Well that's alright,' and then it gets to the point where it's ridiculous. It got to the point I was about saying 'It's alright' all the time, and I got just downright disgusted and mad.

"I can't say I haven't looked at another man, but as far as going with him and doing anything with him sexually I don't think I could, even though I don't think there is any feeling there between my husband and me anymore. We don't go anywhere, don't do anything together. I have my bowling Thursday nights and that's about the only thing I do. . . .

"My husband doesn't know that I am here. I told him I had a trip to take to Chicago because I have been going to school in connection with my job. I am a supervisor for AT & T.

"Maybe I'm not being fair in not telling him because he does love the three children that we have now, and he's a good father when he's there. But he is not there much. And the circumstances at home are such I just couldn't bring another baby in. Money always entered into it because the money was always spent for what he wanted with his drinking and this type of thing. . . .

"I don't want anybody, like my bosses, to know I was pregnant and came for an abortion. It's nothing shameful, there's nothing the matter with it, and I wish that we had the laws in my state. It's not that I think it's shameful, it's your outlook, I guess. I'm conscious of what people think of me. You know how the rest of the world is, and they may hold it against you for the rest of your life like you killed somebody. I know how I felt when I had my cat spayed when she was pregnant and I didn't know it. It really upset me. 'Mrs. Douglas did you know that your cat was pregnant?' 'No I didn't.' 'Another two weeks and it would have been too late." I was really upset, because like I told him I would have let her have the kittens and then had her taken care of.

"Maybe I didn't think about the abortion long enough. Sometimes I feel like it is murder."

## Miss Susan Browne, Age 23, Single

### *Twenty Weeks Pregnant*

*I am present when Doctor Szenes inducts Susan. The procedure is uneventful until he attaches the syringe to the plastic tubing connected to the three-and-a-half-inch spinal needle stuck into Susan's belly. As he withdraws the plunger, instead of the usual yellow liquid, blood appears. "What the hell," Szenes says. He disconnects the syringe and jiggles the needle. "I don't want to stick you again, young lady," he says, "so you might as well let me fool with this for a minute." Susan remains impassive. Szenes reconnects the syringe and suctions again. He gets another bloody tap. "Oh, shit," he mutters to himself. Turning to her and flashing her a brilliant bedside smile, he says, "Don't worry now. This happens sometimes. It doesn't mean a thing. Just gives the doctor a little more work to do, that's all." "What's going on?" I ask him in Hungarian. "How the hell should I know," he answers in Hungarian. "The needle stuck something it shouldn't have. I hope it's the fetus. That's the least problematic possibility."*

*Except for becoming several shades paler, Susan makes no overt response. After one more unsuccessful try Szenes finally gets his yellow liquid. There is an almost audible relaxation of muscles in the little room. The nurse smiles. Susan closes her eyes. Szenes winks at me. I lean against the wall and take a few deep breaths.*

*After Susan leaves, inducted and reassured, still not having asked a single direct question of anyone, I corral Szenes. In Hungarian. "Okay, friend, what happened?" He laughs. "Nothing, as you see. She's on her way." "You know what I mean." "Oh, you mean what could go wrong? Lots of things. But they don't fortunately. Not in my hands." "Give" "All right, lady." I think he is getting back his own for the émigré game I played with him months ago. "Several things can go wrong. At two stages. First, when the needle is introduced, instead of entering the fetal sac, it can hit the fetus, or some part of the mother, including an artery, which is big trouble. Mostly you tap blood in all these eventualities. Sometimes not. That's worse. Because then you proceed, and infuse the saline solution into the wrong place, as for example into the maternal vascular system. That poisons the patient a little. On occasion, fatally. But not here, thank God." With his bent middle finger he knocks on the little wooden table in front of him.*

*"How do you mean poisons?" "Well the saline solution enters the patient's bloodstream, instead of the uterus where it is supposed to go. You've heard me tell all the patients to report sudden thirst, flushing of the face, or tingling and numbness of the body. Those are the symptoms. If that happens, you must determine serum electrolite balance at once, and immediately administer intravenously at least a liter of hypotonic fluids, such as five percent dextrose in water. This usually resolves the crisis, unless you are unlucky. Or rather, the patient is." "Did that ever happen here?" "Not really. Listen, I'm sorry but I've got to get back to work." "Right. Thanks very much."*

*I wait several hours then go to Susan's room to interview her. She makes no mention of the induction procedure.*

"Well, the man I'm going with told me he had a vasectomy. He's had it for almost a year, but something went wrong and I got pregnant anyway. I didn't have my periods so I went to the doctor and I said the fellow had a vasectomy, so he was treating me for fibroids for sixteen weeks. Then he sent me to the hospital for a D & C, but before they do that they give you a pregnancy test. It wasn't fibroids, it was a baby. I just couldn't quite make myself believe that I was pregnant and I put off going to see about getting an abortion. I do feel that the doctor should have found out sooner. I mean, after all the years he's gone to school and stuff, he should know."

*Susan Browne is a polite, placid girl. This is her second out-of-wedlock pregnancy. The first one took place when she was nineteen. That baby she kept. Her account of the experience is presented in the same laconic tones with which she discusses her hometown physician's shocking error.*

"I've always liked kids. When I found out I was pregnant the first time. my first thought was 'Oh goody, I'm going to have a baby, finally.' Now I think I've grown up and I realize that it's probably not fair to the child to go ahead and raise it without a father. At first he tried to say it wasn't his. Then he admitted that it was. He said he couldn't get married and I said I didn't want him to. I just wanted him to help pay some of the expenses. But he didn't. He skipped out. I've never heard from him since. . . .

"My mom was more upset I think this time than she was the first time. She kind of knew it. She confronted me before I had a chance to say anything to her. She just asked if I was pregnant and I said I thought I was. My dad, he never said too much either time, but he wanted me to keep the first one and he didn't say anything about this one. He just wondered if Pete and I were gonna get married and I told him no, he didn't want to start a family now. My mom didn't want me to keep the baby this time but she didn't want me to come here either. Neither one of them thought too highly about abortions. . . .

"I graduated from high school. After I had my baby, I started going to beauty school. I wanted to do something. Every time you'd talk to anybody connected with the beauty school, they always said that you made money. And I like messing around with hair, so I thought I'd try it. And after I'd been doing it for awhile I found out that you don't make that much money, at least in Kansas you don't.

"We have an ABC program. The county pays so much a month and I'm on that. I'm trying to live on $150.00 a month.

"About Christmas last year we had talked about getting married and we talked about it ever since. He just didn't want to start another family now. I think that in time we will probably get married. He said that he would pay for this when I get back, he'd have his paycheck by then."

## Mrs. Ann Wilder, Age 41

*Mother*

"All I had to do was look at her face. I said, 'You're pregnant.' She said yes. I said, 'And you don't want to marry Charlie?' And she said, 'No, I don't want to marry him.' At that point I was so relieved to hear she didn't want to marry him. I was more relieved than I was worried to find out that she was pregnant.

"His family knew it for a while and never told me. This bothers me too. How blind can I be that I didn't see it on her? Twenty-four weeks she is. Her boss knows about it. In fact, some of those people at work knew about it. The men watch the girls and they noticed it, but her mother didn't notice it. You know it kind of bothers me that I was so stupid.

"My husband was so hurt. He kept saying 'Oh my gosh.' He didn't yell or anything. Neither of us did. . . .

"I want what's best for her. Where we live isn't like New York, she would have been pegged as a bad girl for the rest of her life. She isn't a bad girl, she's a good girl. It isn't as if she goes around a lot. Some of her girl friends do. They're on the pill. The ones that work with her they'll never get into trouble like she did. It seems like all her life she's had to pay the hard way with everything that happened. I think what it is with her she doesn't have any confidence in herself. She doesn't, how can you build it up? Someone else has to help build it up, I think, maybe. My telling her isn't enough. . . .

"She's slower, I don't know. She's not as smart as my other daughter, Mimi, and that's been hard on her all her life, the middle child. The younger one, a boy, is even smarter yet. It's really been hard on her. . . .

"We're a pretty close family I think, but this one keeps things inside. She doesn't tell you much. I wanted her to talk to me, and then if I would try to talk to her a little bit, she would clam up. I couldn't say things to antagonize her, about that I thought that she wasn't in love with him.

"She said the reason she didn't tell us for so long was that she didn't want to ruin Mimi's wedding. I said, 'Well, allright, after the wedding, that was August 19th, why didn't you tell us?' 'I don't know, I could never find you together.' That isn't really true. . . .

"When they refused her at that other hospital because it was too large, that started from four-thirty in the morning. She was admitted over there, and everything was going to be all right, and then they X-rayed her and said, 'It's too large.' I really don't want to think about it. I don't know if I'll be sorry. It's her life. I think she should have another chance, right? If it was too late, I'd say give it away, but when the time came I don't know. I wouldn't be able to look at it, I know. I had to really fight to keep from thinking about it as my own grandchild because I want them, really want them. I think I'm really in two.

*Mrs. Wilder and I talk for a very long time, much beyond the taping. She tells me of her ruined childhood, bare and full of losses.*

*Of her adulthood, of small contentments, time-to-time joys, and making-do. Contrapuntal to everything she says is her un-self-conscious total involvement with it.*

*Mrs. Wilder is not pretty, not elegant, not well educated. Periodically she is grossly inattentive to her surroundings and to the people who populate it. Nevertheless, her presence adorns with light the social workers' small office, where we sit. Her resonating, vibrant being and many-leveled responsiveness brings the world alive and certifies it as real.*

## Miss Victoria Wilder, Age 20, Single

### Twenty-four Weeks Pregnant

*She weeps often during this interview, but never openly for the baby she meant to have, which currently is drowning in her belly, in a saline-saturated solution.*

*Vicky is unlucky. Because, although she has considerable charm and unwitting humor, I find myself angry with her for her bland self-righteousness. The saline doctor who inducts her gives her a hard time and also seems angry.*

"When we first found out that I was pregnant his first reaction was that it was the worst thing that could ever happen to him. Of course it was bad, but I didn't personally like the way he wasn't too much help to me. I was going to have an abortion then. That was back in June. I didn't think I could tell my mother. I thought that she was completely against abortions. But then we never really talked about it anyway, because there was no need.

"He was completely against it. He said if I had one then he could never marry me. Then I guess it was both our decision that we would get married. . . .

"Nobody knew until about two weeks ago. The people at work were the first ones that found out. I don't know how they found out. I couldn't understand it. My boss called me over one day, and he was talking to me. I asked him, 'How do the people at work know?' Because it was the men that first started saying anything. I figured it would be the girls, but it wasn't, it was all the men. He said, 'Men don't look at men, they look at girls.' I'm skinny anyway and they noticed as soon as you put on a little weight. As soon as they have something to talk about, they'll talk about something. . . .

"Charlie wanted me to tell my parents right away and I kept saying, 'No, I can't ruin my sister's wedding for her.' Then after the wedding he'd call me up like every night and ask me if I told them yet. 'Did you tell them yet, did you tell them yet?' And I kept saying no. I didn't want him to tell them with me because I figured it was up to me to tell my parents. He told his own parents and I didn't want him there when I told mine.

"He's going to school now to become a minister, he's going to Bible college. We talked it over and we decided that he wasn't going to go this year so we could get enough money to at least get a place. It's bad enough you have to start out being pregnant, but I didn't want to live with anybody's parents right away. The next thing I heard, I hadn't seen him for about two weeks, he went to school anyway. I was thinking if we can't get along now, how are we going to get along after we're married. . . .

"Then Sunday night, I said, 'This is my last chance, I have to tell them now.' I just kept saying, 'Vicky, you have to say it, you have to say it.' I just sat there and nothing came out. So I got up and went to the bathroom and like I gave myself a pep talk. Then I just said, 'Mom I have to talk to you.' Right away she goes, 'You're pregnant.' She knows everytime I say something. I said, 'Yeah but that's not all.' She said, 'What?' And she told me. She goes, 'I know, you don't want to marry him.' I said, 'Yeah.' She was glad that I didn't want to marry him because I don't think she was too much in love with him either.

"I was shocked how they both reacted. I was expecting screaming and yelling and my father kicking me out of the house. I used to get hit. My mom, she always did the hitting. She did the yelling for the both of them. My father just sat there on the couch and said, 'Oh no.' I thought my mom was completely against abortions and my dad too. He said, 'Can she have an abortion?' I just thought, 'Wow! If I knew they were going to say that I would have told them a long time ago.' She said it's up to me whatever I want to do. She said she was just glad that I didn't want to marry him. I said, 'So am I.'

"I don't feel like I'm really killing anything because it's not breathing yet. I would rather get rid of it, then make it suffer it's whole life. If I had to keep it and I couldn't afford it, and get harassed by other people, you know, 'Who's your father,' and all that.

"I was planning on having it you know, so the first time it moved, I was excited and I was going to tell my mom, 'Mom it moved,' but then I remembered I didn't tell her yet that I was pregnant. . . ."

*Vicky Wilder is far from the simpleton her mother thinks her. Her naïveté is seasoned. Her guilelessness is in the service of self-preservation.*

## Miss Rose Lucas, Age 21, Single

### Twenty-three Weeks Pregnant

"I met a fellow and at least I thought I was in love and everything. I haven't seen him since after I told him I was pregnant. He immediately left. He went to California.

"I have a baby eight months old, so you know it's too soon to have another one. I haven't even got myself all together from the first one."

*Disorder, dismay, and detachment are the chief characteristics of Rose's life.*

*Her mother has been married several times, but she believes herself to be illegitimate. From time to time she sees her natural father, who, she says, "looks at me with disgust, I don't know why."*

*Her half brother, two years older than Rose, is hooked on heroin. Of that situation she says, "My mother just won't face it. I don't know why. He's OD.'d twice and the ambulance had to take him."*

*Her eight-month-old baby is illegitimate. The father skipped town before the boy was born. Now, she is almost six months pregnant by another man, who also has left. She is on welfare.*

*There is no trace of emotion in her voice as she tells her story. True, life is a mess, but it is like that everywhere. She does not perceive her lot as different from that of her neighbors.*

*The one thing she minds, and her delicate, black face crumples as she speaks of it, is getting "nervous" and hitting her son.*

*My reaction to her is a prayer of thanks for the wisdom of abortions, up to any weeks of gestation, I don't care.*

"All my life I hated children, and I said I'll never have any and at first I did try to get rid of it. I took pills. Darvons and just anything I found in the medicine cabinet. I wouldn't even tell my mother what was wrong with me, I wouldn't let her call a doctor, because I didn't want to tell her that I took pills. Then I walked out in front of a car and it didn't help. It stopped. He got out and said, 'Did anyone tell you, you're crazy.' I was like in a daze. I didn't want any kids. . . .

"Right now I have a lot of problems with my son. Like I'm not the perfect mother, I know. I'm not a mother by all means and when the baby's crying I just feel like murdering him. And I take out my faults on him which I know I shouldn't. I can't go anywhere and when you don't have kids you can go out. When you have a kid you have to say, 'Well, I don't have a babysitter' or, 'He's sick' or, 'I can't go.' I just scream at him, I know he'll probably resent me when he gets older. But then I make up for it. I talk to him easy, like I say 'I'm sorry' and 'I don't mean to take it out on you' and at one time I did hit him.

"I had a headache, a real bad headache and he just started screaming and wouldn't shut up. And kept on screaming and screaming, so I hit him. And then my mother said she's going to take him away, if I couldn't cope with him. Then I said, 'No I'll be alright.' That really got next to me. I broke down crying. I can't cope with another child. . . .

"It don't help to scream because I found out the more I screamed the worse they was. When I had my baby I just kept my mouth shut, I did. I didn't scream not a once and I was hurting. Now, too, I'm just going to sit and take it quietly."

## Mrs. Joan Wallace, Age 26, Divorced

### Twenty Weeks Pregnant

"I'm divorced. I was married twice. The twins are by my first marriage and they're nine years old. My little boy is by my last marriage. This is by someone that I met and I was going with.

"He didn't want to get married because he has a child by another marriage and he just feels like he doesn't take care of it, so he couldn't afford to take care of another one. . . .

"When I finally broke down and told my mother, she wanted me to have it and give it away. I figured I couldn't go through the nine months and then seeing it, naming him, and give him away. I would care for it if I have to have it. The only way that I wouldn't keep it is not to see it.

"There was someone in our town who would do it for $250 but he was a veterinarian. This guy offered to help, to get some money together, for me to go to him. He even talked to him. I said, 'That scares me,' because I wanted to be safe, because of my other three kids. It wouldn't be worth it. I'd rather have it than lose my life because I've got to take care of them. So I just kept waiting. That was about three months.

"I have been all nervous and upset from it. Like, I just stayed away from people. Gotten into real bad moods over it, and everything, because I knew that the only place to come would be New York and I knew I didn't have the money.

"The fellow I was going with he didn't give me anything. He doesn't even know I'm here. I didn't tell him, 'cause I figured he didn't want any part of it.

"The welfare department is helping to pay for some of it. They have that Medicaid program. And the lady bought my ticket for me, the social worker herself, and then the man, the clergy, gave me money for food and for if I had to stay in a hotel or anything. Everybody pitched in. I couldn't have made it on my own, so I would have ended up having to have it and then that would have been worse for the baby, because it just would have been another child for me to have to take care of.

"I talked to some of my girl friends. They worried about me coming all the way here by myself, but nobody really could afford to come with me. That's why it would be so much better if every state had it, because it's so hard when you have to go away from home. If I was home, it would be over soon and I'd just be at home. Now I know I got to face the trip and everything. . . .

*The saline induction has failed to work and at the time we speak, Joan has been confined to bed for three days with an IV in her arm. She keeps complaining of pain and hunger, cramps and cravings. "If only someone gave me a box of chocolates," she sighs again and again. "I've had nothing in my stomach since I got to New York." She does seem in bad shape. Exhausted and washed out, sweating buckets.*

*The interview is interrupted because Dr. Bender arrives to resalinate her.*

*When I return the following afternoon she is in labor. The railing on her bed is up. Her drained face is indistinguishable from the white sheet on which she lies. She claws at her bedclothes, tosses her body about, and wails in agony. Alarmed, I inquire about her from the nurse on duty. I am told not to worry. "She'll be all right. She is just hysterical. A screamer."*

"I've been here since Monday now and had eight bottles of that stuff. I really had a bad night and a real bad day. Oh, this pain is coming again and it just drives me crazy. I can't lay here anymore. I'm hurting too bad. I hurt all day. They haven't given me anything. They gave me one shot and it wasn't very powerful. She said she was going to see if she could get something stronger. If they would just give me something to knock me out and let me rest a little bit and get some of the pain out of me, but they haven't. I ripped my gown off twice today and pulled the bed apart, up and down. I just can't stand it."

## Mr. Dorian Grant, Age 41

*Father*

*The Grants' predicament is peculiar even for this hospital. Jessica Grant, fifteen, and Angelica Grant, fourteen, are each twenty-three weeks pregnant. For Jessica this is the second saline abortion in less than a year's time.*

*The girls are accompanied by their father, a long-distance trucker. Mr. Grant is an easy-going man with a soft drawl and a quiet voice. He chews on an unlit cigar stub while we talk. Neither this evocative behavior nor my knowledge of his trade succeed in reversing the aura of bewildering passivity he emanates. He has no notion how this happened to his daughters or why. He blames himself, he blames the girls, he blames the world, he thinks there is no one to blame. He has seven children, all of whom he loves dearly, but he can not recall the exact ages of either Jessica or Angelica. He has no feelings toward the fetus, but he is against contraception. When confronted with the fact that Jessica might have been spared a second abortion, he says, "I didn't think she'd do it again." His plans for the future of the girls are to take away their privileges, maybe even to lock them in the house at night.*

"Actually I can't tell you about them because I don't know that much about them. I mean I'm a long-distance truck driver and I'm gone two to three weeks at a time and we've got seven kids altogether. . . .

"Well, the first time Jessica got that way happened a little under a year ago. I got up one morning to go to work and so on the television screen a letter was in an envelope tied to the screen by Scotch tape, and it said 'To Mom and Dad.' So I just pulled it off the television screen and walked back into the bedroom, sat down on the bed, and said, 'Here's a letter.' My wife said, 'What do you mean?' I said, 'Well, it says to Mom and Dad'. I'm interested to find out what it is,' so I opened it up. And it said, 'Well Dad, you and Mom have always taught me and all of us that if one of us ever became pregnant that you'd beat us half to death.' So, she said, 'Now I'm that-away and I just didn't feel like coming to you and talking to you about it. I know I did wrong but I love Paul and they won't let us get married, and I just don't know what to do.' Well, that hurt me so bad, I mean I wouldn't even go out to work that day I just stayed home. I didn't get angry because I felt that I did wrong somewheres along the line by maybe not giving them the right counsel. It's hard to try to counsel a kid, I mean I know my father and mother they always beat the tar out of me, but I believe that there's a lot more talking and not enough whipping going on. Maybe I goofed up at it, I didn't whip them enough maybe. But I don't know, it's just a guess. . . .

"This time she didn't tell me at all, her mother told me all about it. I don't know why she waited so long. I don't know exactly what all took place, but I know that my wife told me about both of them together. I was gone I think for about three weeks. Well I was so mad, two o'clock in the morning I woke those two and I said, 'What in the world do you think we're running here, a whore house or what?' Both of them sat up and cried about it, told me they were sorry and all that, and it wouldn't happen no more. But Jessica, this makes the second time she's told me that. Well, I feel I've done wrong somewheres. There's a lot bigger families than I've got and their kids don't do that. . . .

"The thing of it is her and her boy they were suppose to get married when school was out this year, so it backfired and his parents wouldn't let him get married. He's a real nice boy. He said, 'If it was left up to me I'd like to get married,' but he said, 'If you'll take her and take care of this I'll pay the bill.' Which he did both times, he paid the bill. . . .

"I run twenty-seven states and I never know from one day to the next where I'm going to be. I don't haul nothing but steel, from the steel mill. They ship all over the United States. I sleep in a big truck with a sleeper on it. Most generally I pull into a rest area or maybe into a truck stop. You get lonely. You know, lots of times I'd like to be home but I don't know, it's just what you get adjusted to, I guess. A lot of rest areas I pull into that there's always a bunch of girls come down, knocks on your door once in a while wants to know if you want a date or something. So they spend maybe an hour with you for ten dollars. Well, they'll say ten, but you can always Jew them down to five dollars or whatever you want to give them. It's strictly business that's what they're there for. You can't turn around and tell your wife about it, no. . . .

"Well, I figured that a son, he's got to learn to take care of himself, and which it wouldn't surprise me him getting a girl in the way. If he takes after his dad, I know he will. Well, I wouldn't want it to happen, I think it's wrong myself, but still yet a lot of it goes on. I mean you ain't going to stop it, not by sitting and talking about it. The way I look at it a girl can really get messed up, but a man can do something like that, and in one ear and out the other. . . .

"Well, my wife is pretty well shook up, she has to go to the doctor two or three times a week to get nerve pills. She's really disturbed about it, and she know that somewheres along the line we've not done what we should have done maybe, but I don't know what. . . ."

DR. D.: Are you going to get them some birth control now?
DG: I haven't made my mind up to adjust to that.
DR. D.: Are you Catholic?
DG: No, I'm not. I'm Baptist, and I think I'll just keep them locked up, just don't let them out.
DR. D.: Why are you against getting them birth control?
DG: Why? Well, for the simple reason if you'll nail down to it and allow 'em to get birth control, then they are going to just keep on going. You know they are never goin' to stop. You allow them to get birth control pills, so what's the use.

## Miss Jessica Grant, Age 15, Single

*Twenty-three Weeks Pregnant*

*I speak with Jessica about half an hour after she has delivered her fetus. At the time we talk, the placenta has not yet been ejected. Although this fact preoccupies me throughout the interview, Jessica does not allude to it at all.*

*The passivity of her father is transmuted in Jessica into total will-lessness. At three months pregnant she confesses to her parents, who forbid her to abort. She accepts. Two weeks later her sister makes a similar confession. Two inexplicable months of alleged deliberation pass. The parents order the girls to abort. Jessica accepts.*

"Well my parents knew, but they didn't want me to have an abortion again. But when they found out my sister was they decided to, and it was this late. I found out when I was in my second month. I guess I was scared. I knew they'd probably kill me, two times. They didn't want to go through with it again because it's too much on 'em. I wanted to finish school, I had things planned.

"My dad wasn't home, I spoke to Mom. When Dad came home Mom told him. They didn't like it. They didn't want me to get an abortion. Dad thought it was a risk. They told me to get married. I told them I didn't want to."

DR. D.: Did they talk to the boy?

JG: No.

DR. D.: They never called the boy and asked him if he was willing?

JG: No, they didn't say anything.

DR. D.: So how did they imagine you were going to get married?

JG: I don't know, maybe they really didn't plan on me getting married.

DR. D.: So then the weeks passed and you weren't getting married, what did they say then?

JG: Nothing.

DR. D.: How did you feel?

JG: I was all mixed up. Then when Angelica found out that she was, we just packed and came up here. Mom said that since both of them were 'There,' she says, 'there is only one thing to do now and that is come up here.' I told them if I couldn't have the abortion, I'll just have it and forget about school. But I don't think I could take care of it. I wouldn't give it for adoption, but as young as I am now, I don't know. Then when they said I could that's when I started planning on finishing school. . . .

DR. D.: How do you feel about the abortions?

JG: It's okay.

DR. D.: Did the baby move before you started this?

JG: Yeah, I could feel it moving.

DR. D.: Did that give you any kind of sense about it?

JG: Uh, uh. No.

DR. D.: Do you want to have any kids when you marry?

JG: Uh huh, a lot. I guess seven. He wants a big family too.

DR. D.: Do you blame him at all for all this?

JG: We were both to blame.

# Miss Chris Barris, Age 25, Single

## Twenty-one Weeks Pregnant

"I think my mother sensed it. My mother's a nurse and she was aware that I had missed at least two periods and then she noticed the weight gain, but not a very substantial weight gain. And actually about a month ago she said that she would have been glad for me to go ahead and get a physical, but I kept saying no, for really no rational reason. I was very depressed. I probably reached the stage where I couldn't talk, I was so depressed about being pregnant. I really didn't think that I could get pregnant. This came as such a shock to me. I think she probably sensed my anxiety.

"She knew I was sleeping with someone. She also knew that we had broken up. I hadn't seen him for a while, and he doesn't know that I'm pregnant.

"I didn't love him. I didn't want to marry him. I don't feel that he should have a responsibility financially, but I do feel that he could have been more conscientious, because he was fully aware of the fact that I wasn't taking birth control pills because they made me sick, and he said that he would be responsible. Well, for two weeks I thought that he was using condoms and he wasn't."

DR. D.: How come you weren't aware whether he was or wasn't using them?

CB: I wasn't aware that he had to have an erection before he could put the condom on. I just thought that he had it on.

DR. D.: Didn't you ever touch him?

CB: Well, it was always dark and I couldn't see it. I mean you couldn't tell. . . .

*Chris Barris, college student, daughter of a physician (deceased) and of a registered nurse, beneficiary of liberal views, product of permissiveness, enriched in environment and opportunity, child of her class and times, is cool. Very cool. She is also self-indulgent, narrow, neurotic, and unresponsive to everything outside her whims.*

DR. D.: When did you first start having intercourse?

CB: When I was nineteen.

DR. D.: Do you remember the first boy?

CB: Yes I do. He was a physician.

DR. D.: What was it like?

CB: It wasn't particularly enjoyable. I just wanted to lose my virginity. It was sort of a technical thing. I think we might have slept together two or three times, because he was going with somebody else at that time.

"The next person I was a little more involved with and we considered marriage, but nothing came of it. But it did hurt when we broke up. I hope I don't sound promiscuous. Oh, I loved one, thank you. I got involved with someone who was not good for me at all and I didn't realize it until it was too late. He was a criminal really. I didn't know it, but through him I started experimenting with drugs. I tried LSD with him I suppose six or seven times. It was interesting. I can't say that I'd do it again, but I never had a bad experience. All my experiences were very spiritual, very beautiful."

DR. D.: Any other drugs, by the way, besides LSD?

CB: Well, if you consider grass and hash drugs, but not a heavy user.

DR. D.: Is this fairly common at the university?

CB: Uh-hum.

DR. D.: Was it readily available?

CB: It was to me. I never even had to pay for it. It was provided by so-called friends. . . .

DR. D.: Did you consider at any time keeping the baby?

CB: Never. I didn't even consider it. I couldn't take the responsibility.

DR. D.: And yet you delayed very long.

CB: Yeah. Maybe I was rebelling.

DR. D.: Against what?

CB: I don't know. Maybe things in general. A combination of things.

DR. D.: Like what?

CB: My father's death. . . .

DR. D.: Have you any feeling toward the baby?

CB: No.

DR. D.: Has it moved?

CB: Yes. I felt it in the past two weeks. I thought maybe it was premenstrual cramps.

"I really just can't feel anything for it. In fact I was talking to the pastor who helped me to get here and he asked me what my conception of life was. And I said, well, I suppose you know just right off the bat the baby is born, you pat it on the back, and it starts breathing. That's life to me. But before then it's nothing. Kind of like a growth."

The rest is echo's echo. Meaning whittled down to bone. Bone decomposed to marrow.

Oh yes, these people lie, they kid themselves, testify falsely, confess in bad faith, shirk responsibility, only pretend to honor, bracket the past, and invent their lives. And who among us does differently? Especially in times of crisis. Especially in times of irreversible choice.

But I do not wish to speak of them as if they were the subject of philosophy or art. That too would only be a handy escape from the fact of their palpable being: bloody, sweaty, mean, frightened, confused, yearning, merciful, generous, willing to stretch beyond their size, loveless and utterly desirous of love —and perhaps deserving of it, like all of us, purely on the basis of devastating need.

From time to time, when the ordeal is done, letters arrive. Notes of gratitude. Dark missives of lingering remorse. On occasion a shattered cry from someone lost and dangerously compromised. The four reproduced here are typical, insofar as one can claim that of any human expression.

First, a white, folded sheet with red borders, addressed to "The Entire Staff of the Hospital":

*Dec. 19th*

> *This is a letter that is long overdo.*
>
> *I am very sorry in my heart that the situation ever arose, that of me needing an abortion. I felt guilt, ashamed and I still do. I guess I always will. I am very afraid that God will never see fit to let me every conceive again. This is one of my only regrets. The other is the horrible feeling that I have interferred with another human beings chance at life.*
>
> *What do you do with the remains?*
>
> *In spite of it all I want to say "Thank You" for your understanding and help, and just plain being there. If God approves of what you do I'm sure he blesses each of you at least 1000 times a day for the comfort and understanding each of you gives.*

*Please, always believe in what you do so those who need your help will always be able to find it.*

> *Tearful but*
> *Thankful*

Next a personal note addressed to Suzy Lindstrom:

> *March 27*

*Dear Suzy,*

*Hello!*

*I'm really feeling great. You know that if you wouldn't of been there with me I don't know what I would of done. You really helped me out alot. Saturday nite my breasts got real swollen so I went & got some pills from the doctor so I feel better. He checked my breasts & stomach for infection & there was none, so that was good. I did'nt have as much homework as I thought I would of, but enough. Suzy, mom remembered that she never got that $70.00 back from if you got the abortion done you would get it back, we were such in a rush about things, it slipped our minds, so could you please see about that? Thanks!*

*This is really going to be short because I have some homework to catch up on. So I'll catch ya later'*

> *May God Bless*
> *All My Love*
> *Mary*

P.s. *If you send anything from the hospital do not put on envelope because we know all the mailmen.*

Undated, there is a Thank-U-Gram. It is a two-by-four soft, yellow piece of paper made to look like a telegram. On its back there is a long, printed legend explaining the rationale of its sales value:"THANK-U-GRAMS ARE DESIGNED TO DEVELOP THE FAC-ULTY OF AWARENESS. . . ." It goes on at length. On its reverse the handwritten message reads:

*Hi!*

*All of you are Super!! Keep up the good work. Wish you all luck. Thanks.*

*Sincerely, Julia*

Finally, a lined sheet from a loose-leaf notebook. The careful childish scrawl reads:

*Dec. 22nd*

*Gentlemen:*

*I was admitted to your hospital August 26. For my own record I would like to know all of the possible after affects after having the saline. Literature of which I have gotten a hold of states my chances for ever having children again are very slim. This is just an example. I would be at great peace of mind if you could give me all of the facts after having such an abortion. Also for my use only I would like the sex, weight when it was aborted and approximately how much it would of weighed if I carried it full term, when I would of delivered, healthy or not, and blood type. Please, you must help me in giving me this information. It will ease the pain so much more. Please.*
*Thank you*

*Sincerely,*
*Mary Lou Burns*

Attached to this letter, by paper clip, there is a two-by-three index card. On it Suzy has written:

8/26     Mary-Lou Burns
          Rte 4 72nd St.
          Kansas City, Miss.

12/25    [*Note:* Four months have passed] received letter—
          upset after ab.; asking re: fetus; effects of S.I.

12/25    checked chart
         uneventful procedure
         Fetus del: 8/28 2:40 AM.

[*Then follows:* sex of item, its weight, weeks of gestation, and
"no abnormalities."]

1/4      Reached pt. by phone—Discussed her concerns
         (gave no info. re: fetus) referred to counseling.

"Gave no info. re: fetus." It sounds like a foreign language
if one says it fast enough. If one says it fast enough perhaps
one can evade its deadly impact. Not that I question the professional validity of the decision. Not at all. I question our
predicaments.

━━━

In a month's time I acquire a sort of wooden torpor to the screams that periodically shatter the humdrum noises of the floor. Tears cease to unsettle me. I am unmoved by wailing. I take it for granted that we are in the business of death here, and the tenor of each day will be heartache.

My attention wanders. I am caught by the horror of helplessness and apathy that lies at the core of most of these lives. I am astonished at the meaning of being female. To be impregnable suddenly looks to me the heart of vulnerability, the very essence of dependence and limitation. On this unit, womanhood appears the bedrock of martyrdom, and sex seems like the torturer's wheel on which selfhood is broken.

I exaggerate, of course. I am shell-shocked, as it were, stunned by being spoken to. Staggered by these readily revealed dramas, whose plots are loneliness, whose resolutions are defeat.

Ultimately nothing under the sun has greater significance nor is more problematic than a life and the convoluted network of its relatedness, close and distant, to other lives. It is clear there can be no joy or hope, no meaning at all, beyond personal connections.

To find this truth in the shadow of death is fitting—for it is by our own finitude that we measure the worth of our existence, day by gray day.

"I had no choice" these women say. "I had no choice." A truth perhaps. Perhaps a lie. In any case a testimony to our ties of childhood, where excuses could redeem.

"I had no choice." Who cares, my lady? It is your seed, your blood, your loss, your nightmare—your ledger of sin and expiation.

But is it? Aren't we all responsible for all, and accountable for every desperation?

Well, yes. But only on this floor. Only in extremis. Only when the air is filled with the dust of doubt and death. Otherwise, some of us are rich and others are poor. We take cocktails at six, go to the shore, and abortions ought to be banned or administered at will, because they are, like the pulling of a tooth, easy business.

Not even breathing is easy business if you are human.

# Chapter 4

# D & C Floor: Staff

And death i think is no parenthesis
e. e. cummings

In comparison with the saline unit, the D & C floor appears a haven. This is a false impression that is nevertheless very strong.

Partly, the error is due to the quiet, to the absence of agonized screams, calls for "Mother" or "pity" or "God" piercing the air with embodied pain at the end of which, one knows, there will be a death. No one here probes—"Nurse, what was its sex?" "Can it be baptized?" "Will its immortal soul be saved?" This floor is quiet. Immortality is finite and lasts only while memory speaks.

There are no women here heavy with child, and almost no children carrying children. The D & C floor is civilized.

Getting off the elevator I find myself in physical surroundings that duplicate the seventh floor except for the absence of the television and treatment rooms—those areas are ordinary rooms here, housing patients. There are altogether twenty-two beds on the floor, six in single rooms and sixteen in the eight doubles.

As I walk around exploring I realize that my awkwardness has returned. I am again a stranger, again alone, again the intrusive outsider eyed by the nurses with ill will as I pass. I begin to wish fervently that I were back on the saline unit.

Not knowing exactly what to do next, I decide as I come to

each room to knock, to poke my head in without waiting for an answer and say "Hi." The women inside answer back, "Hi." I withdraw. No one seems surprised, and no one demands an explanation. There are no shouts of "Hey, come back. What do you want? What do you mean 'Hi?' " Patients captive in their beds become divested of their self-assertion. Hospitalization forces one to abdicate control over one's destiny; others take charge. In that situation, each new face becomes a potential source of vital information regarding one's immediate fate. No confined patient can afford to turn anyone away. What if the person saying "Hi" will talk next of a rising fever or blood test results or discharge time or simply produce a permissible goody to eat.

Saying "Hi" has soured. Anyway, the next room I reach has its swinging doors propped open, and I can see that it is unoccupied. The small brown tag on the door frame says 402. I enter.

Crossing the threshold catapults me into bracketed worlds I have not visited for many decades. It is late afternoon, and the light filtering through the slightly dirty windows of 402 bathes the genteel decay of the room in the gray-blue colors of oceanic depressions at dusk. Strings of seedy hotel rooms, dilapidated rooms to let, elegant sanatoriums into which I fit only through the one commonality of tubercular lungs, pillage-wrecked abodes covered with the omnipresent dust of war, all converge in 402. Like ghosts at a wake.

More disciplined looking reveals two regulation hospital beds placed lengthwise about three feet apart from each other. Between them, at the head of the beds and in front of the faded-pink-fiberglass-curtained window, stands a beige night table, badly chipped, betraying previous incarnations in green and white. I pull out its drawer and find an aqua-colored plastic disposable emesis basin. The color half insures it being put to use. Underneath the drawer there is a door, behind which a washbowl and a bedpan are stored. These also are aqua-colored. In fact these three objects represent the only matching items in the room. Everything else is one-of-a-kind functional junk. Over each bed stands a rolling adjustable bedside table. The one on the left is formica-covered, with a drawer and a hidden mirror in it; the other one is plain wood, hiding nothing. Both are hand-painted beige and chipped.

In the right corner there is an old white washstand with its enamel cracked in intricate patterns like rivers on a map of a foreign country. Above the washstand hangs a single glass shelf topped with a pock-marked dead mirror lit by one bare bulb. Next to the mirror, attached to the wall, there is a white metal disposable-paper-towel holder. I remove a towel. It is rectangular in shape with two folds. I unfold the folds and discover that in fact the towel is square. It is becoming increasingly evident to me that sooner or later I will have to leave this room. I notice that the floorboards are painted a beautiful wine color, marred only by intermittent drips of beige that some careless painter splattered on them while doing the walls. I step back into the corridor.

Out here the scene has radically changed. There are four or five stretchers lined up, each manned by an orderly, and several nurses are bustling about with loaded syringes in their hands. Patients receive, just before they are taken to the operating room, one cc of atropine to dry their mucous membranes. As each nurse enters a different room, I hear the same sentence repeated at imperceptible intervals, creating the impression of one speaker followed by a reverberating echo, becoming less and less audible with distance and time: "Okay, dear, they have come for you."

I look at the orderly nearest me. He is a corpulent, middle-aged man with enormous hands that he rests on the edge of his stretcher. He wears a white coat below which green OR pants show. On his head there is a green cap pulled down to his ears and covering half his forehead. His eyes are astonishingly blue. He stands slouched with an air of utter boredom. Suddenly he turns and catches my eye before I can look away. He smiles, but his face remains unchanged. I smile back against my better judgment. "You no wanna done it," he says, "you scare." He has the sickening look of pointless evil. "No, I no wanna, I mean I am a doctor." The information electrifies him. The leer on his face collapses into a mask, his eyes narrow, he straightens up, he turns himself as if by magic from devil to robot. "Sorry, Doctor, very sorry." "Okay," I say and walk away.

At the elevators there are two women waiting, lying on stretchers, wrapped in white sheets, each accompanied by an orderly. The orderlies stand behind the heads of the women, ready to push them, feet first, into the elevator. One woman is staring into space at middle distance, her eyes rounded and unfocused with fear. The other one has her eyes closed. Both seem very pale under their light-green-paper shower caps, which all patients must wear into the operating room.

The elevator arrives, and as its doors open, the woman who has kept her eyes closed begins to weep. She screws up her face as large tears squeeze through her still-closed lids and roll down the side of her head onto the white sheet, making it wet and causing small plopping sounds like sparse rain at the seaside on a quiet day. The slow patter of water hitting wet cloth sounds inexpressibly forlorn. The elevator man looks at the orderly. "Que le pasa?" he asks. The orderly shrugs, "Quien sabe." The stretchers are passed through the threshold, and the elevator doors bang shut. I turn around. There are several other stretchers approaching the elevator from both sides of the floor. For a wild moment I am overcome by total panic. "Dear God, please." I pray for no one and to no one in particular. Life, American-enriched, suddenly seems at a vast distance as my eyes grapple with white-clad women full of sorrow and solitude, here being wheeled, like a stricken army, toward the bloody resolution of internal wars. Enough.

Next morning, I am back on the floor, by duty possessed.

I arrive in the middle of a major brawl between Rachel and Dr. Rodrigo. They are inside the nurses' station. Rachel, pink with fury, legs apart, her hands on her hips, neck thrust forward, screams. Rodrigo, louder and more vicious, is perched on the edge of the nurses' desk facing away from Rachel in a three-quarter turn. He keeps slapping the desk with the flat of his palm, making the metal surface crackle each time with the sharp sound of a pistol shot. Between explosions he shouts, "Shut up, bitch." Bang. "Shut up, bitch." Bang.

Just outside the station, at the little desk on the corridor, Nurse Brown is in the middle of an admitting procedure. Seated with her back to the quarrel, her face impassive with years of practice, she rattles off items on the patient's clothing list: "Bag. Bathrobe, blouse, brassiere." The patient, a good-looking, well-dressed woman in her mid-twenties, is less accomplished than Nurse Brown in shutting out the world. "Yeah," she says vaguely. "Couldn't we go do this somewhere else?" "We have to finish, dear. Coat, collars, dress, fur coat, garter belt, girdle, gloves, gown, handkerchiefs." "Who are these people anyway? What do you mean handkerchiefs? Why do you have to mark down whether I have a handkerchief?" "Take it easy, dear," Brown says. "I am just following the rules. You do want to leave with everything you came with, don't you now?" The patient laughs. "Well, not exactly." Brown ignores the joke. "Hat, hosiery, kimona, overshoes, panties, pajamas, purse." The racket behind them increases. "Rubbers, scarf, shorts, shoes, shirt, slippers, socks, sweater." The patient is suddenly fed up. "Nurse," she says, half shouting, "I want to see my doctor." "Your doctor is not in the building, dear." (Evidently this is a private patient. House cases have no personal doctor; they are assigned on a rotational basis to the staff physicians. The difference is about one hundred dollars in cost and a negligible increase in courtesy.) "The house doctor, then." "The house doctor is busy now." "The supervisor." "She is tied up at the moment." "I want to see somebody, Nurse." Brown looks the woman in the face for the first time. "I am sorry, I will take you to your room now, but first you have to sign here." She hands the woman the clothes list, on which I can see scattered checkmarks indicating the items the patient owns. I am not clear on how Brown compiled the list, since I saw no overt response to the litany. It seems nevertheless to be okay, because the patient signs and they both get up.

By now a discrete crowd has gathered around the station, all with averted eyes and busy postures. There are two patients standing at the public wall-phone, looking in the yellow pages. An orderly is picking up butts, one by one, from the sand-filled ashtray in front of the elevators. Two nurses huddle over a slip of paper that, from where I stand, looks very much like yesterday's menu.

Rachel and Rodrigo are still at it. Rodrigo has slipped off the desk, which makes his arm more maneuverable so that the slaps now come louder and more often. He has also added the word "dirty" to his phrase. "Shut up, dirty bitch." Bang.

Just as I am beginning to worry that one of those slaps will land on Rachel, Dr. X arrives. "A quarrel again" she says, in her precise declarative manner. "Please, it is very unprofessional." "You have no work on the floor?" she asks, turning to the nurses. "Yes, doctor," one of them answers, as both walk quickly away. I notice that the orderly has disappeared into the elevator. "Excuse me Ms. Stern, but I want a word with Dr. Rodrigo," X says, turning back toward Rachel. "Certainly, Dr. X," Rachel answers with exaggerated friendliness. To Rodrigo she says, "The board, I assure you, will hear of this outrage." Rodrigo says, "Shut up." Rachel takes a few steps toward the elevator when she notices me. Before I can open my mouth she says, "I am sorry but I have no time for you now. I am very, very busy. Perhaps coffee later." "Okay," I say, and turn my back on her, not wanting to see her cry.

Dr. Rodrigo is chief resident. He and Dr. X share the responsibility for all floors, and consequently have the most extensive contact with patients. One of them is always on duty, except at night, when moonlighting interns from other institutions take over. Both do medical intakes, Intravenous placements, deliveries, discharges, and attend minor emergencies. Neither is permitted at this hospital to perform abortions.

Rodrigo is a thin, dry-mannered Filipino, with prominent cheekbones and a bushy black moustache. He gets along poorly with people and makes a cult of this impediment. He especially dislikes women and among women most especially those who work and those who get pregnant. He is married and has a child. One time I ask him what would happen if his wife got pregnant again. His response is succinct: "Scrape it out, throw it away." He shocks me often, but two of his performances continue to linger in my mind. One: an altercation between him and Dr. Jesus, the other house doctor. Voices rise, accents get worse, especially Rodrigo's. Finally he screams: "And another thing. You had better learn English. Nobody around here can understand you. Least of all me, you foreigner." Two: I am interviewing a young saline patient who tells me she has been stuck in bed for three days waiting to deliver. Rodrigo appears in the middle of the interview. He checks the girl's IV, listens to her abdomen with a stethoscope, walks out. Two minutes later he returns with an amplifying machine. He plugs it in, places the receiver on the girl's belly, and turns up the volume. The room fills with the steady sound of the fetal heartbeat. "That's it," he cries triumphantly, "that's it—the induction didn't work. Sturdy fellow you have in there, eh?" He gives a loud guffaw, and his broad obscene wink darkens the room.

During the weeks I spend on the D & C floor I become aware again and again of the hidden quality of the unit. On the surface the place is deceptively still, while it is suffused with an underlying dread of things to come soon and later.

Not that it is not busy. On some days as many as a hundred women wait for abortions here. It is rather the meaning of the activity that becomes subjugated to hospital routine, as the fear of personal physical danger temporarily overshadows more complex concerns.

"Will it hurt?" "Can it maim?" "Does anyone die?" are the crucial questions. No, no, no, the nurses shake their heads kindly, with comforting and comfortable patience. No, no— these are easy questions, nice questions, that distract everyone and let everyone off the hook at least for a while.

There are exceptions. One is a young girl barely sixteen. She is scrawny, Puerto Rican, uneducated, poor, and headstrong. Some say she is crazy. I love her as she takes off down the corridor, screaming, her white gown flying in a blaze of glory. "Let me outta here. I won't do it. It's my baby." Six weeks pregnant—afflicted with an abstraction, one might say—she leaves triumphant, with two sulky parents who have been hastily summoned by Dora.

Will this madness cost her her life? Opinions differ on the floor. I have no opinion except to observe again that the question of which life, whose life, is a frequent and unanswerable dilemma in this hospital. To note also that after her departure, all the women—patients and nurses—set their faces a little tighter.

There are opposing exceptions as well. I meet a bright young woman—with fat dirty knees, which she keeps uncovered in bed—for whom this is the fourth abortion in forty-two months.

"How come?" I ask, enfeebled by my disapproval. "Oh, it just happened." "Don't you mind, don't you wonder?" "No, it's okay. I can afford it." "How do you mean?" "I make enough money." "Yes, but what about otherwise, can you afford it otherwise?" "How do you mean?"

We have, up here, boss, a failure of communication.

The hospital is of Night, but not of Sleep; to paraphrase the poet James Thomson. "There sweet sleep is not for the weary brain; The pitiless hours like years and ages creep," to quote him. I interview at night fairly often. The patients like it, the staff is less busy, and I am accustomed to and comfortable with vigils that crises engender. Hospitals at night are a special experience akin to states of siege, to waiting in a bunker for the second, predictable air raid, to hiding in a small place during search and seizure, to traveling by force toward unknown destinations. In short, everyone in a hospital at night is a "displaced person."

There are a number of consequences to this altered state of being. The primary one is depression, frequently compensated for with a reckless, giddy, to-hell-with-it attitude. If one is not very sick (as the patients here are not) and if one is very careful not to puncture the balloon (as everyone here is), the hospital at night is a gala event.

The world outside—indifferent through its sleep—recedes. Those uninvolved are hard to remember and solitude begs company. A kind of solidarity springs up on the floor, a vast, involuted compassion for this castaway crew of miraculous survivors from that worst of human diseases: guilt.

Friendships are quick and short. But they last the night. Tongues untie, hearts open, charity flows by way of coffee and cigarettes. A small redeemed universe blighted only by self-pity and fatigue.

One late night, two black women take over the floor. They are dressed alike, in striped silk turbans and long multicolored robes that flap about their feet as they sway in the semidarkness to the sounds of a little portable radio set at red-hot rock. Before anyone can recover, all the women have come to see the show. The pair (postop D & C's scheduled for an 8:00 A.M. discharge) dances. The whole scene is over in less than three minutes. It ends when someone yells, "Quick, the head nurse," and the performers duck into their room. One tossing behind her the mystifying remark, "The poor thing, I am a nurse too."

Discharge is a ceremony of graduated steps. Barring complications, those women who were under twelve weeks pregnant may leave four hours after they come back to the floor from the recovery room. Those who were between twelve and fifteen weeks must wait until the following morning when they are let go at around eight. In either case, first they are returned to their rooms and transferred to their beds, half-asleep. All through the afternoons, from this room and that, one can hear again and again hoarse, drugged voices mutter in anguish, "Is it over?" "How much longer?" "Has it been done?"

"It is finished," the nurses answer. "It is finished."

When they become fully conscious the women are served a light meal. Toast and tea. Perhaps jello or ice cream. Sometimes soup. All of them grab at their food and devour it. No one leaves a crumb. The relief of survival generates large appetites.

By and by, Rodrigo appears, or Dr. X. Either one palpates the patient's belly, checks her sanitary pad for the amount of bleeding, takes her blood pressure, asks her how she feels, and if it all looks in order, signs her out.

A "Certificate of Termination of Pregnancy 24 Weeks or Less: Confidential Medical Report" is also filled out at this time. (The form states, "Only for scientific purposes approved by the Board of Health; not open to inspections or subject to Subpoena.") Death certificates are not required except in cases of live births.

Shortly after the doctor leaves, the nurse arrives. She brings with her the patient's belongings and the sheet of paper on which they were noted. Together they check off one against the other. The patient signs a receipt and receives her things.

It is now time to go. Time to discard the sheltering anonymous gown and dress, the battered body again in self-chosen garb. The commonplace reasserts itself as the crisis recedes. Life-affirming conceits build again the phrase "I am" and forge a measure of meaning.

The nature of the animal is to be self-absorbed and through that to construct and reconstruct its fate. The nature of the animal is to be absurdly vulnerable to the fixed look of one of its own.

▬▬

The D & C doctors, unlike the saline physicians, do not spend much time around the hospital. They come in, change, scrub, operate, change, and leave. Their cases are scheduled one after another, so that even if they spend six or seven hours working, all of it is uninterrupted operating room time. Their contact with the house patients is cursory and occurs only after the woman has been placed on the operating table. "Your name, dear, is Joan Dutch." (I often root for some brave soul to say "I know.") "Yes." "You are ten weeks pregnant." "Yes." "You'll be discharged this afternoon." "That's what they told me." "Okay, doctor," addressing the anesthetist, "let her go." The patient is put to sleep and the doctor starts to work.

To catch the D & C doctors for interviews is therefore difficult. I spend a considerable amount of time stalking them, until I realize that it is a waste and I must wait for the odd lucky chance of a cancellation or a scheduling error, which leaves the doctors irritable but free.

# Benjamin Kalish, M.D., Age 47

*Dr. Kalish becomes enamored of my tape recorder and spends half an hour of our total possible ninety minutes discussing the damned thing and examining it in great detail. He also worries for me about the cost of having my tapes typed and insists on giving me instructions on how to get a grant. "I don't want a grant," I say. "I just want to ask you some questions." "You should have a grant. For research it is more intelligent to get a grant." "Probably, but now I just want to talk with you a bit." "We are talking." If somewhat literal, his logic is nevertheless unassailable.*

*After a long while we do get down to business. The readiness with which he admits his guilt feelings about abortions surprises me, especially since he distorts most other facts that are unpleasant for him. At forty-seven he refers to himself as a young man. To have never married he attributes to his poverty during his student days and to his wealth later: "When you make a great deal of money, everybody is out to marry you off. It becomes very difficult." About blisters that appear on his right arm and hand after about two thousand abortions and that remain undiagnosed by the orthopedic surgeon he consults, he says, "I am sure it was muscular in my case, I've never had any adverse psychological reactions."*

"I was trained very strictly. I was a resident at a major hospital, and you'd lean over backwards not to disobey the law. We had a therapeutic abortion, but it was very difficult to get a case by. So when I first started to do abortions I would secretly feel guilty even though it was now legal. I almost felt as though someone's going to put the hand on my shoulder and arrest me. But today I'm sort of acclimated to it and I look at other parts of the country and I say 'Well they're very backwards, they don't do abortions there.'

"I do D & C's here in vast quantities. And I do salines in another hospital as my own private patients. I have done about 4,500 cases, since the law changed. This is true of about five men here, who've all done about the same amount.

"This helped me indirectly, because basically I was always

a shy introverted bookworm, research, teacher-type person, and this has forced me to be more outgoing, more talkative, more able to quickly size up a patient. When you do a lot of abortions it's always nice to know who's going to get a bad psychological reaction. And out of necessity you evaluate the patients right away. So in a sense it's improved my interview technique.

"Most women seeking abortions are young and they're single, and before the law changed they would come to my office crying and there was nothing you could do about it. And now you can take care of them, you can solve their problems so really there is a great need for it.

"Occasionally you look at the fetus and say 'Too bad this could have been a living person one day.' When I do a D & C, I do a real D & C, I don't do suction. Now if you do suction, you put it in and it schooches out and you don't really see it. When you do a D & C most of the tissue is removed by the Olden forceps or ring clamp and you actually get gross parts of the fetus out. So you can see a miniature person so to speak, and so even now I occasionally feel a little peculiar about it, because as a physician I'm trained to conserve life and here I am destroying life. But overall, I'm happy about the law because basically these girls would be in a terrible problem if not for the change of the law.

"I guess I feel guilty because according to the Hippocratic oath you're not supposed to do abortions, and according to the Maimonides oath you're not supposed to do abortions. So how could you be trained and raised one way, and suddenly be told it's okay to do it. . . .

"Well, the saline is even more grotesque and unpleasant. And I'm sure it must be terribly unpleasant for the patient. When we do D & C's it's under general anesthesia, so the patient comes in and the doctor does the dirty work. And she wakes up, and it's his sin, and she's cured. But with a saline she's participating in this sin, because she's awake, she knows what's going on, she feels it coming out. She hears the nurses rushing over and saying, 'Oh look there's the baby,' so I'm sure the patient suffers more, physically and emotionally.

"Now I am usually called, after it is expelled. I arrive on the scene and I see the fetus and the placenta in a bucket, away from the patient, but even then it's an unpleasant sight, because it's already big and it looks more human obviously than a little teeny fetus from a D & C. . . .

"The patient can feel movement, but it's interesting she doesn't talk about it. She doesn't say, 'I stopped feeling movement a half hour after the saline.' It happens that there is another little thing which I've never read about or discussed with anyone else. But on a number of occasions with the needle, I have harpooned the fetus. I can feel the fetus move at the end of the needle just like you have a fish hooked on a line. This gives me an unpleasant, unhappy feeling because I know that the fetus is alive and responding to the needle stab. When you put in the needle, theoretically you go in the sac and take out fluid and put in salt water. But there are times when you hit the fetus and you can feel the fetus wiggling at the end of that needle and moving around which is an unpleasant thing. No one has ever mentioned this, but I've noticed it a number of times. You know that there is something alive in there that you're killing. . . .

"I was aware of a physical disability. About a year ago, myself, and one or two colleagues mentioned this also, noticed that something was happening to our right arms. We got blisters. I went to an orthopedic doctor and he x-rayed my arm because the muscles were tense and swollen and I had blisters on my hand and an aching feeling. But that's a mechanical reaction simply from using your hand in a strange movement for long periods of time. This was a physical reaction to the heavy volume of the work. In my own case I never had any psychological adverse reaction. Except an occasional feeling that one was destroying life. But in my own mind the issue had already been resolved that this is necessary because otherwise these poor girls are going to risk their own lives. . . .

"As I get older I get more communicative and I talk more and I'm happier, so I'm different in that sense. Most of my colleagues are happy when they're young, and as they get older they get unhappier. I am the reverse, so I'm unusual."

141

DR. D.: How is it you never married?

DR. K: Well, you see, first of all, I got through school very young. I did four years of college in two and a half. And I was elected to Phi Beta Kappa and was an officer of all the societies. So I was always very busy. And then I went through medical school, and I was always very conscientious. You see in the United States there is a certain amount of discrimination. Like today, for example, medical schools are opening their doors to black students, but years ago it was accepted that there was a quota on Jewish students, so if a Jewish boy got into medical school he kissed the ground, he was so happy. Therefore, I worked very hard all the time and never went out.

"Also, when I was a resident for five years I lived on fifty dollars a month. Getting married was out of the question because I couldn't support myself, much less a wife. Then before I realized it, I became busy and was very affluent.

"Then one becomes a target of different matchmakers because they say, 'Oh, he's very well to do, so let's try to hook him.' You see. It's a different psychology. One goes from one type of situation to another type, before you realize it. Without boasting, I am relatively young and yet I'm nationally known for the research that I've done. And not only that, but it's easy to build up a good practice."

## Michael Christie, M.D., Age 45

*My first impression of Dr. Christie is that he is a matinee idol from the provinces. He looks like a lady killer. He does not, however, trade on his handsomeness. His impact flows like static, noisy and uncommunicative.*

*Mike Christie is an embittered man, and although we speak for a long time, I do not learn why. My experience again is visual. I feel, as we talk, as if I were looking at a photograph in double exposure. The wealthy, educated physician superimposed on the laborer's hungry son, whose idea of honor is vengeance. The idealistic* doctor, who refers to entering the profession as "I got the calling," superimposed on the money-grabber, who, as gossip has it, exploited the abortion-season more than any other doctor here.

"I do D & C's. I don't do salines. I don't like them. My personal objection is that it's too messy. It's difficult to wait for the lady to abort in two or three days. I like it done fast, finished and out. I don't have time to come back and check and so forth. It's a physical impossibility for me to do it. I am with two major hospitals. I'm senior attending at both places. I see about 300 patients a week. And of that, I have probably two requests a week for abortions. Prior to that I'd been sending all my cases out of the country. Then naturally with the abortion law change, I started trying to find a place that would do it, at the most efficient and most economical manner. I picked this place because it was closest to my office. . . .

"In the beginning I was mixed up because I was taught by the Hippocratic oath not to take a life. But I mixed up my feelings about the fetus as an entity versus just as a procedure, and when life begins. Does life begin at the moment of conception or does life begin at viability, which is twenty-eight weeks? Or does it begin at the moment of birth? So, with that in mind, I had to resolve my feelings. And I resolved it like this. That since I've been in practice for more than ten years and seen what criminal abortion can do, people have forgotten what criminal abortion can do, in those ten years I've seen everything. From crippled patients, to infections, to death. Directly traceable to criminal abortions. So long as there is a money factor and criminal abortions exist, and they don't do it at an established hospital, by certified and competent doctors, you're going to have that tragedy occur over and over again. I felt that this was detrimental to good medical practice, and it was also a condemnation against women. Since women are the ones that get pregnant and not men. I feel this way. I don't think women should be a second minor sex, I think they have just as much right to their bodies as men do. If men could get pregnant they would have had abortion on demand ten centuries ago.

"But it took even me to wrestle with my conscience. Because I had never done abortions before the law was passed, never.

"I come from a Catholic background. And not only did I have to wrestle with it ethically and morally, but I had to wrestle with it spiritually. I'm not a practicing Catholic. Never have been. Nevertheless, I still believe in the sanctity of life since I'm a physician foremost before I'm anything else.

"I don't feel that anything above twenty weeks should be done. There's always a holding back to do salines. I don't particularly like it. I feel guilty doing it. Because I think the baby is more alive. The baby is more toward viability, more towards compatibility with life than it would be at twelve weeks. I've seen them, I've done them, I have done hysterotomies, I've done multiple procedures on them. Including salines. And I just decided it's not worth it to do, because I have had such terribly strong feelings that it's turned me off. I feel that I am destroying life. I feel that I'm actually killing them. And that kind of feeling I don't like to live with. And I rationalize by saying to myself that from one week to sixteen weeks is to me the upper limits of what I would do. Because the system, and the fetus as an individual doesn't become that, until after that time. Then after that time I leave it to others, more radical than myself, to do whatever they want to do.

"And I know that lots of my colleagues feel that way too. They're not Catholic. They're all religious denominations. Jewish, Protestant, all walks of life. And they don't do them at all. . . .

"It's not a purely altruistic aspect either. The money that's involved is also a big factor in why I do this. And I think that most doctors who do abortions also do them for the money's sake. It's a big motive, and certainly it's nothing to be hypocritical about. It's a fact of life that is present with us in society. . . .

"I went through lots of relationships before I married my wife. It's my first marriage, and I hope it will be my last. If anything happened to her, or if we did divorce for some reason or other, I would never marry again. I can live within myself.

**144**

Without all the vicissitudes and all the responsibilities of a marriage. . . .

"My wife also has a Catholic background. But neither one of us are very strong Catholics. She is anti-Catholic, and I am nothing. I don't believe in anything. I came from a very poor background. My father was a laborer, and I worked for a long time to go to medical school. I was a writer. I wrote a comic-strip for five years, and I was in advertising, and I wrote for television and radio. I was going to write for Hollywood, and all of a sudden I got the calling. And I got out of that life and went into medicine. . . .

"I think I have a good marriage. We have two children. I think we have a very good life. But it's not a happy life. Too much pressures. It's seldom we see each other. We don't take enough holidays. We are constantly being deluged with telephone calls. The life of an obstetrician is very bad, very bad. And we have financial trouble since I support nine people. Her family and my family. I would make a good Mafia member, because I honor my friends and destroy my enemies. I never forget a slight, I never forget an encouragement. Those who helped me when I was younger and struggling up, I've lifted them up when they were going down. And those that stepped on me, I stepped on them and crushed them while I was going up."


## Robert Harris, M.D., Age 30

*Dr. Harris is one of the house doctors at night in this hospital, and a third-year resident elsewhere. He is a tall, handsome black man, a little overweight, with a great deal of presence. He is very busy, and I have to hound him for quite a while before he consents to be interviewed. It is worth it to me to keep after him, because he is the only black physician I know anywhere.*

*I learn as we talk that Dr. Harris is extremely bright, rather matter-of-fact, considerably detached, a little depressed, and slightly sardonic at all times. Contrary to my expectations I do not feel that in meeting him I am getting to know the representative of an unfamiliar genotype. In fact, he sounds to me very much like myself, and like all of us uprooted and suspect emigrants who have come to an alien world and made good.*

*But success under these circumstances is always a little blighted. "I made it, yes," he says, "but I haven't found the answer. I don't know why." I am in complete empathy. Achievement provides a lot, but it fails to substitute for not belonging, and it also fails to make one feel at home.*

"I don't like abortions over five months basically, twenty weeks as a rule. This is, of course, a compromise—a cop out. Because it doesn't make any difference. What's the difference between twenty-two and twenty-six weeks. One is as much a fetus as the other one. It's not rational, it's just an arbitrary point to allow some sort of moral outlet, guilt outlet. I've tried not to make it a moral issue, but a social issue without moral overtones as much as possible. But I think from a straight moral point of view I probably would object to abortion. Because I love kids. From that point of view every fetus is a potential child, and morally I just really don't think that should be done. Socially there's a great need for abortion, purely because there's a large group of women, who for various reasons will get pregnant and they don't want a child. I feel that they should have a right to allow themselves a choice, to have another chance, so to speak. Of course, there's abortion that gets abused. Women that come back three, four, and five times. This is another one of the boundaries I place in my own personal feelings. I would just not do it, I would probably refuse to do the abortion after two. I would begin to wonder, this woman is probably unreliable, once is a mistake, twice—

"Abortion from my point of view must be coupled with family planning. That is my real interest. If a woman comes along for an abortion, she should have at the same time proper advice on family planning, proper advice on an available method of contraception. It should be made clear to her that abortion is not a form of contraception as such. There are women who say 'What the hell, I can get an abortion.' . . .

"The saline in fact is easier to do to a certain extent. You're putting a needle into a fetus which you don't see. You don't necessarily have to be around for the outcome. The doctor is very rarely there, the nurse has to take the brunt of the saline problem. You go home. I may get a call for one or two a night. The nurses will deliver eight, nine, or ten. A D & C you're actively doing the abortion because with the suction and curettage it makes life less easy. With induction you don't have to face it at all. . . .

"I suppose that if you want to go below the surface, and thinking about it, I do feel you'd be an abnormal person if you could really honestly say that abortion didn't bother you at all. It goes against all things which are natural. It's a termination of life, however you look at it. It just goes against the grain. It must. . . .

"The argument that abortion is being used as a tool to eliminate the black race—the doctors, being representatives of the establishment, encourage black girls to have abortions, whereas they probably don't encourage white girls the same way, because they don't want to cut down on the white population—I don't think this is a valid statement at all. The reason black girls have more abortions is that unfortunately the black population make up the lower border of the socioeconomic group, and from this group always comes a higher amount of abortions.

"Here for instance most patients are white, by far, many, many times. This is probably because it's private, and whites can afford the fee more than blacks. But up at the other institution it's just the opposite because there again the patients are ward patients, public patients, and there it's mostly blacks.

"I've seen more prejudice in the ward services than in the private service. I think I've had more problems with black patients to some extent than with white, because of the reverse sort of prejudice. For so many years black patients have been coming to the hospital and just never saw a black doctor, who actually works there. And I think they tend to expect a sort

147

of preferential treatment because they are black and I am black. Which I'm not accustomed to giving, because I don't make a distinction. I don't make any attempt to establish a greater rapport with a black patient than white.

"I just can't sit down and feel the bitterness that American blacks feel because I haven't experienced it. No matter how I try to gain rapport in that respect, I can't walk along the streets of Harlem and say, 'I know what you're feeling,' because I don't know what they're feeling. I can see it, I know it's there, and I can understand now the bitterness. But I am West Indian and, particularly, British, and I have a very strong British upbringing. I've been in England for a large number of years.

"I was trained in Scotland in a totally white society, where there isn't even a small black community. The only blacks in Scotland are the students, and very few. For six years of dealing with white people I suppose I've got a bit immune, to some extent. Although the prejudice existing in Britain and Scotland is a little different than here. It's less overt. It's less obvious. The British way of life tends to make it, you know, you must never be nasty to anybody no matter how you feel about it. It makes life more easy. Here it happens every now and again we get a difficult black patient and somebody will say, 'Why don't you go and talk to her.' So I say, 'Look she's from Carolina and so are you. You probably have more rapport than I have, even though you're white. You are closer to what she knows than what I know. So you go and talk to her.' That's the way I feel. I have more problems with black patients than white. It gets so bad, the black/white situation, that if you shout at a black they say it's because I'm black. If you tell a black maid, 'Go and do this,' she'll say 'If I was white you wouldn't do that.' And it becomes ridiculous.

"My wife's attitude is totally different from mine. She makes a distinction between having a black friend and having a white friend. She has acquired the sensitivity of American blacks to a large extent because she's experienced it. She went to school here, she's been through the ropes of prejudice in colleges and jobs. . . .

"I am successful, yes, but I don't know, I still haven't really found the answers. At one time I was very close to being a priest. People say this is the answer. . . . I wasn't terribly religious then, as such. I went to church more than I go now, but my interest was in theology, not in religion. You know theology is the ultimate study."

DR. D.: What decided you not to become a priest?

DR. H: I like girls. I love women, in fact, I always have, and I just could not see myself abstaining. . . .

"I enjoy being married at times, but it's no big deal. I'm not fascinated by marriage."

DR. D.: Do you have extramarital affairs?

DR. H: Strictly for sex. Short-term things. Two, three months. If the woman gets involved with me, I break it off. I do try to spend most of my free time with my family; therefore, any woman I have an affair with sees very little of me. It's no big deal.

DR. D.: Why do it at all?

DR. H: It's a very good question. Why, I don't know. I think again it comes back to the male ego bit. And surely not because I particularly want to. Most of the time I'm bored as hell. I think it's just you get the feeling that something is available.

———

149

*D & C Floor: Staff*

For months no nurse will talk with me. An aide here and there consents, but the registered nurses steadily refuse. "No comment," "I'd rather not," "Sorry," are standard answers. "Okay, don't talk to me. But would you tell me why you don't want to?" I ask again and again in desperation. "Sorry," "I'd rather not." Their muteness acquires in my mind the proportions of a mystery.

Nursing altogether appears to be a profession of extreme psychic hardship. Trained in a context of rigid hierarchies, nurses are required to meet various contradictory and mutually exclusive demands.

They are made accountable for the welfare of patients without being permitted to assume any major responsibility in relation to them. A good nurse, like a good private, never makes decisions.

Nurses are to succor and to comfort their sick, at least in theory. A difficult task when they are not allowed to reveal to the patient any item of information about himself, however innocuous it is. "Nurse, I feel terrible, what is my temperature?" "Ask your doctor, dear." "But, nurse, the thermometer is in your hands." "Doctor will tell you, dear." "Why won't you?" "Regulations."

Under these circumstances, nurses inevitably develop into bullies. They scrape to the powerful and kick the weak. They become capriciously cruel, aggressively contemptuous, in revenge and in doomed imitation of their "betters." They contribute greatly to the peril that it is, for any sick person, to enter a hospital.

Eventually I interview the few nurses who are willing. Even they say little of value, because they mouth the job-saving party line, or otherwise fall back on the safety of personal platitudes.

I speak with Frances Castle, head nurse. She is a soft-voiced black woman of great sweetness. She does not want to say no to me, but she also does not want to risk free speech. The result is a disastrous series of banalities and cautions. I throw the tape away.

I speak with Lucinda Fernandez from the Philippines, seven

months pregnant. "How does it feel carrying the baby and seeing these abortions?" I ask. "I can't say," she says, "because I am not against abortions. My best friend had an abortion last year." I groan and thank her, and we part. Much later, in casual conversation when I am not taping, she says, "It's pitiful for the baby. It's ready to be born and then they just take it out. It's a sin."

Nurses' aides are a little bolder. Probably because they are less visible, more embittered, and don't have much to lose. They stand lowest on the totem.

Sue Mora, 39, single, from Korea, says in heavily accented, broken English: "I'm working first time, girls here, all hate them, I hate them. Now I understand because American custom is free. Some girl and boys met, make love, it's custom, free, so I understand, but if came in a Korean girl in this hospital I don't understand. I hate.

"See these things I am disgusted, yeah. Almost one month I'm so sick because baby come out. When I saw it I can't eat. Nausea sometimes now. Because sometimes I am guilty. Because Catholic custom, it's a rule, is abortion bad. I help now, so I'm guilty for help."

She is on the verge of tears. I try to comfort her, but it is obviously the wrong move, because she starts to cry. In embarrassment and guilt, I look away and take stock of the contents of the serving kitchen where we sit. Besides us, it contains a sink, a refrigerator, an instant-coffee maker, an oven, two chairs, one small table, many cups (both styrofoam and waxed) for coffee and water.

# Maureen O'Neil, R.N., Age 42

*Director of Nursing*

*I interview Maureen O'Neil toward the end of my research. She is a flaming redhead, quick to anger, slow to regrets. Her archenemy in the hospital is Rachel Stern. During the months I know them they have many major clashes. The rest of us think them very much alike.*

"When you meet them afterwards and you talk with them, you sit down on the bed and you're not talking on a professional basis, sometimes they'll open up and say 'I don't know whether I did the right thing.'

"I think a lot of us discount religion, which you shouldn't do. Basically religion does play a bigger part then we're giving it credit for. We're saying, 'Oh, they're all atheists, they don't believe.' They tell you they don't. But when it's a big fetus, you will hear them asking a lot of questions: 'Is it a boy or is it a girl?' 'Will it be baptized?' We've had many requests for that too. We do it, it doesn't mean a thing. But if it rests somebody's peace of mind, you baptize a fetus. I mean for the psychological effect. It's not recognized by the church, how can you murder a fetus and then baptize it? I feel if it makes the woman happy, why not? If it satisfies her psychological hang-up, whatever it is.

"In some ways it is very boring these abortions, the same thing day after day after day. In fact the nurses are excited about complications because it's something different. . . .

"I feel that after eighteen weeks I think we're getting a little high. When you deliver a three-pound infant, as we've had quite a few, I think that we have to be a little careful on our dates. Probably the most tragic thing I have seen is a woman that has a live fetus. She's completely shocked, completely devastated. We've had one poor thing that came from Chicago, didn't even have an abortion. She went into labor and delivered. It only lived an hour or something. She wanted to hold him up, have him baptized, she really went bananas. She was about twenty weeks, but it was breathing and had a heartbeat."

DR. D.: Was oxygen given to it?

MO: Sure, I mean it's too immature to live. But she had to go through this business of making up her mind did she want it buried. You know you get into all this once they're born alive. Have it buried or have a city burial or what. Also, if they're born alive you have to make out a birth certificate and a death certificate.

"Anything under twenty-four weeks goes for incinerators. I hey ask you what you're going to do with the fetus, you can't say incinerate it. I tell them it goes to city burials.

"I feel it's up to you. Each one has to decide for themselves. I feel we are not doing enough afterwards. I think there should be a place where they can contact the doctor who did it. I don't think they get enough from the actual doctor who does the procedure. He doesn't visit them afterwards, he doesn't talk to them. He sees them in the operating room just before they go on the table. I feel it's not really a very close patient-doctor relationship. I mean, do you really feel a twelve-year-old or fourteen-year-old understands all this, all the ramifications?

"I don't think the staff I have has ever been known to be gung ho. I had quite a lot of problems with the nurses' aides over this thing. On several occasions I heard comments, you know, as I walk around, that were derogatory. That deep down they're against it, but they will not admit it. But just because a patient's demanding, she's 'a bloody nuisance' and 'it's not my fault she's here for an abortion, so don't take it out on me.'

"I had some who just walked out. Walked right out the door. 'Thank you, goodbye,' didn't discuss it further. 'I didn't know this is what you were doing.' Now I have a mixture of some staff for whom a D & C is okay but a saline is not. And I've lost a number of good staff members because they would not work on the saline floor.

"I feel that up to twenty weeks you really push an abortion. Personally. And if they had modified that law I would be all for it. Because after that stage they are getting pretty big. I mean, have you seen the twenty-week ones? And I must say it turns my stomach, and I agree with the staff in one way that they feel a little repulsed when you get a big fetus. It is very traumatic for the staff to pick this up and put it in a container and say, 'Okay, that's going to the incinerator.' "

## Jeremiah Adam, Age 32

*Porter, Orderly*

*Jeremiah Adam is the only orderly who agrees to be interviewed. I try with several others but run into an impenetrable wall of distrust and suspicion.*

*On one occasion, I address two men in Spanish. It is their native tongue, which they speak among themselves. They stare at me blankly and remain silent. I switch to English. One of them, clearly speaking for both, announces: "English no good. No speak, no understand." The joke breaks them up. It is one of the very few times I find that a common language in an alien land fails to become a bridge.*

*Adam, as everyone calls him, although other orderlies are addressed by their first names, is different in one more respect. He permits me to talk with him while he is eating his supper. I learn in this hospital that unlike my middle-class and academic habits, whereby meals are considered prime time for conducting verbal business, laboring people take their food with greater ceremony. Eating and work (and they consider speaking about work, work) are not to be mixed. I shock several persons with my ill-mannered ignorance of this self-evident rule.*

*Jeremiah Adam laughs often as we talk, and he calls me madam. He is a guileless, unpretentious man whose life emerges with vivid color in all its accidental formlessness. People are kind to him, he is obliging, another day passes without trouble.*

*His physical presence tells another story. Whenever possible, he wears a gleaming-white, well-starched doctor's coat with the collar turned up and the cuffs folded back. He looks dashing, and the razzle-dazzle of his movements reflects the explosive joy he takes in that.*

"Sometimes they got me down in central supply, sometimes I run a little messenger work, just when nobody is around. Sometimes I do orderly work too, with the patients.

"Everybody likes me here in this place, all the white faces upstairs like me. I don't go back running and squealing on this and that, but they like my work, they appreciate my work. Do you know, you mighten believe this, I never said no yet in the two years I'm working here. I was tired, they give me a whole lot of work, and I never said no. And I hear other people refuse things but I never did refuse yet. I could have been fired many times, you're suppose to get three warning slips and then you're out, I must have gotten about forty-five. For coming in late, staying out. I don't mean to do it, but, I can't say—women is my weak spot. I like too much women that's why.

"When I first went to OR work my reaction was I didn't know they were going to put me in the section of operations. Well, a naked woman, it doesn't mean much to me, because I have several girl friends. But when I went up there I didn't know that they were going to allow me to see what's going on in the area. So one day the boss upstairs told me, 'Come.' And I had to go in the area, so as I stretched up my head, I saw the operation with the patient's legs wide opened, and I was a little shocked. I said, 'Oh, man, look at this,' to myself. So I stuck around to see how the operation would be, because I never seen it before. It was the first time. It was kind of frightening to tell you the truth. With the cutting up of the baby and everything, I said, 'Oh, man.' It was a shock to me. I don't know how to explain it. If I go to a dance, for instance, I don't tell nobody about the abortions. I keep my mouth shut and say I'm a porter. I don't want to discourage nobody.

"It really was exciting to me, it was very exciting to see how this abortion is. I was like thinking about the abortion all the time, but it was very surprising to me. I could write a book about this place, if I had the sense to write a book. . . .

"When they give the saline with the big needle, she's awake and pushing it in her belly, that I don't like. I don't go for that. I think it's a sin. When they reach that big, they should go through with it, have the baby.

"But I can't tell them, 'Hey man, don't do that, that's not right.' They want to make money, I need a job. I really don't care. I want to work. The patients come, they have the abortion, I need a job. . . .

"Sometimes the patient is very scared. Comes in here mostly with a big problem, having the abortions. Sometimes they tell me things that sometimes they shouldn't tell me, but I come experienced and I'm accustomed to that. I just try to cool them off, to make them happy, say something to them not to discourage them from men. Sometimes some of them talk in a way that men is the worst thing like a animal, and I try to cheer them up.

"Sometimes they'll ask me a question whether, how long will it take, if it will hurt, when do they put you to sleep, do they bleed much, simple things. Simple things to me, but it's a big thing to them, because they've never been through it before. I tell them like the doctors know what they'll be doing, they'll be in the corridor for a while until they get the call to go inside. The doctor will put them to sleep as soon as they reach the room, the operation will take about, say, six to ten minutes. I cheer them up, I tell them good things. . . .

"Now I have heard some people say it's a sin to have an abortion, it's a shame. But I look at it this way. If you don't need a kid, why have it? Sometimes some of them want to change their mind. I talk to them, black and white, I talk the same thing to. They say, 'Mr., what's you name?' I say, 'Adam.' They say, 'Adam, you know you're so kind, I don't feel like having the abortion.' They say, 'Is it too late now?' I say, 'No, do you want me to call the nurse and tell her you don't want it anymore?' Sometimes they change their mind—. . . .

"I have a kid. My kid is down South. A girl she is, four years old now. I always wanted a kid. I always wanted to see what a kid of mine would look like, and I really cared for the woman anyhow, I still do because she's very nice. That's why she left, she said I was too swift.

"I seen my kid twice, when she first born and when she was one year old, then the mother left. I am going to marry her. She's coming to me next month in August. Right now we're talking the plans about marriage. My supervisor could tell you. I send money sometimes once a month, sometimes three times a month, sometimes monthly. . . .

"I'm not afraid to talk to nobody. I mean if I was a technician probably I could tell you more."

———

The numbers game is the opiate of the D & C floor. Everyone plays, although the particular number varies from person to person. Dr. Harris places the magic figure at twenty. Another doctor at ten. The favorite of the unit is fifteen. New York State bids for twenty-four.

The numbers represent weeks of gestation above which the act of abortion is said to qualitatively alter, and to be transformed into—let us not mince words—murder.

There is no logic to these numerals. They are arbitrary choices in the struggle against guilt; they are bones thrown to the savage dogs of conscience. Some of the figures make medical and procedural sense. None are valid as arbiters of the moral issue. They evolve from and affect subjective reality based on degrees of self-deception.

Theoretically, pregnancy is calculated from the first day of a woman's last menstrual period, although conception as a rule does not take place until ten days to two weeks after that day. In practice, because many women are unreliable in reporting the date of their last period, doctors compute gestation time by fetal size. It is known, for example, that a fetus of five hundred grams corresponds to twenty weeks of pregnancy.

Twenty becomes a magic number for some physicians because classical textbooks have placed fetal viability outside the uterus at five hundred grams. The estimate is grossly inaccurate. Even with recent dramatic advances in the postnatal care of premature infants, survival is virtually impossible below eight hundred grams of fetal weight (about twenty-two weeks of gestation).

In the State of New York the legal limit for abortions is set at twenty-four weeks. The figure has no medical significance. It merely represents a political compromise between warring factions in the controversy.

Eighteen weeks is another favorite red herring. It is the time of pregnancy when the fetus generally quickens, which means that its movements become perceptible to the mother. Many people assert that abortions are defensible before that time but not afterwards. Although this stricture makes very good sense in terms of the mother's subjective experience, in terms of fetal life it is an irrelevant dimension. Quickening does not bring the fetus to life. To name one contradicting fact among many, the fetus has a detectable heartbeat from twelve weeks on. What perceptible fetal movement usually does do is to change the woman's attachment to her pregnancy. In line with that, most saline patients, for example, contrary to medical evidence, claim that their babies have not moved even as late as at twenty-four weeks of gestation.

The numbers game in the abortion field is an absurdity. Extrauterine viability of the fetus as a deciding factor in doing abortions is a position of ignorance or of extreme bad faith.

Abortion fetuses, after all, come to be outside the uterus by force and not by mishap. To argue, therefore, in favor of abortion exclusively on the basis of viability is logically akin to maintaining that to drown a nonswimmer in a bathtub is all right, because he would have drowned anyway had he fallen into the ocean.

There are more numbers. Ten, twelve, and fifteen stand out. Ten weeks of pregnancy is the safest time for D & C's. It carries the least risk of perforations. For hidden as the facts may be, perforations of the uterus are a permanent risk. Statistically the chances are very small. They are about one in two thousand cases in the hands of experienced surgeons at a well-equipped legal hospital. The trouble with statistics, however, is that they do not predict the specific fate of Mary or Jane. So each has to take her private chance of becoming the casualty.

Twelve is the number of weeks at and below which suction aspiration is applied, and the patient is discharged within four hours of being brought back from the recovery room. Suction curettage is a modern and, in relative terms, very safe technique whereby the uterus is vacuum-cleaned in a matter of minutes, without it being subjected to the potentially more deleterious process of pervasive scraping.

Fifteen weeks is the cut-off point between D & C and saline abortions. At fifteen weeks the fetus is too large and its bone structure too hardened for it to be surgically removed through the vagina, without running a very high risk of massive damage to the cervix and uterus.

Fifteen is a particularly charismatic number, in that all the D & C doctors claim that beyond it abortion is very nasty business.

# Chapter 5

# D & C Floor: Patients, Parents, and Boyfriends

Suffer us not to mock ourselves with falsehood
T. S. Eliot

I follow Jeanette Buday, sixteen, fourteen weeks pregnant, to the D & C floor. I choose to follow her, I guess, because her name sounds Hungarian. My aim is to observe the routine process of checking a patient into the unit.

On Jeanette's arrival, Nurse Norton says, "Hello. Sit down, dear." Next, Jeanette's blood pressure is measured, her temperature is taken, her clothing list is checked off. She is handed a shopping bag, known as the patient's kit. It is white plastic, decorated with pink-centered blue daisies. It looks rather cheerful, I think. I watch her examine its contents. She removes, inspects, and replaces, one by one, the following standard items: a green plastic water pitcher of 28 oz. capacity; a bar of Dial soap, one ounce in weight; one washcloth of blue and white checks, manufactured of fibrous paper, rather like Handi-wipes; one large soft paper towel with a design of blue and green mythical flowers; one white regulation heavy-paper hospital gown; one pair of disposable beige slippers with green striped trim around their edges on which is printed, in large black letters, "PRO-TEXMOR Disposable Slippers"; and three obstetrical pads wrapped in white paper with a blue-flower design. The pads appear larger and thicker than those

161

one might purchase in a drugstore. A white elastic sanitary belt is wound around one of them.

The last item is a brown waste bag, with two one-inch adhesives attached to it at one end, to enable the patient to stick it to the side of her night table. The waste bag is also decorated. Printed on it is a blue vase with pink flowers. On the vase itself, a blue bird is perched on some green grapes. In front of the vase and a little to the right, there lie one apple and one pear. Both are depicted in their natural colors. With each, the colors overflow a little the borders of the fruit. The waste bag is flame- and moisture-resistant, according to the legend printed on its lower left-hand corner. Its dimensions are six inches in width, twelve inches in length.

The kit acts on me like a conditioned stimulus. I hunch my shoulders, I shorten my neck, I inwardly bemoan the absence of a human carapace.

I know about kits. One is issued them at the beginning of journeys and at the end of roads. At times of descent. On those occasions when the haves leave and the have-nots stay to face the music. The music is usually their own howl of pain.

"I'll show you to your room now, dear," Norton says to Jeanette. Jeanette nods. Valise and plastic bag in hand, she follows Norton. I follow her. We are led to 609, double room, companion bed empty for the moment.

"Undress yourself, dear," Norton says, once we are all inside the room. "Take a sponge bath, change, and get into bed. I'll return in half an hour." "Okay," says Jeanette. It is the first word she has uttered since I met her.

Norton and I leave. She to attend to other duties, I to rest my feet.

In one half hour we are both back. "Okay, then," says Norton, "I want to know, did you give urine?" "Yeah." "A blood sample?" "Yeah." "What do you want with your dinner, coffee, tea, or milk?" "Milk." "Have you eaten anything for the past twelve hours?" "No." "Good. You're not supposed to. Let me just go through this preop check list," Norton says. I know she is taking the patient's time. This is supposed to be done as clerical duty. But the patient doesn't know that, and I do not interfere.

"Premedication," Norton reads, "not yet. Consent signed, yes. History and physical charted, yes. Lab work done, okay. Patient voided—did you void, dear?" "Yeah." "Okay. Do you have any dentures?" "No." "Caps or jackets on the teeth?" "No." "Any wedding ring to be taped?" "No." "Any jewelry on your person?" "No." "Wig, hair pins, false eyelashes, contact lenses, lipstick?" "No." "Let me see your hands. I will have to remove the nail polish from four of your fingers." "How come?" "So the anesthetist can see how you are doing." "Okay."

Norton produces a piece of cotton soaked with nail-polish remover and cleans the nails on the middle and ring fingers of Jeanette's hands. "Are you allergic to any medication?" "No." "Show me your identity-band." Jeanette thrusts her right arm forward. "Your name is Jeanette Buday." "Yeah." "You are sixteen." "Yeah." "You are a house case." "Yeah." "Very fine dear. We are all set. Good luck. See you when you wake up." "Yeah." Norton leaves.

Jeanette and I stare at each other. "Are you Hungarian?" I ask. "No, my father was, but he is dead." she says. There is a pause. "Are you scared?" "Yeah." "I am sorry. It isn't bad, you know. I mean, it won't hurt or anything. I mean, don't go by the kit." "Yeah." "Do you like Hungarian food?" "My father didn't cook." "Right. Good luck. Goodbye." "Yeah."

I need a vacation from this place. I am seeing too much. Too many dilemmas, paradoxes, absurdities, circumlocuted hardships of Being; too many undistinguished dramas, everyday tragedies, gray martyrdoms come to my attention.

There are too many Jeanettes. Too many others. Faces blur, voices merge. Not two the same, and all alike.

Humanity, I love you in small doses and from a distance. Because from up close your maggot-eaten, vulture-picked wounds stink to the high empty heavens.

## Mrs. Merl Afilides, Age 25, Married

### Ten Weeks Pregnant

"I'm back for the second time. They did one originally three and a half weeks ago, but there was a hole in my uterus caused by an IUD so they couldn't complete it. So I had to come back. Now I'm ten weeks pregnant, I mean I was. Now they just did it.

"The first time I came right away. I mean I knew that was what I wanted to do. I just had a baby five months ago. And I didn't want another child. I was using an IUD. But the sperm were determined and they crossed over the IUD. I didn't know that the IUD had perforated me until I went up there and they started to do it and then the next thing they knew they had some of my intestines.

"The vacuum doesn't accept anything but the matter it's supposed to, so it just put it right back in place. I had no complications.

"I had a very good doctor. It's very important to have confidence in your doctor. I don't know that I would recommend just going into a clinic, and just using anybody because it's sort of supportive to have someone to talk to. Someone that you know. . . .

"At first my husband wanted the baby and then when I said I didn't, he said whatever I wanted.

"I had time to think. They didn't take enough out the first time that there was any damage to the embryo. So I could have kept it. I didn't have to come back to have the abortion. But I definitely wanted it, and there wasn't anything to fear in the procedure."

DR. D.: How did they treat the perforation between the first and second D & C's?

MA: There's no treatment. They just told me to stay off my feet, and that was mostly for internal bleeding. Because of the intestine, that they were afraid of. It wasn't actually for the perforation. The perforation heals itself, they figure in a week, but to be sure, they waited three weeks. . . .

164

"My husband is a pharmacist. I am a school psychologist. I'm also a speech pathologist. I got a few degrees. I liked going to school, let's put it that way. I wanted eventually to become a psychologist for the deaf. A specialty. . . .

"I had one illegal abortion in 1969. It was just before I got married. I had two parents that were cardiacs, and I didn't want to upset them. My father has since passed on, but I knew that any kind of shock, it was like forget it. And believe me, this procedure is nothing in comparison. I so strongly say, you know, like if it's a plane trip, or whatever it is, take it. Spend the extra money and get it done legally. It was done on a kitchen table. I mean it turned out that the doctor was very competent. He was a Cuban physician who could not be licensed here, he didn't want to go through all the schooling and things of that nature. He was an older man, but he did a fantastic job. But, it wasn't under sterile conditions."

DR. D.: Were you asleep?

MA: No. I was awake through the whole thing.

DR. D.: Were you frightened?

MA: Yes.

"When it got painful I couldn't moan or anything because the people in the next apartment might hear. He lived in an apartment house, and it had to be done all hush-hush.

"He used archaic equipment, he used very dangerous drugs which my husband knew the name of but I didn't. When we came back and looked them up, we found that the FDA has not approved them for use in the United States. I would have liked some anesthesia. He did everything manually. The procedure upstairs took ten minutes, but this procedure took over an hour. Plus he tried to dilate me, and I have a condition where for some reason I just don't dilate. The whole thing was a mess. I was thirteen weeks pregnant, and there was no nurse there. He just had a tray of equipment and a bucket and it all plopped into the bucket. He had a pair of rubber gloves and he boiled everything on the stove and he used two kitchen chairs for the stirrups. So it was quite an experience. But I would have died rather than have my parents hurt. That's the way I felt.

"It was very expensive. It cost about $1,000 and then I had to go back for a second time to be cleaned out because he didn't finish the first time."

DR. D.: You had to go back to him?

MA: Yes. Because no one else would touch me. I started to have an infection, but my husband, as I said, is a pharmacist, and he had me on a high dosage of antibiotics which were combating the infection. It was mostly pain and bleeding and this went on for two weeks. Heavy bleeding. So I went back again. The same setup. It wasn't as painful the second time, it was uncomfortable."

*There can be no better argument in favor of legalized abortions than the story Mrs. Afilides tells.*

*She is dead wrong about the machine not accepting intestinal matter and "putting it right back in place." But that is not important. What matters is the crucial question: Would she have survived this time, on the kitchen table, the ministrations of an unlicensed, Cuban abortionist?*

## Mrs. Emma Kennedy, Age 29, Divorced

### Ten Weeks Pregnant

"My boyfriend is beautiful. He gave me the money. He brought me here this morning. I've spoken to him already today. He says he loves me so I don't think the abortion will matter.

"I went off the birth control pills in May because I was having horrible cramps in my legs and everything like that. June, July, August, I bled constantly on and off. I figured if I were bleeding I couldn't get pregnant. But I did. . . .

"I have two children at home. My own. Eight and nine. Having this child just wouldn't be right for them. We weren't going to get married. He's married. He's got his own children.

But I love him and, like, we broke off and we've always gone back to seeing each other."

DR. D.: What does he do?

EK: What does he do? Okay, he has an automotive business. A front.

DR. D.: For what?

EK: Okay, he has an automotive place and this is what he does.

DR. D.: What is it a front for? Now you can't tease me like that.

EK: He's being paid. He works with Carlo Gambino. He's a nephew. And he's married and, like, it's not very right before that walk of life to get divorces and things like that. . . .

"He's a very busy man, very busy man. Weekends he's usually home unless he can run into the city and see me. Friday nights he stays with me until Saturday morning whenever we wake up. Eight, nine, ten o'clock. And I call him everyday. He sees me after work, even if it is just to run in and give me a big hug and kiss.

"At times I am jealous of his wife. Like I carry on and I cry and I say 'Why do you have to be married?' and he says, 'You know I can't do anything about it now.'

"He is trying to make enough money so that he can get out of the marriage. You know it's all a bunch of lies, but you try to believe it. Like the holidays come along and you die. That's the part that hurts."

*The last thing Emma Kennedy looks like is a Mafioso's moll. Although that may just be my unreasonable reluctance to link clean-cut looks to corruption. Corruption ought to be greasy, or big-nosed, or fat-hipped at the very least. I don't believe that for a minute, of course, but it reassures me. The prejudice protects me from what I have seen: urbane murderers, mundane sadists, assassins disguised in the habit of friendship.*

"Thanksgiving is not so bad. I'm working Thanksgiving. But Christmas will bother me and New Year's Eve will bother me. Other than that I'll survive. Like last Christmas he bought the tree and he bought the kids all their gifts."

DR. D.: Why don't you find another guy?

EK: Happily single?

DR. D.: Yes.

EK: If you can find me one that's beautiful and nice and loves kids, you have my address and my name. But I got to find somebody like him. I compare every guy. I've gone out nights, you know, looking around, and it's horrible. The places are horrible. All everybody wants to do is to get laid, and I don't want that. I want a love affair. I want a relationship that might go into a marriage. And like most of these guys are married anyway. You don't see very many single guys around. They are separated. Oh yes, they are separated for this night. My wife is home and you're here, so we're separated. It would be beautiful to find somebody single. . . .

"I'm happy, at times. I'm not happy when he has to leave me. He cuddles me in bed, tucks me under the covers, kisses me good-night, 'I gotta go home.'

"Sex with him is beautiful. I haven't found anybody better. Neither has he. We're compatible. This abortion is going to kill us. This is going to gently kill us. I told him at least two weeks. 'Two weeks?' I know it's going to be longer than that, but I told him two weeks. 'Okay, but you're going to have to learn a few things in the next two weeks.' I said, 'Oh really?' He said, 'Yeah really.' He said, 'You're going to be laying on your belly a lot in the next couple of weeks.' I said, 'I'm not going to turn greek for anybody.' We've done it but I don't like it particularly, but I'll please him. And I love sex. I could have it every day, three, four times a day. I could do it all the time. Psychoanalyze me that. I think I am a nymphomaniac.

"About five years ago, right after I got divorced, I went very wild. I went very crazy. I was doing it to everybody and anybody. Like a machine. I could not get my fill of it.

"With my husband it was horrible. No comparison. He's from a very staunch Irish rich Catholic family, and I guess they didn't think much of things like that. . . .

"My boyfriend said, 'I knew you were pregnant. I knew that

night, that I did it, I knew you were going to have it. That's a love baby,' he said, 'definitely a love baby. Keep it as long as you want, until it's safe enough. You can't keep it forever. You know you can't keep it.' "

## Mr. Victor Marks, Age 41

*Father*

*Mr. Marks is a very likable man. He has big rough hands and a quick fleeting smile. He is Catholic by birth and belief, but his anger is not based on dogma.*

*He is very disappointed. Personally, not in principle. He feels that Linda has let the family down. She has been self-indulgent, and she has incurred an unbudgeted expense.*

*Toward the boyfriend he harbors no grudge.*

"I don't know what happened. Her and her boyfriend came and told us that she was pregnant. Of course you can't have an abortion in our state. This was three weeks ago."

DR. D.: What took you so long to get here?

VM: It was just the system. We had to go through Planned Parenthood and they send you to a doctor and this doctor sends you to a preacher and then he set an appointment. We came to a clinic over here last Thursday, but maybe we goofed up over there. They said she's too far along. But here they said she wasn't. So there's three doctors and all three of them was wrong. One doctor said ten weeks, this other one said twelve and a half weeks, this doctor here says no, she's twelve weeks. I don't know who is right and who is wrong.

"Anyway, we had to come back today, to have her done here.

"I believe she was scared of telling me, not my wife. She told both of us together. I was kind of disappointed in her. Oh, not that I hold it against her. I'm not that type of person. But that's not the way we had brought her up. We came up Catholic, brought them up Catholic, and anytime they ever had a question we always answered it honestly. No beating around the bush, we told them where it's at. Sex, intercourse, everything. We told her the truth about the whole works. I was disappointed in her when she told me but I mean I wasn't mad or nothing like that. . . .

"They wanted to get married, and I told them it was foolish. To me it's a poor way to start a marriage really, because of all the people I know who started a marriage like that I'd say 80 percent are divorced. I think this will be a lesson to her. Her boyfriend Barry is a nice kid. At least he had nerve enough to tell. He was going to come with her, and then I told him I'd come.

"I'm going to have a little talk with them. I'm just going to tell them I don't approve of it and if they think that much of each other surely they can wait until she gets out of high school to get married. That's the way I look at it.

"I know she knows she hurt me and her mother, and I honestly believe she won't do it again. But if she does, what can I do about it? She's eighteen. But I told her 'Well, this time I'll foot the bill, but this is it.' I work too hard, my wife works too hard, to give them the things that they have, and something like this comes up, I believe she's depriving the rest.

"I don't think it's right for any parents to buy pills or diaphragms or stuff for their kids. I mean before one's starting into college and she's on her own. That's a different story. I believe if you're doing this, then you're giving them the right to do it. I mean they're saying 'Well, mother bought them for me so she must say it's okay.' I don't agree with that.

"My next girl is seventeen. I have more confidence in her. I've always had more confidence in her than I have in this girl. This girl was the oldest, and she's kind of babied and pampered. My other one won't fool around. She knows about this and she was rather disappointed too. . . .

"My state just turned down the abortion law, and I know they came out with a lot of propaganda and all this bull. I talked to a doctor about this and the way he talked to me, this is all bullshit what they're putting out. I voted for the law.

"To me everybody should have his own right to make up his own mind. That's just like me coming to you and saying 'Why, you can't do this, or that, because I don't like it.' To me this is not right.

"Japan has had for years abortion and when you see those people over there, how some of them live, you're pretty glad they've got something like that. A law where they can have abortions. . . .

"Me, I work seven days a week and I don't have time to hang around no place. I am an electrician. Usually I'm gone from home probably ten hours a day. When you get off work a lot of guys hang around bars and stuff, but I don't. To me I'd rather have more of the things that are good in life at home, then hanging around bars. That's just the way I've been brought up.

"We have our fights but I've honestly got to say that I've never laid a hand on her and she's never laid a hand on me. Oh, you have your words, your differences, maybe you don't speak to each other for a day or two, but that's with everyone.

"I believe you could hurt my wife with words. Sometimes maybe I get on her about something and maybe she'll cry, but she's worked at the plant too long for this. I think when they work in a factory they tend to change. I don't know, I guess they just get harder. Like probably when a lady works in a restaurant or something, maybe she'd tend to cry quite a bit. If you ever worked in a plant you'd know what I'm talking about. After a while you become where you get an attitude of 'So what.' . . ."

DR. D.: Did you ever have sex before you were married?

VM: Oh yes. One in Japan, Hong Kong. A prostitute, but they're under medical supervision. That's the only ones we ever messed with. Every two or three weeks they had medical inspections. And in California. Not a prostitute in California, that was just a girl. She was a nurse.

"This is their livelihood in Japan or, say, Mexico. I mean I've been in Mexico probably a million times, Japan, Hong Kong, the Philippines."

DR. D.: How about the nurse, did she mean anything to you?

VM: Nope.

DR. D.: Could she have meant anything to you?

VM: I don't think so.

DR. D.: Why is that?

VM: I don't know. . . .

"I go to school quite a bit. I take everything, anything I like, electronics, dance classes, whatever appeals to me. See we can go there, we don't pay tuition. It's what they call 'Citizens for Books.' General Motors pays for us. To me if you like a course why shouldn't you take it, you're helping yourself."

## Miss Linda Marks, Age 18, Single

*Twelve Weeks Pregnant*

"I feel like I just closed my eyes, they just stuck the needle in and I went to sleep. I was scared. In the elevator I covered myself all up. I don't like people looking at me. I had a green hat on. The guy that was taking me just kept looking. I didn't like it. When you just got here, you're scared.

"Then they took me through these doors, and they put me aside and told me to wait there until the doctor came. Then this guy came in and took me into an operating room. There was two doctors, and they asked me if I ate or drank anything. I said no. And that one doctor, he, I guess, stuck an IV needle, and that's what put me out. After that I can't remember what happened. It seemed like it just got done real fast and some nurse kept calling my name. I had cramps, not bad, but they were not cramps that you feel on the outside, they were more like on the inside. I heard somebody talking, they said, 'Move over,' and then they left the room for a minute and I guess I opened my eyes. . . .

"I didn't tell my parents until I found out for sure. I missed two periods. I was about seven weeks when I told my mom and dad.

"I went to the doctor, but my boyfriend called and found

out for me, if I was or not. They told him I was and he came and told me and he told my parents for me. I was standing there when he told them. One thing, I thought my mom and dad were going to be really mad, but they weren't. They were kind of upset but they weren't like most parents who sometimes get really mad because the kids did it. All my dad said was 'I told you' and stuff, but since it's all done with now, he didn't get mad.

"I think I was more scared about my mom finding out than I was myself, because I didn't want to hurt them. My mom said it was up to me if I wanted this abortion or not, nobody else. My dad didn't like people saying, 'You've got to get one.' They just told me it was up to me. . . .

"I had been brought up the right way. You know, if you're a nice girl, you don't go out and get into trouble. My dad was upset, he's just thinking of what his parents would say and stuff. Because all my cousins ended up pregnant and had to get married or didn't even get married. And he was just thinking about them. But my ma said it was okay, that he'd get over it. At first, like for two days, he didn't talk to me but then he started. You know how fathers are. I'm kind of like his little girl, even though I've got two other sisters. My ma tells me I am his favorite, that's why he was so hurt. . . .

"I wanted the baby at first. I was going to get married, but then I started thinking he wouldn't be making enough money to support us, so I said we'd better wait until we were planning on getting married. He agreed. He didn't want me to have the abortion, but then he said that he understood what my mom told me and he told me to figure everything out for myself. He said if we got married, he'd have to borrow money and stuff and then after the baby was born we'd have a lot of people to pay back, so that's what started me thinking. People to pay back. Then I'd end up like some of my relatives. Poor. They're not poor, but they're not middle-class. I mean they're always owing people and stuff, and I couldn't see being that way all the time. That's what got me started thinking about the abortion.

"I think I would have dropped out of school, then I figured

if I dropped out now, I'm sure I wouldn't go back next year because I wouldn't be able to get through all the hard work and everything.

"I knew I was pregnant but I acted like I wasn't. Some say you get attached to it. I didn't get that attached to it because I didn't really know it. I knew it was a baby but I didn't feel like it was in me or anything. Now I feel okay. I don't feel guilty or anything like they said. The radio said it. If you commit murder, you would be guilty the rest of your life and stuff. If I felt guilty I would have felt it before I got here."

*On the night table, next to Linda's bed, there stands a painted, battered, plaster statue of the Virgin Mary. In the Virgin's arms is the child. Her red lips smile. Her blue eyes shed brown, bumpy tears. Her pale skin and multicolored clothes are pockmarked in white where the paint has chipped.*

DR. D.: Is there a story to her?

LM: No, just somebody to have around. My aunt gave it to me. At home I keep flowers by her and light a candle. It just seems whenever I pray to her, you know, things that I want, tell her to help me out, something happens. I don't know about now. I had a feeling God was going to punish me for what I did. My dad said God has to forgive murderers once in a while.

DR. D.: Do you think this was murder?

LM: In a way, because it was alive. I'm Catholic, but I believe in abortion and all that stuff. Like in my state they didn't pass it because they put out a bunch of garbage about it. Have you seen those pamphlets? It was awful.

"Kids in my school tell me it's murder. Well, I know if they were in my position right now, they would have got one too. But if I would tell them, they would probably turn against me because I done it. I'm not ever going to tell them because I don't think it's anybody's business. . . .

"I'm not going to go to confession either. I'll get yelled at for missing like three years. They don't come around telling us everything they do, so I don't see why we have to go around telling them. . . .

174

"I prayed before I got here. Then now, when I was hurting, I told her, 'Make it not hurt,' and it doesn't hurt anymore, not a lot. That's before they brought me those pills, and it stopped kind of.

"I just tell it things, because I don't know what to say. I just treat her like a person. At night I talk to God. Like when I didn't know if I was pregnant I used to talk and ask Him that I wasn't. I was."

*In someone older, better educated, more introspective, more convinced of her self-importance, and therefore feeling more entitled to doctrinal rebellion, the last two sentences would augur an impending crisis of faith. Linda merely shrugs and smiles a little sadly.*

———

It is not often that patients are accompanied by their husbands or boyfriends. Even those men who do come along deposit their women in the waiting room and leave, to return later when the deed is done. Unlike fathers, mates do not remain in the waiting room to sit on the benches in somnolent detachment and to check their watches at short nervous intervals. They do not stay to pace, as fathers do, nor to make frequent trips to the water fountain to wet their dried lips.

This is a world of physical danger for women only, and that goes against the masculine grain. It makes the men awkward and shamefaced as they attempt simultaneously to apologize for and to deny their complicity in all that led to this, to this circumstance of uneven consequence, where mutual actions have ended in one-sided risk.

Male guilt, private and ontological, hovers here below the ceiling like a self-consuming predatory bird. It hangs on the walls among the printed notices. It carpets the ground on which stricken couples stand kissing each other goodbye in haste.

With each departure a silent covenant is made to reaffirm customary trusts. Not to go mad, not to revolt, not to pluck out eyes or tear at the flesh, in fact, not to mention at all the enormity of this anatomic injustice—never to be altered—that permits one partner to go for coffee, while the other one goes elsewhere, to be stripped, spread-eagled, and have done to ordinarily unspeakable things.

There are exceptions. It appears that sometimes relatedness, like isolation, is a problematic state. It appears that the glory of love is often a burden. It appears that the vertigo of falling free in space, which loneliness produces, can be matched in horror by the claustrophobic restraints of domestic bliss. It appears that neither this nor that but always the other is the preferred human choice.

Once I watch a woman take leave from her enterprising husband, who has managed to deliver her unto the D & C floor. It is a strictly forbidden practice. She is fair and blond, he is red-haired and ruddy.

"Okay," he says, "You'll be okay. But now I must go."

"Go?" she asks. "Go? Where will you go?"

"Don't start again," he says. "Don't, just don't."

They are standing in the corridor, in front of the nurses' station, but they speak to each other as if they were alone in their soundproofed, drapes-drawn living room. I feel I am spying on them, but the tension they emit acts on me like a magnet. Inside the nurses' station Norton obviously feels the same way, because instead of interrupting the scene and admitting the woman, she continues to shuffle charts and to look away.

"I won't do it," the woman says, in a dead monotone. Whatever strength she might at other times possess, it is not discernible now. She looks like one about to die.

"But you will," he answers, "you must." He, too, speaks in a monotone, but his atonality is of determination and not of defeat. "Don't go crazy on me Laurie," he says. "We have been through this eighty-four times. You got pregnant and I am sorry. It does not change the situation."

"What situation? Tell me what is the situation. I love you. We are about to have a child. What situation, Steve?" She is weeping, and I judge the rising note of hysteria in her voice as dangerous.

"Laurie, please. Please. Don't make me go through it again. Let me go."

"I don't know what the situation is. I don't know why I am here."

Suddenly he is very angry. His hands are on her shoulders, and he is shaking her back and forth. "Be-cause-I-am-through," he shouts. His speech is broken into syllables, in rhythm with his enraged assault on her. "Be-cause-I-do-not-want-you, or-this-ma-rriage-or-this-child. Be-cause-I-want-out. Out. Out. And you knew it. I have told it to you. You came to me that night. I didn't want it. I want out."

He is brutal beyond belief. Yet there is no way to ignore his desperation. His ruddy face is beet-red now, and he has started to tremble with bone-shattering violence.

"Laurie," as he calls her, is silent. Her pale, pinched face has the look of imminent madness.

Norton steps out into the corridor. "Sorry, sir," she says, "you have to leave now. No relatives are permitted on the floor." As she speaks she pushes the button to call the elevator. Her manner has no hint in it of anything amiss. I begin to wonder whether perhaps she had been really occupied with the charts. But, of course, that is not possible.

The elevator arrives, and the man enters it. "Goodbye, Laurie," he says.

"Goodbye," she shouts as the doors clang shut. "I hope I die."

Norton raises an eyebrow. "Did you say something dear?"

"No," Laurie says, weeping. "No. I have said nothing in years."

# Mr. Peter Mason, Age 41
## *Maria Bella's Boyfriend*

"I'm a state recovery agent. I recover bail jumpers. I arrest them and return them to my state. To the county prison. Everyone's not pleased to come back, so it's sometimes dangerous. But then I subdue them in any manner necessary. It gets interesting at times, providing you don't get involved in the people's personal problems. Because, you see, everyone has a problem. They always justify themselves. They always have a logical reason why they ran away. So they try to beg me to let them off. Including female prisoners. They've used different methods. They say, 'Why don't you say you couldn't find me' and things of this nature. It doesn't work.

"I get paid a salary, but there is a bonus connected with the insurance company. Which is sort of unofficial. I carry what they call a body warrant to return the body to this state once it's left. 'Dead or alive,' but that's back in the wild west, usually that's not necessary. But I do carry a gun. I've been doing this work for two years, but I studied criminology. I have a very good manner doing background investigation on the individual.

"In broken love affairs, women always want to help. If you can convince the woman that it's for the man's betterment that he returns, 99 percent of the time she'll fall for it, unless they take the standpoint that you're a pig. Any peace officer is a pig to them. Sometimes they're abusive in their talk. They talk down to you like you're a piece of garbage. That you're going to do an injustice to somebody, and they know somebody who was mistreated by a police officer. They're just justifying in their mind that you're no good. You're not doing the right thing. But you see one thing that you can't do is set yourself up as judge and jury. I never participate in whether a man's guilty or not. I just carry out the order, that's it. . . .

"Before this, I was a production superintendent in a ceramic factory. I studied that. I've studied many things, but never

179

really pursued anything to any depth. And that's how I met this girl, she worked for me."

DR. D.: How long have you known her?

PM: About two years, three years maybe, three and a half years.

DR. D.: Have you ever been married?

PM: Have I ever been married? I'm married presently.

DR. D.: I see. Do you have any kids?

PM: Two.

DR. D.: Do you live with your wife?

PM: Yes.

DR. D: Does she know about this?

PM: No.

DR. D.: Does she suspect?

PM: No, I don't think she suspects, I don't really think it makes any difference.

"My son is thirteen and my daughter is eleven. And they crave constantly, maybe because it's developed through my wife. I love my children very much, and to separate I couldn't afford to keep them like that. I've went through the affairs of my wife, and I think that's partially why I've begun to seek out an affair of my own. As a matter of fact she had about seven of them. Right now I think she's gone into some sort of shell as a martyr, her conscience I think has bothered her, and now she has turned this into a complete uprising, totally against sex. . . ."

*Peter Mason is a shortish, wiry fellow with large workman's hands, shrewd eyes, and some secret sorrow that unbeknownst to him intermittently surfaces on his bony face.*

*Above all, he yearns for power, and he evidently gets it. Over Maria Bella (currently in the OR aborting his baby), whom he labels a child, and over his wife (currently at home minding the children), whom he labels a cheat.*

PM: I've had other affairs aside from Maria, but Maria hasn't.

DR. D.: Since you are together?

PM: Yes.

DR. D: Does Maria know?

PM: No.

DR. D.: How come you did?

PM: I think it was just pure animalistic lust with these relationships. I mean the sure need of man to maintain being a man. But nothing other than possibly a girl and a good time, that's all.

DR. D.: How about Maria, is she something more than a girl and a good time?

PM: Yes, definitely.

DR. D.: How much more?

PM: Oh, if I could straighten a few of Maria's ways out, I think I probably would marry Maria, if I was free.

DR. D: What do you think the abortion is going to do to your relationship with Maria?

PM: I don't know.

"I don't think it's really going to destroy it. I think that the relationship would be destroyed without the abortion. She did make a statement downstairs as much as saying that she's going to give up the only thing she ever wanted.

"It upsets you emotionally. Then again, how would I feel if the families were to be exposed. My children, her father, all the people that she knows, to a child out of wedlock. And we come from a community where everyone knows everyone, not like New York City. I think she would shame her parents, which are very funny Italian people. Her mother is aware of the abortion and agrees with it. . . .

"I don't think it's the child as much as it is something that is a part of me. That's more the feeling, that she's losing something that's a part of me rather than just the child itself. But you see it's nice to say 'Have a baby' and then after the baby comes, the things that come behind it. Then what?

"And Maria has lived at a standard as a single girl, spends a lot of money on clothes, fancy car, and I would say she's living beyond her means even as a single person. She hasn't saved a dime and she's thirty-one years old.

"See, Maria's led sort of a sheltered life. She really wants the baby but due to the circumstances, number one with her father who would never accept the situation like that. Of course my status, I just don't think that regardless of what might develop at a later time as far as Maria and I go, this wouldn't be a good situation to force it. I mean because it would sort of force an individual or force a decision on someone's part that might be hasty.

"She has to be a realist. She's still a child basically and very sentimental and not a realist like myself. . . .

"You see I wouldn't even go for something like this, but you see in certain times in life I think this should be able to be done, depending on a situation. I don't think it should be a common thing that every person who just wants to have it done should have it done, because they just don't want a child. I think there are extenuating circumstances involved here, but I do believe that if the circumstances are such it should be legalized because it's only going to be done anyhow."

*"There are extenuating circumstances involved here," Mr. Mason says.*

*He says it straightforwardly with no trace at all of irony. He has forgotten his earlier contempt for his bail jumpers who all, according to him, claim for themselves special circumstances.*

"I've tried to look at it as the baby doesn't exist. It hasn't taken its first breath. That's when I feel a baby is a baby. If I would have known what I know now, I probably would have wanted my wife to have an abortion. It would have been better for both of us, because here we are two miserable people living together because of children. I'm sure she feels the same way about it."


## Mr. Morton Fitzsimmons, Age 40

*Margaret Dunbar's Boyfriend*

"I was referred by a doctor in Philadelphia, and I brought Maggie here for an abortion. She had been pregnant before, and her symptoms, the underneath of her breasts they feel sore, which is one of the signs. Plus her just not feeling right. We figure she is about five weeks."

DR. D.: I take it from your names that you're not married?

MF: That's right.

DR. D.: Are you yourself married?

MF: I was. I am in the process of divorcing.

DR. D.: Do you have any children?

MF: Yes. Two. Boys. Sixteen and fourteen.

DR. D.: Did you consider keeping the baby at all?

MF: No, I never wanted one.

DR. D.: Does Maggie have any children?

MF: No. She had an abortion before. I had known her for eight years.

DR. D.: That was during the time you were married?

MF: Yes.

DR. D.: Are you planning to remarry?

MF: To Maggie, yes. But I didn't consider keeping it, because I feel I don't want to be burdened anymore. I mean my two boys are old enough, but I just don't want to start over. I'm going to be forty, and I don't appreciate the fact of raising children again. I am considering a vasectomy.

DR. D.: How about Maggie, how old is she?

MF: Twenty-eight.

DR. D.: Is it all right with her never to have kids?

MF: Her feeling is she wouldn't want any either. I think it was her rearing. She came from a large family, and her life was miserable, etc., etc., of raising a family because she was the youngest child. I think this had a lot of stress and strain on her, I don't really think she wants any, not even her own.

DR. D.: When Maggie had the previous abortion, was that from you?

MF: Yes.

DR. D.: That was when it was still illegal, I take it?

MF: Yes. It wasn't hard to find a doctor. And as far as going through it, we sat down and we talked about it and we went through it. About six years ago.

"Six years ago I wasn't in a good position. I was only building my way up at the time. I didn't have the time to put into it. Also, there were certain elements in my marriage which at the time I couldn't consider because I was doing something, I had too many irons in the fire. Financially I couldn't break away, it would become too costly. I am in investments. I didn't want to split fifty-fifty. . . .

"The sex part I don't know about my wife. As far as her companionship, her companionship was her two boys. I think this is one of the things that could have turned the tide for me. That I was the one put aside for the boys. I mean that I couldn't go out with her, or do anything with her without taking along the boys. She wouldn't consider a baby-sitter. She felt they were her children and wherever she went they should come. I didn't feel that I could live with this all the time.

"Certainly there was a resentment, I mean because you can't do what you want. Everybody likes to more or less show a little of their emotions when they go out to a party or something like that. You know, even in a nightclub you'd like to stay 'til one or two in the morning, not stay 'til ten o'clock and come home.

"She felt a family is a family. She would always want togetherness, which I felt was overdoing it. One of the reasons I may have stayed a little bit longer was to see that the boys were brought up to where I knew what they wanted to do. I think that they've made up their minds now as to what they want to do. What college they want to go to, etc. Everything is taken care of. . . ."

DR. D.: I notice you still wear a wedding band.

MF: Yeah, so does Maggie.

DR. D.: That's her ring, so to speak?

MF: Yeah.

*Mr. Fitzsimmons is a stocky man. He is pot-bellied, barrel-chested, bitter-faced. It is not pleasant to talk with him. I feel puzzled by and sorry for Maggie, whom I never get to meet.*

184

# Mrs. Gina Ricardo, Age 43, Married

*Fifteen Weeks Pregnant*

*When I stop my introductory declamation, Mrs. Ricardo says, "I don't know that I want to. Do I have to talk to you?" "No," I say. "No. I would just like it. I mean it would be useful to me. But you don't have to." As I deliver this reply, I shift from foot to foot, I shrug my shoulders slightly, I shake my head from one side to the other, I look the picture of long conditioned resignation, unconsciously replicating the historical message of her face.*

*"Okay then," she says. "It might be okay."*

*The more we talk, the more her appetite for talk grows. She becomes giddy, she has the giggles, she acts high. Her face unwrinkles, her voice drops its cut. She is a hidden addict to attention, like all of us, all bribable by interested eyes focused on the dull bones of our bare existence.*

"I have four children. From five to ten. This was a slip-up, I guess. For five years I was just careful and it worked. I didn't use nothing. We thought of having the baby. But the more we thought about it, the more we thought of our age and my nerves were getting bad, and we decided it would be best to have this done. The overall situation with the kids we have, and I'd have to quit working, and one income, you know, nowadays isn't very much on a regular pay. I'm a helper in a delicatessen. My husband works for the highways.

"We have one graduating high school this year. And he may want to go to college, and that'll take money. And our daughter, she's in different things at school, and it's so much money for that, and it just seems like if I had to quit working we'd just exist on his pay.

"You know, when you first get pregnant, you're disappointed of course, especially after a long time. The more I thought about it though, it worked on my nerves. I could see myself getting more nervous by the day. I thought this was the best thing. Of course, he didn't right away, but then he finally did. He said if it was gonna cause my nerves to go bad and that, why, it would be the best thing to have it done. It isn't far enough yet that I felt life or something. Now if I were far enough, where I think I felt life, then I don't know if I would go through with it. Like a lot of these girls, they come in here six months pregnant. Well if I went that far, I'd go the whole way. Because the baby's formed then I think. . . .

"I'm going to try to teach my daughter that she shouldn't go out and do those things until she's married. That's all you can do. If they go out on their own and get in trouble, well, then it's something else.

"Of course, if something happened and if she wanted to go ahead and have the child, I'd go along with her."

DR. D.: Did you have sex before you were married?

GR: Yes. I was engaged to somebody else, before.

DR. D.: But you are saying something different to your daughter.

GR: You try to teach them that way.

"I think it makes for a better marriage if girls run around. I really do. Because when they settle down they are ready to settle down. Whereas a girl, maybe she only goes with one person, she is more apt to want to run around later, because she has never done it."

DR. D.: In that case, why would you advise your daughter not to do it?

GR: Well, you're supposed to advise them to do the right thing, right?

DR. D.: But you're saying the right thing is to run around a bit, so you can find out what's what.

GR: Well that's her prerogative. But I wouldn't tell her that it's right to do it.

DR. D.: Why ever not, when you really do think it's right?

GR: I don't know why I wouldn't. I wasn't brought up that way, I guess. I come from a large family. My father always had the attitude if we were going out, it was to get in trouble.

"It wasn't that I was taught it was all right. I mean, really you feel guilty down in, because you do these things. Maybe that's why I wouldn't want her to do it."

DR. D.: Did you ever tell your husband that there were others?

GR: Oh, he knew when we got married. Well, he went out with other people too. Men do. That's an accepted fact. He knew I was no angel. He accepted me for what I was and we took it from there.

"I can't say that I just like sex 'cause I don't. There's times when you just don't want to be bothered. Like I work out, and then I come home and work, and then I'm tired when I go to bed, you know. Which statistics say that you should still, if your husband wants to. You should as an obedient wife do it, which I don't agree with unless he pitches in and helps with the housework afterwards."

DR. D.: Does he?

GR: No.

DR. D.: Do you think that it's going to make any difference in your marriage, this abortion?

GR: No. It would have, had I done it on my own. And he hadn't agreed to it. But since he agreed it's just going to be like something that happened and that's it. We'll go on living. He worries more about what would happen to me, than me having it done. . . .

"Really, I don't get much out of life. Just to see my kids grow up happy. But I want to give them things, and if I don't work to earn a little bit extra money, I can't do that. Because I come from a big family and we were poor, and I had to go without a lot of things."

DR. D.: What delayed you for fifteen weeks?

GR: Well, I didn't get to the doctor before the first of October, because he was away and then they were filled up. I couldn't get an appointment.

DR. D.: And you knew you were pregnant?

GR: I figured it, when I missed. He referred me over to this Dr. R. He said I was too far and he gave me this number. That's how I got here. Now I am going to have my tubes tied.

"I think that if a woman is able, she's the one that's going

187

to have to do it, because they're more strong than a man when it comes to things like that. They can take more than a man."

## Miss Erika Ney, Age 42, Single

### *Eight Weeks Pregnant*

"I don't want the child, and it's inappropriate for a number of reasons. He's a married man. I don't see him anymore.

"It was at the end of a very difficult relationship and it was an impulsive sort of thing. I guess if I really thought about it, I would no longer have been involved with the man. It was sort of a last coming together, and I just took a chance. This is my first pregnancy. The more difficult thing was ending the relationship with the man. The sad thing for me was that he wasn't the kind of man I wanted to be with always. I don't think he'd be a good father and I don't think he's the person whose child I would really want to have.

"I think that I wanted to have children at a much earlier point in my life than right now. I'm terribly involved in my work, and I would want to feel there was a father, or somebody who was responsible with me for the child. So now I don't want the child."

DR.D.: Does he know you're pregnant?

EN: No, he doesn't.

DR. D.: Why is that?

EN: Well, I haven't seen him in two months. It was very difficult for me to end the relationship and it would be terribly upsetting for me to see him. And I feel he would use this to pull me back again into something that I struggled to get away from. Also he'd be terribly upset by it, and he couldn't handle it very well. I think I can handle it better than he'd be able to.

"This is an ironic aftermath. It's never happened to me. I was incredulous that it happened. I considered keeping it, but not seriously. I played with many aspects of it. Like what sex it would be. Why I haven't had children? What it would be like to have a child, etc. But it just seems so unfeasible in my life style, and without him or a man.

"I really feel I'm too old at this point to have a child. It would be sort of risky at forty-two, for the first time. Plus the fact that he's not a person who wanted children. He never had children and never wanted them. He's quite a bit older than I am. I think he sees me as having much more life, and he was more involved with me physically than he'd ever been with anyone, and I think all that would have touched him but I don't think he could handle any of my distress. He is a kind of child himself. I guess that's the problem. . . .

"This is uncomfortable but I'm not terrified. I'm the kind of person who mulls a lot afterwards. I have experienced other things that have upset me more, and I just feel more sad about this, that's all. My whole work is involved with kids and with little children particularly.

"I was a teacher once, and I have spent a good deal of my time with little children. You know, there's a whole strange thing about all this. I mean in some ways I was rather pleased to feel pregnant. I have felt at other times in my life, a lack of never having been pregnant. So I can't really say that I have experienced all this as something terrible.

"The way I got pregnant, part of my own irresponsibility taught me a great deal about the relationship with this man. I hope this whole experience will lead me into something new, into another kind of a relationship with some other man, that's more productive. . . .

"It's not that I want to be married particularly, but I would like to be with someone consistently that I feel very good about instead of sort of repeatedly being in situations that end up as a mess, which I've been in more or less most of my adult life."

DR. D.: How is it that you never married?

EN: Well, now you're asking me four-cassettes worth. It's such a long, hard story. I guess I've been busy sorting out and finding out and doing too many things. Not feeling the need of the stereotype of marriage. But experiencing different people and doing different kinds of work and changing my life in various ways. One person I was involved with for a very long time was married with kids. It was an impossible situation for him to get out of. Another person, much earlier in my life, I never felt was right to marry even though we were very close. I still believe it was a very wise judgment on my part. Although we lived together for several years. So I mean it's complicated. . . .

"I don't feel I've been coerced into any decision. I mean, what I wanted to do is clear to me. I won't regret that. I regret some of my own foolishness, in not taking care of myself. But those things happen. Who is ever so rational all the time? You know, I've done more stupid things in my life. I hope I'll be more careful in the future, but I mean who is that careful about everything? . . .

"I've been sorting out the difference between spending my life looking for the lost father I never had, or someone to solve certain problems in my life which I didn't want to solve myself. In particular, certain kinds of identity from the man, rather than establishing my own. And I feel now at the point where this is no longer necessary.

"I'm a little concerned about all the feelings after the abortion because I tend to get into periods of moderate depression and mull around."

*The loneliness of Erika Ney creeps into my bones. Has she decided well, I wonder. Will she not regret tomorrow losing this last chance to have someone of her own to love?*

## Miss Jane Ballantine, Age 17, Single

*Fifteen Weeks Pregnant*

*Jane Ballantine, 17, IQ 70, cute as a button, is done-for in this urban, industrial society, where the most prized item of barter is brains.*

190

*Neither she nor her mother acknowledges this fact. That is good. It gives Jane a small fighting chance.*

*But I, as the observer, become once more befuddled at the rulelessness of this world, at the mightiness of its disorder. In one case truth damages, in the other it heals. Sometimes acquaintanceship with reality makes people sane, at other times it drives them mad. Who is to say what is the right path? Certainly not anyone with a heart.*

"I know where it happened. With Tommy Town, but I'm going with some other guy now. I loved Tommy, though, see, he put great big bruises on me. With his fist. Finally I told on him."

DR. D.: How about making love? Did you know what you were doing when you did it?

JB: No, I didn't.

DR. D.: You didn't know that you could get pregnant?

JB: No. I don't like it now, because my mom won't let me see him and all this. My mom went over and talked to his mom, but he wasn't there. But he knows I am pregnant. I think he was shocked.

"My mom said, you know, he was responsible but there was no way he could support me and all this. So I don't want to have it. . . ."

DR. D.: What do you want to do when you graduate high school?

JB: Go in the army.

DR. D.: The army?

JB: Yeah, my plans are all worked out for that.

DR. D.: To do what?

JB: To join the navy.

DR. D.: What do you like about the navy?

JB: I don't know, I'd just like to travel.

DR. D.: Have you ever traveled?

JB: No.

## Mrs. Ruth Condon, Age 34

*Mother of Jane Ballantine*

"She began getting sick in the morning. She did not tell me, so if I hadn't figured it out myself, I would not have known until probably too late to do anything. She just was, I guess, afraid to say anything. But I noticed that she was getting sick every morning. Throwing up. That usually means just one thing. I asked her, and she denied it at first, but it wasn't really a very emphatic denial, so I told her that I was going to take her to the doctor and see.

"She's a junior in high school and she's in the same class with this boy and they went together. . . .

"I told his family Wednesday evening. I only spoke with his mother, but she was equally shocked as I was. I don't know why you're always shocked. You always think somebody else's kid is going to do it, and not your own. And I don't know why people take the attitude that they do. It's medieval really, but she couldn't believe it either, and I assured her it was true. I told her what plans I had made, and asked if she had any constructive ideas. If not, that was the plan I was going to take. It's not a realistic thing to say these kids can get married and make a go of it. I would give them two years at the very most for the marriage to last. There's a personality clash that they've always had, and I was hoping that she would see this long before she did. I jumped on the bandwagon early this fall when they were sort of having a little fight, and I just said, 'I forbid you to see him anymore,' and I just think it's a ridiculous situation to try to force a marriage like that, and it would just be a matter of time.

"They are both slow learners and he's a little slower than she is, and I think emotionally it would just wipe them out.

"If she went through with it I think there would be enough social feeling there, that I just don't think she would ever go back to school to finish. And I don't think he would finish now. To me that's prime. You can't do anything anymore without getting a high-school diploma, and I was pretty insistent on that.

"The only alternative to this would be for her to have the child and then put it up for adoption.

"Jane's IQ is in the low seventies. So I think they said she was a borderline slow learner. She really can't keep up with the regular class, but at times I felt I made a mistake by putting her in the slow-learner class because of the environment. The kids in there that she has to choose her friends from. I have felt at times that I made a serious mistake. I wish there was an intermediate thing to put her in, because she really does not belong in either one. It's too much of a struggle for her in a regular class because she feels terribly inadequate, plus the fact that she's not getting the lessons. So she just withdraws more and more and she says nothing. And in the slow-learner class there's no competition because these kids really are slow, most of them.

"Tommy is a little bit slower yet. He has a terrible complex. I mean he's a weight-lifting type, and physically he's a very mature guy, but emotionally I think there's a really a big problem with him. And I think he takes it out by dominating her, and she lets him do it. He used to punch her black and blue as a game. Then I said, 'Hell, it has to stop.' . . .

"Basically I don't know if his mother agrees with me or not, but of course the thing was, I hit her cold with it. She had no idea. I wanted his parents to know before I came here, because in hindsight people can come up with some glorious stories, and I thought, well I'm going to ask her going in what she thinks about it, and if she disagreed violently we'll go from there. But until somebody comes up with something that is a workable solution I just couldn't see any other way."

"I've been married and divorced twice. She was very small when her father and I were divorced, but they were close anyway. I think that this time it probably tended to upset her more than the first time, although towards the end they weren't really that close but I do think it bothered her some.

She calls him Daddy even yet but she doesn't see him or anything.

"Her real father doesn't come by either. As a matter of fact the last time she saw him was probably seven or eight years ago and then it was probably like a five-minute thing. She does see his mother. I don't object to his mother picking her up, because I mean it's her grandmother and she loves her and Jane loves her, but I'm not going to force the father to come and get her. You don't want to do that.

"I think he's still married to his third wife, I'm not sure. They do send support payments if they're forced to. They're always way behind and they skip a lot and stuff like that. I made an issue of it two or three years ago and we settled for some miserable portion of it. He never sees her, he never calls to see how she is.

"She fell on his mother's steps a few days after last Christmas. She hit the back of her head and had a terrible concussion, and we spent three days in the emergency ward. And he knew it because his mother was very concerned, but even knowing the fact that she might permanently be a vegetable, he never sent a card. Didn't call, he did absolutely nothing. . . ."

DR. D.: How old were you when you first married?

RC: Seventeen. Yes, when I saw that, I said, 'Oh, a repeat.' It really rattled me.

DR. D.: Were you pregnant?

RC: Yes, and I guess that's why I panicked. I said, 'Oh, she's going to do the same thing.' The funny thing is this summer I started to see some likenesses in her father and in this boy and suddenly I took the most intense dislike to him. . . .

*Judging by Mrs. Condon's history, life is a precarious event. Things happen through some inexorable law of repetition, independently of choice. Children fulfill unrecognized parental yearnings, repeat the repudiated pasts of their elders, and err in a demonic mold.*

*Balance is maintained by way of elaborate shams until a critical event interrupts the conspiracy for a while. That is made into "bad times," when truth has surfaced, when being alone and a stranger is factual and suddenly real in the forced privacy of pain.*

"With my second husband I realized that he was running around with ungodly numbers of women and stuff, and it just seemed like I was waiting forever for nothing. He had plans to leave and marry one, and I even made it my business to see what she looked like and it absolutely wiped me out. She worked in a bar, and there's nothing wrong with that, but I couldn't believe the caliber of woman he had chosen to leave me for, and egowise it just flattened me right out. She just looked as cheap as anything I have ever seen. He had bought her a car and he was paying her housing and and everything. And let's face it, what I made was going in on this too, so I considered I was paying half of it.

"He has not married her though, and we are still friends. We speak on the phone. . . .

"I have told Jane that rather than have this happen again, I'd rather she take pills. But I'm not by any stretch of the imagination suggesting that she just indiscriminately have sex with anybody going or coming. I wasn't sure what to do, but I felt I should say something, so we talked about it like that, and she was very quiet again about it.

"I hope she looks at it in the right way, what I'm trying to do. I'm not willing to run the risk of this again. . . .

"I have not allowed myself to think about the abortion as such. I try not to think about it as a person. I'm trying to look at it more on the overall outcome of the whole thing. As opposed to the life of a little person. And when I get it that personal, I'm not sure exactly what I feel about it. I think it's better to have the abortion than to have the problem that it's going to create. Because I would be terribly concerned for the child if it was born. So I prefer the abortion to that. I think it would be very tempting to try to keep the child if she did have it. I think once it got that far along, I would start thinking in terms of grandchildren, so I decided not to have that risk."

———

## Mrs. Sylvia Austin, Age 26, Married

*Thirteen Weeks Pregnant*

"I wanted to have the child but my husband is sterile, and I have two children and that's what split us up, you know, the pregnancy. He said it wasn't his and we were separated for a year and we were going to go back together and I told him I was pregnant and he knows it's not his child, so I decided to have the abortion. I felt I wasn't ready to have another child anyway. My first son is five and the other is two and a half, and they are a handful."

DR. D.: Are they your husband's children?

SA: Yes, both of them are his, but we were separated for a year and he got syphilis. And it made him sterile, that's what he said. And we stayed separated. And then finally he was coming to see the children and we decided we would try to go back together.

"I told him I was seeing someone else, he didn't want to believe it and it hurt him a lot and then when I came home pregnant he was really hurt. The fellow I am seeing, he's much younger than I am and he's a junior in college, and I didn't want to rush him into anything. So he and I talked about getting an abortion. He was very upset but he said he thought it was the best thing. He's more understanding than my husband.

"At first I was going to have the child and keep it. I wanted my baby. I didn't care if I'd made a mistake and had gone to bed with another man, because I wasn't planning on going back with my husband. It's like a weekend thing with him. He works up here in New York all week, and comes home on the weekends.

"He manages a bar for his father, he keeps the books. It's a fast life. Plus he likes to gamble a little bit too. He's pretty lucky in that. I don't like that, I just want to have a nice home with my kids and raise them. . . .

"I care for my husband more. I admit that. He has a lot of faults and everything, but the feeling is still there. He's still the kids' father. Like the other guy, he's got so much that my husband doesn't have, yet he's lacking in what my husband has. Like if I could put them both together it would be a perfect man. . . .

"The first fellow I ever had I went with him for two years. And then decided to, well, I was high one night. We were drinking wine, and we were in the car, and my girl friend, I could punch her in the nose right now if I ever saw her again. She and I were very close all through high school, and she was telling me how nice it was, and how she felt when her boyfriend made love to her, and what he would do to her and how beautiful it was. Well, she filled my head so full of sex that I had to try. So I tried it and it wasn't great.

"It just like gave me cramps in my stomach and I thought he was a monster. I looked up at him and he was on top of me and I said, 'Get off me.' I don't like to look at a man's body. I really shy away. I think a woman's body is beautiful, everything about a woman is beautiful. I couldn't talk to my mother about that either, because she would say, 'Don't be silly.' She'd say, 'When you meet the right person you'll know it.' Well, when I met Joe I thought I knew it. But it wasn't true. With my husband I had a climax if we had oral sex. But if he should just have intercourse with me I would never get a climax, never. I never have and I always thought there was something wrong with me. That's why I tried to talk to my mother and find out if there was something wrong with me, and she said, 'No, there are so many women that never know what a climax is and they never feel it.' So how could they possibly think that they love this man? See, I think that sex is part of showing someone that you do love them.

"I tried it with a woman once. It was something completely different. I mean she was hard as a nail. It was a year ago. I met her through friends. I found myself wanting to do things for her.

"If I didn't have any children, I think I would be much happier. That's funny. I think I was holding back because of my children. I found her beautiful and she hates men and she doesn't like anyone that likes men. Yet she dresses like one.

197

And she kind of looks a little like a man, yet she's a woman.

"I found being with her, I felt like she knew what I wanted and I knew what she wanted. She knew how to get me aroused and I knew how to get her aroused too, because I feel that a woman knows what a woman wants. If I didn't have any children I think that I would have pressed the issue with her.

"I still think there's something wrong with me. I think I'm what you call a bisexual. Because I enjoy being with my husband and there's a feeling there. I was raised to think that a man and a woman is right, and that's the only thing that's right. Two women together isn't right. That's queer. That's the way I was raised and that's the way I look at things. But then when I met my friend she was just different. She was human, she was warm.

"But my children mean more to me than anything, and I wouldn't know how to raise them with me living with another woman. If I was smart enough, or if I had counseling or something like that, maybe. But now I'm afraid that it would hurt them. Change their life in some way that would be wrong.

"I don't feel anything about the abortion because I didn't feel the baby moving or anything. I think if I had felt the baby growing inside, I think I would have hesitated. This way, I made the right decision.

"Marriage is a risk and having children is a risk."

*Sylvia Austin is a large-boned girl, of plain countenance and a crew cut.*

*The most lively thing about her is her voice. Like a well-used instrument it provides the variegated sounds of mournful dirges, marches of revolution, and romantic tunes sweet and cheap as penny candy.*

*Love and sex are big items with her. But the doctor in me becomes concerned with other things. With the silence behind her voice, with the hooded nightmares hidden in her eyes, with the hopeless collapse of every smile she attempts.*

The most threatening pitfall in this hospital is a creeping conviction of absurdity. Daily, terror and desolation dictate decisions, the meaning of which are obscure to everyone. This life against that. Why? That life against this. Why again? Because patients can speak, and fetuses are mute?

And what of these histories? What of these forsaken, neglected, lonesome lives, whose principal light—as reflected in their speech—shines forth from cultural platitudes, from which they learn what they ought to want and what they have missed.

Things happen. Situations arise. We do what we can, which is not much. Will, God's or otherwise, appears an obsolete notion. The most frequent gesture is a shrug. The most prevalent phrase is "I don't know."

And yet, these beings are a far-flung parcel of nature's most dignified and complex best, I say. And I say that saying that is not worth a damn. Because that is not what they know. What they know is the monotony of day-to-day hope, the soul-corroding acid of recurrent disappointments, the nausea of life, the fright of death.

And one more thing. They know, even when it is not conscious, the muscular, visceral, sensory, total joy of breathing, of having a heartbeat, of being alive. They can flex limbs, use minds, grind pelvises, yearn with their spirit and weep for grief and gladness, private and collective. That sight makes mincemeat of absurdity. At least for a time.

# Chapter 6

## *Surgery*

The sun has fallen and it lies in blood
The moon is weaving bandages of gold.
Oh black waves take me down with you
Gian Carlo Menotti

Rachel takes me to the Operating Room Floor quite early in my work at the hospital. It is here that I meet for the first time Mr. Smith, the chief OR nurse, and Dr. Bender, who works primarily with salines.

They are drinking coffee. They offer me a cup, which I gratefully accept. We sit, and talk, and drink, and smoke. The door of the room is closed, and there is an atmosphere of great coziness inside. I feel very reassured. The fact is that I have worried a good deal about coming to the OR floor. Operations frighten me. The sight of blood makes me sick. The smell of ether sends me into a panic of accidental inhalation and unexpected death. I ask about ether, and I am told, again to my great relief, that it is used here very, very rarely.

We are interrupted by a knock on the door. A nurse sticks her head in to say that it is time for Mr. Smith to scrub. Mr. Smith says, "Okay." Dr. Bender says, "I have to go too." All three of us get up. Mr. Smith opens the door for me, and I am about to step outside but I am prevented by a passing stretcher. On it is a sleeping woman covered with a white sheet from neck to mid-calf. Her naked feet form a pale and callused vee. Next to her right foot there is a small, transparent plastic jar filled with some kind of bloody substance, like chicken innards. I know, because when I was a child my grandmother used to buy live chickens, have them killed according to ritual by the *schochet*, defeather them herself, burn their skin over a fire (another ritual), and disembowel them. I used to watch her—in fascinated motionless horror—as she reached deep inside the animal and then, slowly withdrawing her hand, scooped ahead and downward the innards. Layers of newspaper had been spread on the table into which the stuff would fall. She then folded the paper, all four sides, and carried it to the garbage with her right hand, holding her other hand under the package, palm upward, to catch possible drops of blood that might soak through during the short trip. They never did. Her left hand always remained immaculate.

"What is that jar?" I ask. By now the stretcher has passed us and we stand in the corridor. "Parts of the fetus," Mr. Smith says. "For the lab. To see if there is pathology. The law requires it. Well, goodbye now. Nice to have met you, doctor." "Yeah, me too, thank you," I say. "Goodbye," says Doctor Bender. "Goodbye."

I do not return to the OR floor for a very long time. When I do, it is to the chief's office for interviews, preferably behind closed doors. And even after that, my first explorations turn out to be geographic.

There is not much territory to cover. The chief's office is to the right of the elevators. It is a big, messy room with a large desk, a few chairs, and some cabinets. The surface of every piece of furniture is covered with papers, files, dirty ashtrays, boxes of tissues, packs of OR masks, empty coffee cups, and whatever else anyone has ever put down and forgotten. Nominally the office belongs to Dr. Holtzman who clearly has no proprietary interest in it.

To the right of this room there is a smaller office where the nurses usually hang out and where a clerk makes up schedules, keeps records, and administers the jars of fetal samples for later delivery to the labs.

Next, turning a corner and proceeding west, there is a beautiful, polished, fine-grained wooden door, new and completely out of keeping with the rest of the unit. A blue, printed sign above it says: "Washroom." I open the door and step into a kitchen. It is a very modern kitchen, fully equipped, lined with cabinets. On each cabinet door there are several strips of white adhesive tape on which someone has written by hand, in ballpoint, the names of the medications stored inside. I spend several refreshing days reading these labels. Beyond here, due west, there is only the recovery room.

At the other end of the floor, to the left of the elevators, stands the Operating Room. It has large swinging double doors, with a small square window on each door at eye level. From the base of the doors to just below the windows shiny metal sheets cover the wood, like mirrors. Whenever the doors swing open, as people and stretchers exit and enter, I can see that beyond the doors there is a short corridor leading to another set of swinging doors exactly the same as the outer ones. I have been told that is the entrance to OR One.

Loitering on this floor is not easy. While operations are in progress, which is most of the day, there is a continuous, steady traffic, to and fro, of terrified or unconscious women, depending on the direction from which their stretchers come. Often as many as eight or ten waiting patients are lined up outside the swinging doors. (Their number is many times multiplied in ghostly, infinite regress through their reflection in the metal mirrors.) As soon as one person is taken into surgery, another is brought up from the D & C floor to take her place in line. The process works on the principle of a conveyor belt.

Waiting, the women lie on their stretchers in silence, imprisoned between protective metal bars. Their pinched faces are full of determination and terror. Big-eyed, bird-like, pale, hawk-handed in fright, they seem like lost souls before the final judgment. Although they are pushed close together, each of them is very much alone, isolated in her private world of dread. There is no heroic moment of truth here, only a desperate internal scramble to contain one's self and hold together for another, little while.

I watch them wait, and I watch the staff move among them oblivious to their struggle. The nurses are rushed, harassed, busy, intent on the preservation of the bodies of the women. It has to be that way, I know, there is no time for anything else. Besides, unexpected kindness at such a moment might even be detrimental to hard-won self-control. Still, the sight of these juxtaposed, separate, walled worlds fills me with a kind of total horror to which I cannot put a name.

"Nurse, nurse, what time is it?" one woman calls from her stretcher, holding her bony hand in front of her mouth as if to stifle the escaping words. "Quarter past four, dear," Nurse Mason says, momentarily interrupting her murmured conversation with an aide. There is a clock on the wall, visible to the patient, and all of us know that she is not asking for the time. My stomach fills with ice cubes at my helplessness to interfere with this farce—which I know to be necessary, to be essential for the sake of self-control and routine. What use would it be to run to the woman and say "Please scream your fear," or to shout in rage at the nurse, "Tell her she'll be all right, when she asks for the time." To uncover reality here would mean to turn this place into a madhouse. Therefore I am silent, and clutch my stomach, and go for a walk down the corridor.

As I turn the corner, I find Betsy leaning against the wall in her habitual laconic slouch, chatting with a gray-haired tall man in OR greens. They must have come up the stairs or else I would have seen them sooner. "There you are," Betsy says, "I was just talking about you." "Dr. Denes, Dr. Holtzman." So this is Holtzman. He nods. I nod back. I have heard a great deal about Holtzman from Rachel and Betsy and Edie and several of the counselors. He is supposed to be a notorious ass-pincher and booby-squeezer. He is supposed to be vulgar, loud, rowdy, and a male chauvinist pig. "I'm glad to meet you," I say. He turns toward me, but his eyes fix on some point behind my head. "Whaddayasay your name was?" "Denes," I say, grinning. "Doctor Denes." "Howdya spell it?" "D-O-C-T-O-R D-E-N-E-S." "You are a shrink." It is not a question. "Yeap," I say. "Well, I gotta go. Goodbye. Good luck." He turns on his heels and is gone.

Due to various perversities in my character I like him enormously. For one thing it requires no discerning eye to see that he is very, very depressed and that his manner is at least in part designed to hide the depression and perhaps in some measure to overcome it. For another, except for this one maneuver, he is clearly completely himself.

The next time we meet it is on the food line in the cafeteria. I say, "Hi." He says, "Hello, dear." I shake my head and say, "Wrong." He says "Oh, you are the shrink." I say, "Right." He waits until I sit down and chooses a different table.

Our third meeting takes place on the OR floor again. I catch him as he exits through the OR swinging doors looking gaunt and exhausted. "I am the shrink," I say. "I want to interview you. Will you do it?" "Anything for a pretty girl," he says, obviously dropping with fatigue. There is a quality of games-manship in him, which for a time I aggrandize into the heroic. "Provided you get me a cup of coffee while I change." "Done," I say, grinning again. In ways I completely enjoy but hardly comprehend, he consistently elicits in me the weird sensation of being a six-year-old chock-full of motherly instincts. I bring coffee for both of us and doughnuts and apples. I put them out on the desk in his office before he gets there from the changing room.

He arrives in five minutes. Impeccably dressed, he resem-bles most a very successful Seventh Avenue garment salesman. "Oh," he says, looking at the desk, "I hate apples, and dough-nuts don't agree with me. You could give me a cigarette." "Can we start?" I say, thoroughly exasperated. "It is very late." "So start, start, I am ready."

We talk for an unreasonably long time. The sardonic vulgar beam with which he burns others is turned in on his life, as he illuminates with complete frankness its craggy matrix.

After this, we talk many times, with the tape recorder on and off. We would become friends if he knew how to do that, but he does not know. Women are to treat or fuck. People are to be wary of. I fit nowhere. His warmest feelings are reserved for his children, so he adopts me. Being OR chief, he makes my life very easy on the floor.

Mentorship by the powerful in this hospital is a mixed bless-ing I learn again, as I did before with Rachel. Without it, I

could do nothing, of course. I would be out. But with it, I come
to be seen, by nurses and aides and orderlies, as the agent of
my protector, and I become heir, by association, to all the
attitudes they harbor toward the "boss." I am therefore treated
by various persons in the unit with distrust and semisup-
pressed rage, provoked by Holtzman. On the whole, however,
things go well for me. I get to interview Mr. Smith, the chief
OR nurse; Tom Scott, who is Mr. Smith's friend and an OR
aide; Dr. Berkowitz, the anesthesiologist, and various other
people who work on the floor. I am gossiped with, and I am
permitted to hear the mythologies of bygone days, as when
they were working three shifts every twenty-four hours (before other states legalized abortions) and everybody got rich at
his own level. I am informed of past sexual scandals. And of
scandals of another sort, like the day when one doctor perforated three cases in a row and Holtzman had to be called
back on emergency to fix them up. Like the day when a uterus
detached itself during surgery and practically fell on the table.
Everybody was called in that day, even outside help. The girl
was sixteen. Holtzman, like an idiot, held out for sewing the
damned thing back. He won through sheer lung power. It
worked. The girl now has a chance to bear children and deliver through a Caesarean section.

For several days I stall, then approach the task backwards.
I wait at the OR doors and join the orderlies as they wheel a
woman out and toward the recovery room. It is someone I
know. Jacqueline Renault. Born in Paris. Divorced. Thirty-
five. Twelve weeks pregnant at intake. Mother of two. When
I spoke with her this morning, she wept. Now she lies unconscious, the little jar at her feet.

It is a short distance to the recovery room, and the orderlies
walk briskly. At the entrance, one of them calls to the nurse
inside, "Okay, Rosie, a customer for you." Rosie appears. She
is a short, thin, elderly woman with tired eyes and fading red
hair. She is wearing a blue, knitted cardigan over her nurse's
uniform. I automatically note that she is transgressing one of
Rachel's regulations. Cardigans are allowed, but the color
must be white. "Put her over here," Rosie says, pointing to an

empty spot on the left side of the room. The orderlies do as they are told. "Anyone to go?" the one who has spoken before asks. Rosie shakes her head. "Nobody is ready." The men leave.

I stay, standing at the door, inside the room. Beside Mrs. Renault there are three more patients. The one farthest away from me near the right-hand windows appears to be sleeping peacefully, in normal slumber. From time to time she shifts her body weight. The other two, like Mrs. Renault, look drugged. None of these three have moved since I came in.

Rosie slides out Mrs. Renault's chart from under her head, looks up her name, and begins gently to slap her face. "Wake up, Jacqueline, come on dear, wake up." No reaction. Rosie unhooks from the wall the gray arm-band part of a blood pressure machine, winds it around Mrs. Renault's arm, hooks it to the apparatus on the wall, and, placing her stethoscope in her ears, proceeds to take the patient's blood pressure. I notice that each woman is hooked up to her own machine on the wall next to her. Rosie stops and makes a notation on the chart. "How is it?" I ask.

"110 over 80." "That's good," I say. For once I am not bluffing. Charlie Bender taught me one time that in the recovery room the patients' vital signs are checked every fifteen minutes. These consist of respiration rate, pulse, and blood pressure. If things are going well, respiration in a postoperative sedated person ought to appear normal. Not too slow, not too rapid, and not too shallow. There are, however, several oxygen tanks in the room and two respirators, in case a patient does develop breathing difficulties. Pulse rate ought to be between 90 and 110 beats per minute. Below 90 one would suspect inadequate oxygenation, above 110 the possibility arises of hemorrhage or shock. The same applies to blood pressure, where the normal range is between 90 over 60 and 140 over 100.

Rosie is slapping Mrs. Renault again. "Wake up, Jacqueline. Jacqueline, wake up. Time to get up." Mrs. Renault begins to murmur something inaudible. Rosie goes to the next patient in line, a very young, pasty-faced, blond girl. "Ma-ry, Ma-ry, up-sy dai-sy," Rosie chants to her in singsong, while she gives her a couple of half-hearted pats on the face. "Up-sy dai-sy, Ma-ry, Ma-ry." Mary does not respond. The patient next to her, however, does. With her eyes closed, her arms flailing in spastic randomness, she begins to struggle to sit up. Rosie jumps over to her and with one skillful motion presses her back on the stretcher. "Just a minute, dear, just a minute." It does no good. The woman is dead set to get out of wherever she thinks she is. Her face is a concentrate of effort. She pulls her upper body forward by stretching her neck, while her uncontrolled arms flap about uselessly. But sit up she will. Her determination coupled with her inefficiency is a dreadful sight. To make matters worse, Rosie in her confusion, instead of shouting "Wake up," keeps yelling "Lie down." Each time she does, the patient redoubles her efforts to sit. "Wake up," I scream, but I am too late. The wrestling is over. The patient is suddenly lying down again, fast asleep and snoring.

Meanwhile, unnoticed by either Rosie or me, Mrs. Renault's murmurs have swelled to an obsessive guttural tide. "J'ai soif, j'ai soif, j'ai soif, J'ai soif." The room fills with her mindless demand: "J'ai soif, j'ai soif." Rosie listens for a moment, then turning toward me, announces, "The poor thing, calling for her husband Joseph. She is French, you know." By now I have had enough. To hell with it I think. Let God come down and handle this. Let Him protect all these conflicting interests, wounding no one. I don't know how. "Rosie," I say, "I think she might be thirsty. Her lips look very dry to me." "You could be right at that, Doctor," Rosie says, wetting a towel and pressing it to Mrs. Renault's lips. Mrs. Renault quiets down, sucking. "Goodnight, Rosie," I say and walk away.

In the corridor I meet Mr. Smith walking toward the recovery room. "All of them still asleep, right?" he says looking disgusted. "Right," I say. "Well, what can you do," he shrugs. "The good doctor is so damned slow they get bombed out of their minds—and then they act crazy and don't wake for more than an hour." I know he is speaking of an old German attending, whom I have seen around but have not particularly wanted to meet. "Goodnight, Mr. Smith," I say. "Goodnight, Doctor," he says, looking disgusted.

I have run out of plausible excuses for further delay. Next day I approach Holtzman in the cafeteria while he is eating lunch. "Listen, could I possibly go into OR with you please and tape there?" "Sure," he says. "I wondered why you didn't ask sooner. What are you going to tape, the clanging of instruments? The patients are asleep." "I'll tape you." "What do you think I do there, keep up a running monologue?" "Will you let me come?" "Anytime, annyy timme," he says with a mock-dirty leer. "Oh, for Christ' sake. Tomorrow then?" "Anytime." "Thanks. See you tomorrow." I turn to leave, but I would like to get some pointers from him, a preview maybe. I don't know exactly what. Anything really, to reassure myself that for me to go into OR is not a completely crazy project. Since I am not clear on what I want, I am also not clear on how to ask for it.

"You start at ten, don't you?" I say. "You know I do." "What I mean is, when should I be there?" "Ten minutes before." "And then I scrub with you?" "Only," he says, and there is no hint of a smile on his face, "if you intend to do part of the surgery."

So I goofed. To hell with it. I am sick anyway of the pretense by innuendo I have to maintain in this hospital of being a Doctor doctor. Yet I must do it or else faces shut down, information dries up, charts become unavailable, and my status changes to that of a very undesirable alien.

Physicians are a weird lot with regard to their degree. They treat it as if it were a membership card to an exclusive and closed brotherhood, a learned Cosa Nostra. It isn't even what they do to outsiders with it that stupefies me, although that is peculiar enough. Nor what they do to the nurses, which is terrible. The most astounding thing about MD's is their unassailable fellowship. It appears that a doctorate in medicine is thicker than blood.

Starting with their first-year students, on whom they capriciously confer the title of doctor (the kids are at best six months out of college), all the way to their most senile or inept or renegade colleagues, they maintain an impenetrable attitude of solidarity and specialness toward one another. To say,

"My name is Doctor So and So," insures an automatic, perceptible, positive shift in the other doctor's receptivity toward oneself. The positive regard is independent of age, specialty, or level of achievement. In fact it is quite impersonal, and it is directed primarily toward the shared title. I find the phenomenon inexplicable given how rich and influential physicians are in this country. My only other experience with this sort of fraternal loyalty has come from belonging to a persecuted minority group.

At any rate, I obviously just blew it with Holtzman, but I am too disgusted to correct it. That, of course, is not as daring a decision as one might think, since Holtzman is a *steppenwolf,* and his pack instincts are singularly weak for a physician.

"Okay," I say. "I have told you I am not an MD. Now please, you tell me what I will have to do. Everything." "You don't have to do anything. Just get into the clothes issued to you, come into the operating room and stand somewhere out of the way." "That's all?" "That's all. Don't worry, shrink, you'll make out okay. And I'll show you the rest of it tomorrow."

That afternoon I talk with Mr. Smith, who says okay: "A pleasure, Doctor." I also talk with nurse O'Neil who says okay, provided I get releases from all the patients who are to be operated on. "But I will not interview the patients," I say, "they will be asleep." "I know that, Doctor," O'Neil says, "but I like to be prepared." It seems easier to comply than to explain the facts of the matter to her. So I say, "Fine, thank you very much. Most grateful. A pleasure. Goodbye. Good luck." "Goodbye, Doctor," she says. "Doctor is right isn't it?" "Yeah, it's right. It's right—it is, as a matter of fact, perfect. Toodeloo." I begin to think I had better watch my step, and temper.

Next morning I am on the D & C floor at seven. I speak to all the women scheduled for D & C's between ten and four. I get releases from everybody, even from those whose surgeon is not Holtzman.

At half-past nine I arrive on the OR floor. "I am going in with Doctor Holtzman today, could you get me some clothes please?" I say to the nurse on duty. "Sure thing, Doctor," she says. She leaves and reappears with a green gown, a cap, and some paper booties to put over my shoes. "Strip to your underwear, please, Doctor, except for your shoes, and put these on. None of your hair should show." "Thanks," I say, "where do I do this?" There is a long pause. "Well, we don't have a changing room for female doctors. I am sorry, we have never had a female doctor here. You could use the nurses' locker room." "That will be fine, thanks. Where is it?" "Right there, Doctor." She points to an unmarked door, across the elevators. "Great. Thanks again," I say, and go toward the appointed entrance.

Inside, it is a very small room, crowded with gray metal lockers, some chairs, a washbasin, and a full-length old mirror propped against a wall. I take my clothes off, fold them on a chair, and put on the robe. I have some difficulty getting my arms through, because the sleeves are glued shut with heavy starch. I put the cap on my head and, seated, pull the paper booties over my shoes. Each bootie has a long black plastic strip hanging from it, which one has to wind around the ankles, tie, and tuck back into the shoes, to keep the booties secure. When I am done, I get up and look at myself in the mirror. My sense of unreality, which has been steadily growing since I entered this room, is now total. I am also sweating heavily, although there is a window open, and cold gusts of wind keep rattling a newspaper someone has left on a nearby chair. Outside, it looks like it is going to rain. I hang my tape recorder on my shoulder, take a yellow pad and pencil, and proceed to OR.

As I push the swinging doors open, a nurse I have not met before intercepts me. "Authorized personnel only," she says. "I am authorized," I mumble. "What did you say?" "I am Dr. Denes." I clear my throat. "I am a doctor." Now my voice is too loud. Holtzman notices us from inside. "Come on, Doctor, come on," he booms. "What are you waiting for? We have to get started." Turning to the nurse, he says, "Give her a mask." The nurse takes one from a large pile in a box standing on a shelf near the doors. "Here, Doctor." "Thank you." I don't know what to do with it. It has four strings, and it has to be tied at the back of the head at two levels, but my hands are full with my pad and pencil. Holtzman glances at us. "Tie it on her," he roars again. "Come on, can't you see her hands are full?" The poor nurse jumps. She is a small Chinese girl, and she gives me a well-deserved look of pure hatred. But she does tie me into the mask. I walk without incident the next five yards to the second set of swinging doors, which are now propped open, and I step into OR One. Since the operating table is empty and there is no patient to be seen anywhere, I calm down a little.

I have never before stood up in an operating room. The changed angle of vision that my verticality provides radically alters my remembered impressions. The overhead reflector, for example, is not as large as the sun, it is approximately four feet in diameter. Operating-room eyes brim with buried meaning only because they are bracketed between mask and cap. In fact, no portentous silent signals are sent or received. The staff moves at normal speed, or a little faster, not in the slow, drawn-out, staggered motion I thought I had observed lying down. I am beginning to feel very good at being here. This is after all a secret and forbidden place, where only the anointed go to perform magic or to be its subject. I do not belong, and yet here I stand: a witness to revelations. The fraternity would probably excommunicate Holtzman if they were to learn of his complicity in this sacrilege.

Besides me, pressed with my back into a corner, there are four persons present. Dr. Berkowitz, at the head of the operating table, is checking the oxygen and nitrous oxide tanks and testing the IV hookup. Tom Scott, who has just wheeled in a small table, like a tea cart, covered with a blue disposable paper sheet, is fastidiously positioning it on the right side of the foot of the operating table. He is pushing it back and forth over a very small distance trying to get it just right according to some necessity with which I am unfamiliar. Mr. Smith is fiddling with the suction machine. I have seen the machine before. There is a spare one stored in Holtzman's office. This, too, for some obscure and disturbing reason, or perhaps because shapes, creativity, and associations—both in the world and in me—are finite, reminds me of an implement related to food.

*Surgery*

The machine resembles one of those carts on which coffee and Danish pastries are brought around in office buildings at ten and three o'clock. It is made of metal, it moves on wheels, and it has a handle at each end. On its side there are hooks around which to wind its own electric cord. On top, however, rather than a coffee maker with its outward flowing spigot, there are two identical glass jars, each with 120 cc's capacity. Plastic, flexible transparent tubing, about an inch in diameter, connects the jars to each other and to the machine. Another, rather long tube of the same type, projects from one of the jars. This one ends in a hard plastic elongated tip, and it is the part of the apparatus that is pushed into the vagina during suction. Inside each of the glass jars, hanging from the lid, there is a bag made of gauze. Its purpose is to trap the suctioned fetal matter, while permitting the blood to drain into the jar. During the procedure only one of the jars is supposed to be actually filled. The other one is merely a precautionary standby, in case the first one overflows.

The fourth staff person in the room is the young Chinese nurse whom I met earlier at the entrance. She is busy with the operating table and with things around it, but she is doing so many things so fast that I am unable to identify her specific actions. I also stop trying because Holtzman appears. He walks in, his arms held in front of him, bent upward at the elbows, his fingers spread apart. All eyes simultaneously shift to him. "Let's get going," he says. I look at the clock on the wall. It is five minutes to ten. I have been in the OR for three minutes.

Joe goes to the doors and calls out "Okay." Two orderlies wheel in the first patient. They push the stretcher parallel to the operating table, lower the metal bar, push the stretcher adjacent to the table, and stop. The nurse is now occupied with Holtzman. She holds a large green gown open, which he gets into, front to back. He wears the gown over his OR suit. The nurse steps behind him and ties the gown. To tie it at his neck she has to stand on tiptoe. Next, she puts plastic gloves on his hands, with the familiar movements of a mother readying a small child. Meanwhile, Mr. Smith has moved to the head of the table near Dr. Berkowitz. "Slide over, please," Mr. Smith says to the patient. The orderlies steady the stretcher. The patient heaves herself over, with a little help from Mr. Smith, who makes sure that the sheet covering the patient goes with her and continues to cover her white gowned body. Berkowitz is filling a syringe with a clear liquid. The orderlies start to leave with the stretcher. One of them calls in my direction, "Hi there." By the time I register that he is Jeremiah Adam and that it is to me he spoke, they are out of the room. I note that I have not observed where Tom was all this time. I look at the clock. It is three minutes to ten. I think it might have stopped so I check my watch. It is three minutes to ten.

Someone, probably Tom, has removed the sheet from the little cart at the foot of the operating table. It is full of gleaming, vicious-looking metal instruments. My heart begins to pound. This is for real. These people are not kidding. They may look like merrymakers at a masquerade, dressed all in green with their masks and ridiculous booties; they may move like performers at a happening loosely synchronized around a general idea but otherwise independently engaged; but all that is merely appearance. The blood about to flow will be real. This woman will become unpregnant. Her life will permanently turn a corner, and her fetus will in fact not be born. The magic of this room resides in its power to incontrovertibly alter, for better or for worse, whatever was before. I, too, will never be the same again. The thought terrifies.

Mr. Smith and the nurse have taken up a face-to-face position on either side of the patient at the lower end of the operating table. The nurse pushes the cover sheet up to the woman's belly. Mr. Smith and the nurse each lift one of the patient's legs and place it in the obstetrical stirrups. They tie each leg to the stirrup with leather straps, at mid-calf and at mid-thigh. Mr. Smith drops the leaf of the table, which had until now supported the woman's legs. The nurse throws a small coverlet over the spread-eagled woman, to hide her exposed genitals. Neither of them speaks at all.

During this, Berkowitz is working on the patient at the other end. He lowers slightly the section of the table under her head, so that her neck is stretched and her chin juts out. He takes her left arm and straps it, palm upward, to a wooden contraption that extends from the operating table and that holds the patient's arm straight and level with her body. He winds a rubber tourniquet above her elbow and swabs her lower arm with alcohol. "Have you eaten anything today?" he asks. "No." The patient's voice is barely audible. "Make a fist please. This will pinch a little." The patient curves her fingers inward, and Berkowitz pushes into her vein a 20-gauge needle, attached to a short plastic tube. "Ow, it hurts!" She sobs. I notice her for the first time. It is Stephanie Levenson. Twenty-one, old-fashioned, and ashamed. She has told no one of her pregnancy, not even her roommate at college. "If my parents knew about this, they would die." Her eyes are wet with tears, her lips quiver, her face is crumpled with misery. "Don't cry, don't cry or we'll be in trouble," Berkowitz yells at her, while taping the needle to her arm. "You'll get full of mucus." Stephanie sobs louder. "Come on, now, don't frighten her," Holtzman hollers from the other end of the table. "Don't you frighten my patient." Then very gently he says, "It's okay, honey, I'll be right there with you." The girl quiets down. Berkowitz mutters, and affixes a filled syringe to the tube attached to the needle in Stephanie's arm. He is now ready to put her to sleep at a second's notice.

Holtzman approaches the girl, chart in hand. "Your name, honey, is Stephanie Levenson?" She nods. "And how old are you honey?" "Twenty-one." "Fine. That's a good age. And you are twelve weeks pregnant." She nods again. "Okey-dokey. You'll be going home tonight, dear. This won't take long." I am seeing an aspect of Holtzman he hides everywhere else. "Go to sleep now, honey." Holtzman nods to Berkowitz who pushes the plunger of the syringe. Stephanie opens her mouth to say something, but she emits no sound. Instead, her eyelids fall. Holtzman walks away. Berkowitz removes the syringe and connects the plastic tube to the tube of an IV hookup. I venture out of my corner, near to Berkowitz. "What's that stuff?" I ask him. "A Brevital drip. We prefer it rather than to keep shooting the stuff with a syringe. If you run the drip fast enough, it has the same effect, but it is steadier. Also it gives me greater freedom to watch the patient. That's important, because Brevital, as you know, is a rather strong respiratory depressant. So we have to be careful."

As we talk, I am standing with my back to everything except Berkowitz, whom I face. Abruptly my attention is overwhelmed by two noises. The clanging of metal and the rhythmic horrifying howl of a dog. I turn around. The clanging is easy to identify. Holtzman, seated on a stool between the spread legs of the patient, is slamming down instruments on one side of the little metal cart, almost as fast as Mr. Smith is handing them to him. Take, fiddle, slam. Take, fiddle, slam. From the distance where I stand, which seems to have increased by miles in the past second, the process looks like a game of toddlers. I can not locate the dog. The howling continues. I look at Stephanie. The sound comes from her. Her jaw has fallen, her whole body heaves with wracking hiccups. To me she looks moribund. Berkowitz takes a leisurely step toward her and pulls her jaw up to close her mouth. The hiccups continue, but the howling is muted.

"What's going on?" I have difficulty talking because my mouth is stone dry, although the rest of me is wet again with perspiration. "The Brevital," Berkowitz says. "You know how it is when they suddenly become a little anoxic."

"The noises, the noises, that come from your patients," Holtzman shouts across the room. "Oh, okay," Berkowitz shrugs reluctantly, and straps an oxygen mask on Stephanie. "Is she all right?" I ask, but I do not hear the answer because Holtzman is making some noise of his own. He is using the suction machine, which gurgles in the replica of a slurp but more prolonged and much louder. The room fills with the smell of blood. It recalls vomit and freshly peeled almonds. It recalls crashing into a lamppost and, in the suddenly ensuing lull, the first sticky, sickening taste of one's life oozing out in red.

I start toward the doors blindly. Tom says, from far away,

"Are you all right, Doctor?" I am all right but I have to leave, only I cannot say it. God bless Holtzman, who thunders "Let her go."

I go, not very far, to the sinks where the doctors scrub before the operations. I pull down my mask and splash some water on my face. Mr. Smith, who has followed me out, offers me a cigarette. "It happens to all of us, the first time," he says comfortingly. I am not comforted in the least. I am furious with myself. For Chris' sake I didn't even actually see anything. I ran away from noises and smells. Traffic patterns, furniture, fantasies made me bolt. On the other hand, one has to consider the context, I argue. Bullshit! Coward! Idiot! My rage is bitter and boundless, although somewhere I also know, vaguely, that my Self is not entirely the target and my leaving OR One is not entirely the cause.

Mr. Smith is still talking. I catch his last phrase: ". . . and almost fainted, but there it was just a matter of adjusting to surgery itself. Here this is a matter of mixed feelings because you have probably guilt feelings, probably way back in the back of your mind. You have the surgery, and you also see what's coming through the tubes, or what he is taking out of her. Like it could be a person. It makes you feel bad. All of us here had an experience of that." "Yeah," I say. "Thanks for the cigarette." I re-adjust my mask and decide to return to OR One, but Holtzman is just exiting. I check my watch. It is ten after ten. Time sure does not fly around here.

"Feeling better?" Holtzman asks. "Yes, I am sorry." "Forget it. Are you coming along to OR Two?" "What do you mean? It's finished isn't it?" "Sure. That case is finished, but the next one is in OR Two, all prepared. It saves time. I switch from room to room, so that I don't waste my time waiting for the orderlies to mop up and for the staff to get the patient ready. I can do six an hour this way, easily. If they are real early pregnancies, I can do seven." "I see."

While talking to me he has scrubbed his hands, dried them with paper towels, and now he holds them up in the same gesture with which he had entered OR One. I follow him to

OR Two. As we walk through the swinging doors all eyes shift to him. "Let's get going," he says. I go to my corner.

OR Two is the mirror image of OR One. Everything in it is the same, in reverse. I note that the instrument table is uncovered, the patient is in position, and Berkowitz has finished preparing her arm. Evidently the staff changes rooms while Holtzman scrubs. I look at the patient. She is Maude O'Malley, a very good-looking woman with huge blue eyes. I spoke with her this morning, briefly, but I had interviewed her husband yesterday at length. They have been married for one year. She has two children, from a former marriage, who live with them. He has never had a child and at fifty-one considers himself too old to want one. He thinks they are happy. The idea of an abortion does not bother him at all.

Holtzman is talking with Mrs. O'Malley. "I am Doctor Holtzman. You are Maude O'Malley." "Yes." "How old are you, Maude?" "Thirty-five." "What's your excuse? The fifteen-year-olds don't know any better. Do you have any children?" "Two." "What did they tell you, that you are going home today or tomorrow?" "Tomorrow." "Naughty girl. Two children. Oh well. Off to sleep you go." Throughout this conversation, whenever he is not speaking, Holtzman hums a quiet little tune. Maude O'Malley panics. "Wait a minute," she shouts. "I am not asleep yet. Don't do anything." "How can I?" Holtzman is at his driest. "I am standing next to you." He nods to Berkowitz who pushes the plunger. Holtzman walks away. Berkowitz says, "Go to sleep." Mrs. O'Malley twists her head to look back at him. "But I want to know if . . ." She is out.

Berkowitz straightens her head and hooks her to the IV. "Is she going to hiccup?" I ask him. "Probably. Most of them do. Say, I meant to ask you, my daughter has applied to graduate school in psychology and she has been accepted in three places. At Michigan State, at Storrs, and at Columbia. Where do you think she should go?" The noises start again. "Well, they are all good schools. It depends. . . . What are you doing?" He has picked up Mrs. O'Malley's free hand, and he is squeezing one of her fingers. "Checking. She looks a little cyanotic. The color of the nails is a good indicator. Also the lips, look here." He takes her lower lip between thumb and forefinger and pulls it outward. "See the color?" It looks blue. "Yeah. Is she in trouble?" "Nah, not much. Like I told you. The Brevital can knock respiration out completely for a while. So they don't breathe at all. Well, which school do you think?" "But that sounds terribly dangerous. I mean, you can become a vegetable in a few minutes with total anoxia." "She wants to go to Michigan, but my wife says either Columbia or Storrs. She wants to have the girl nearer home." "I don't think she is breathing." "She is all right. I myself think, she should go to Michigan, provided it's just as good a school."

The stench of blood grows very strong again. "Yeah, yeah. Michigan is fine. It's the best. Aren't you going to oxygenate her?" "You worry too much. She has stopped breathing just this second." He clamps the mask on her and starts the machine. "Watch her fingernails. There she goes, you see? The color is coming back. In another second she'll be breathing on her own again. Michigan it is then, right? That's your advice?" "That's my advice." The magnitude of my revolt is such that I forget that the other end of the table is mined territory and start walking that way.

"Coming to see it from our angle?" Mr. Smith asks, laughing. I stop. "No. No. I think I'll just stay here in the middle." "Oh come on, Doctor," Mr. Smith teases. "You've got to see it sometime. We all did." "I am finished here," Holtzman says. "And anyway don't rush her." "Certainly, Doctor," Mr. Smith answers smiling, but the irony in his voice cuts. He does not like Holtzman.

They joke, they hum, they fight, they are preoccupied with their children's careers. To one patient they are sweet, to another mean, for no discernible reason. Jesus Christ, how does anybody ever come out of surgery alive?

Holtzman stands up. The nurse removes the stool on which he sat and with three quick movements undoes the knots of his robe. He takes it off and drops it on the floor. Berkowitz unhooks the patient from the IV, takes off the oxygen mask, and removes the taped needle from her arm. Holtzman throws his gloves in the wastebasket. The nurse and Mr. Smith untie the patient's legs and straighten them on the table. Tom calls to some orderlies outside, "Okay fellows. Get to work." Four of them enter. Two take the patient, two start cleaning up.

"Let's go," Holtzman says to me. "Okay." We stop at the sinks. "Well? When are you really going to watch an abortion?" he asks. Go to hell, I think. Bastard. "Well, it would be easier to watch a prostate operation from right up front," I say. "I bet," and he gives me a very dirty look. "I'll watch this next one." "Actually, you can take all the time you want, shrink," he says, in one of his sudden changes of mood. "It doesn't matter to me." "I'll watch this next one." "Okey-dokey. Let's go." His arms are up, and we walk to OR One. The time is ten thirty-five.

Positioning myself at the lower end of the operating table, I observe for the first time the preparations that have been performed here. There are several layers of plastic-lined, disposable, blue paper sheets spread on the floor, covering the area where the surgeon sits, and extending beyond the instrument table. The instrument table, also, is covered with a sheet, on which the instruments rest, lined up in a predetermined, precise order. Next to them there is a jar filled with a brownish liquid that looks like iodine. The overhead reflector is tilted to illuminate most brightly a midpoint between the patient's spread legs. Directly below, on the floor, stands a large wastebasket lined with a beige plastic garbage bag.

As Holtzman says "Go to sleep," and Berkowitz pushes the plunger, the nurse lifts off the patient's white cover sheet. The woman is unshaven. Her moist private flesh glistens against the surrounding darkness of her hair. The devastating vulnerability of her exposed nakedness is akin only to archaic nightmares.

"We are running late," Holtzman says. "Let's get a move on." He picks up a small forceps from the instrument table, in between whose pincers a cotton ball has been placed. He dips the cotton into the iodine jar and, with a few quick movements, spreads the iodine on the patient's vagina, entering her a few times, to disinfect the canal as well. So much for the temple of love and its preciously valued entrance. Ain't nobody gonna worship here today nohow, gents. I am in a state of helpless rage again.

The nurse picks up a fresh sheet, in the center of which a square has been cut, and spreads it on the patient. The square fits around the vagina and frames it. Whatever the medical reason for this procedure may be, I find it enormously helpful to my morale. No more spread thighs, veined legs, broken-nailed toes, no more person. I see only a white expanse, in a straight line, from knee to knee, barring my vision beyond it. Only white folds falling around a fenestrated center, which now clearly circumscribe a mere technical problem. Holtzman places his left hand over the sheets and with his right hand examines the patient internally. "Yeap," he says. "Fifteen weeks is correct." Turning his head to the nurse behind him, he says "Stool please." She pushes a little round stool close enough to him, to hit the back of his knees. He sits. Without looking, he extends his right arm, and Mr. Smith slaps an instrument into his palm. It is a weighted speculum, which I recognize as he hangs it on the lower rim of the vagina. From the bottom part of the speculum, there unrolls a limp, transparent plastic glove.

It seems to me that I have given up on my customary functioning a long time ago this morning, so I really don't care whether it becomes known that I imagine things. "There is a glove hanging from the instrument in her vagina," I say. It is also possible, of course, that I am performing a service, alerting an unaware Holtzman to slipshod staff error. "Sure," Holtzman answers. "To pick up the big mess." "I see." He extends his arm, and Mr. Smith slaps into his palm a retractor. He places it on the upper rim of the vagina, forcing the vagina to open into a large circle. "Hey, shrink, are you familiar with the instruments?" I shake my head. Since we are both focused in front of us with total concentration, he does not see my signal. "Well, are you or aren't you, speak up," he says in a fit of irritability. "No," I say. "Well, I'll tell you. I told you I'll teach you, and I will."

What the hell does he think anyway, that I am one of his goddamned medical students? But of course I want to know, and by tomorrow I know I will be grateful. "Thanks. Thank you." I don't sound sincere at all. He doesn't seem to notice. "Look," he says, with a new instrument in his hand, "I grasp the cervix with a tenaculum, and remove the retractor." The tenaculum is a sort of clip, which now pinches an upper portion of the cervix and which he leaves dangling there. "Next, I will use the dilators. We use the curved, graduated English dilators to enlarge the entrance to the uterus. They do less damage. Number eight, please." The last sentence is addressed to Mr. Smith, who slaps a number eight dilator into Holtzman's hand. The dilator is a rather long solid metal tube, slightly curved, with a cylinder at one end on which a number is stamped. The number represents in millimeters the width of the dilator at the base. From base to tip the instrument gradually narrows, making the diameter of the tip three millimeters less than the base. The design permits the surgeon to dilate the cervical canal in minimally increasing increments.

Holtzman pushes number eight into the woman's cervix, which instantly begins to bleed. The fingers of the glove start to grow. Holtzman removes the dilator, slams it on the table, and holds his hand out for the next one. "Number ten, please." Mr. Smith provides it, Holtzman places it, the vagina bleeds, the glove swells. The cycle is repeated again and again with great rapidity. At number fourteen, in addition to blood there is a spurt of yellow liquid. "I broke her water," Holtzman says. "How many of these do you use?" I ask. "It depends on the size of the pregnancy and on how rigid the cervix is. With this one I think I need only one more. Maybe two." "That will make seven in all. Is that right?" "Yeah, that's about right. It's about average for fifteen weeks of gestation." He slams down the last dilator and holds his hand out. "Suction tip, please." Mr. Smith puts it in his palm. "It's really too advanced a pregnancy for suction to work at the start, but I do it routinely anyway. There is nothing to lose and it often clears the way for the forceps."

He has placed the suction tip into the vagina and now connects to it the plastic tube that is attached to the machine. "Okay Tom," he says. Tom, who is standing next to the suction machine, turns a knob on it. Holtzman begins to vacuum deep inside the patient. The tubing is transparent, and I see thick blood swirling and flowing toward the glass jar. "Goddamn," Holtzman says, "I am getting nothing." It does not look like "nothing" to me. There is blood everywhere. The floor is splattered, the table drips, pools spread on Holtzman's green gown, tinting it purple. The glove hanging from the speculum has grown into a full sized inverted red hand, which now, through overflowing, itself bleeds into the wastebasket below.

"Tom," Holtzman calls. Tom turns the machine off. Holtzman withdraws the suction tip, places it for storage purposes on top of the sheet covering the patient, and holds out his right hand. "Forceps please." Mr. Smith slaps into his hand what look like oversized ice-cube tongs. Holtzman pushes it into the vagina and tugs. He pulls out something, which he slaps on the instrument table. "There," he says. "A leg. You can always tell fetal size best by the extremities. Fifteen weeks is right in this case." I turn to Mr. Smith. "What did he say?" "He pulled a leg off," Mr. Smith says. "Right here." He points to the instrument table, where there is a perfectly formed, slightly bent leg, about three inches long. It consists of a ripped thigh, a knee, a lower leg, a foot, and five toes. I start to shake very badly, but otherwise I feel nothing. Total shock is passionless.

"I have the rib cage now," Holtzman says, as he slams down another piece of the fetus. "That's one thing you don't want to leave behind because it acts like a ball valve and infects everything." Raising his voice and looking at the nurse, who stands next to Dr. Berkowitz, he says, "The table is a little bit too high. I am struggling." The nurse jumps to crank it lower. "That's better," Holtzman says. "There, I've got the head out now. Also a piece of the placenta."

I look at the instrument table where next to the leg, and next to a mess he calls the rib cage but that I cannot recognize, there lies a head. It is the smallest human head I have ever seen, but it is unmistakably part of a person. My vision and my hearing though disengaged, continue, I note, to function with exceptional clarity. The rest of me seems mercifully gone.

"Okay," Holtzman says. "I think I have chopped it up enough. We'll try the machine again. Tom." Tom turns on the machine, and Holtzman picks up the suction tip. He is lifting it toward the vagina when his elbow accidentally hits the patient's outstretched covered leg. The suction tip wavers for a moment and is about to fall. Holtzman catches it in midair, but the shock of the catch shakes the tip free of the earlier accumulated blood that has not been fully sucked into the jar. The right side of Holtzman's face is completely splattered. "God damn," he screams, as he quickly leans over the patient's leg to wipe his dripping face on her covers. Tom turns the machine off, and the nurse, cotton pad in hand, starts toward Holtzman. "Never mind," he yells. "I can do it myself." A huge wave of giddy hilarity starts up in me. Aha, I think, "Production in Technicolor of The Revenge of The Fetus." The hilarity stops.

"Turn the goddam machine back on," Holtzman says. He replaces the tip in the vagina and vacuums, moving the tube back and forth briskly. "It's coming along okay," he says. "Up to twelve weeks the machine gets everything out, but beyond that the pieces are too big to come through the tubing unless I take it apart with the large ovum forceps. Okay, Tom."

Tom turns the machine off. Holtzman hands his end to Mr. Smith and says "Sharp curette." Mr. Smith has it ready for him. The instrument resembles a bowl scraper, and in fact Holtzman's arm moves in a manner similar to a cook scraping a vertically held bowl. "We use this to make sure no little pieces remain inside. Once over lightly is enough. That's the difference between an experienced and an occasional operator. The amateurs keep doing the same thing over and over again, not confident that they got it all. Me, I do it once, and save the patient trauma. Some of the guys around here scrape the goddamn uterus for an hour." He slams the curette down and says "Suction". Mr. Smith hands the tip back. Tom turns on the machine.

The vacuuming this time lasts no more than a second. "All

finished," Holtzman says. He gets up. The nurse, who has come around to this side again, pulls the stool away and undoes the knots on his robe. Holtzman steps closer to the patient and, standing, reexamines her with his hands. "She'll be fine," he says. He takes off his robe and drops his gloves into the wastebasket. "Are you coming?" he says, turning to me.

I am sitting on the stool that the nurse has pulled out of the way when he stood up. I feel exhausted. "I don't think so. Thank you. No more today." "Okey-dokey. See you around," he says and leaves for OR Two.

I sit, too tired to move, and watch the orderlies remove the patient and mop up. I watch Jeremiah Adam throw the speculum-glove into the plastic-bag-lined wastebasket, set the basket aside, close the bag, and lift it into the center of the blood-splattered sheets on the floor. He folds the sheets, all four sides toward the middle, picks up the package with his right hand, and carries it to a trash can standing just inside the swinging doors. As he walks, his left hand hangs free.

—

# Abraham Holtzman, M.D., Age 57
## *Chief of Gynecological and Obstetrical Services*

*It is hard to say more about Abe Holtzman. He is what my grand-
mother used to call a* grubberying. *Translated, that means a
roughneck, perhaps even a boor. Yet he also has great charm, a good
deal of honesty, and the kind of vitality for which I can forgive
almost anything to anyone.*

"I went through a lot of introspection as to why I even
became a doctor. For many years I thought I became a doctor
because I was afraid maybe to compete with my own father
and my brother, who are very successful in the family business. And yet, I have a great deal of interest in the business,
financially and also by working in it. Sometimes I think I
enjoy business more than I enjoy medicine. I'm one of the few
Jewish boys who went to his father in 1938 and said, 'I've been
admitted to medical school,' and he said, 'So what?' He looked
upon a physician as a man who made a housecall on the fifth
floor walk-up in the East Bronx for two dollars. . . .

"My father and my uncle were small operators. After my
brother got out of the army I remember when he first came to
the family with the idea of borrowing ten million dollars t
buy an office building on Fifth Avenue and Fifty-eighth
Street. They nearly died, but they bought it.

"I practice medicine not to make a living and yet I like to
make money at it. We made a lot of money in abortions. I don't
really know why I did it. I sort of fell into it. I was the director
of the service here, so when the abortion program came in I
looked at it as sort of a challenge. We did set up a very good
program. But then I could see from the point of view of man-
agement that they were less interested in the best program
than in the best-paying program. For the first two or three
months I didn't do any of the abortions. I just did private cases.
I felt a little above it. Then I suddenly realized I had all the
headaches because whenever they ran into trouble I got involved. I took over gradually and worked two days a week and

225

I found that I worked very hard, but I made an awful lot of money. When I finished paying income tax I said now what in the hell did I do it for in the first place? Keeping twenty cents on the dollar. Then it's the old axiom of being a little bigger fish in a much smaller pond. Whereas at the medical school where I also teach, I'm a very small fish in a very big pond. So it's personal satisfaction I wanted. . . .

"Prior to the passing of the abortion law, I don't think there was ever a patient came to my office in the last ten years who wanted an abortion and couldn't get one, if they could afford to pay for it. And a perfectly legal one. For a hundred dollars the patient went to the psychiatrist and he would say, 'You're going to kill yourself if you don't have this abortion?' 'Yes.' 'Okay, goodbye.' Then he dictates a nice long letter she's suicidal. So. Two psychiatrists, two hundred dollars. It was a farce. By the time you were finished it cost you about fifteen hundred dollars.

"So when it started legally in New York, $575 was considered a reasonable fee. The only trouble is the referral agencies got into the act. Like Richard Harris ran this abortion information agency. He was charging the patients $800, $900, and he was paying the hospitals that did the cases $350, because he gave them volume. And he was taking the rest. But Louis Lefkowitz ran out and got an injunction against him and slapped all his money in escrow so he hasn't been able to pay us for two years. He owes us about $150,000. Lefkowitz feels the money should be returned to the patients. They overpaid. They were robbed. It was fraud. His ad used to say in the paper that he advertised, 'No referral fee,' or a '$25 referral fee.' He made $450 for just making a phone call, and running a limousine out to the airport.

"Today all the clinics are in trouble because it multiplied too fast. Basically when you started out there was a big price war. Everybody started cutting the prices to drive somebody else out of business. Then somebody cut the price again. The women, they loved it. The women-libbers. I remember one came in to see me. She said to me, 'You ought to do it for nothing. You owe it to us.' 'I'm not saying that mankind doesn't owe it to you, but why do I, Abe Holtzman, owe it to you?' 'Because it's my right. I'm supposed to get it for nothing!' It's all up here in the head, you know.

"The business has become bastardized. Too many non-professional people have gotten between the patient and the doctor. The axiom among the referral services—I don't care if it's the clergy council, or it's Reverend Mooney, or whichever one it is—quite apparently like everything else, it's not how good can you do the job but how cheap can you do it. And cheap is cheap, it's not too good.

"The good days lasted—almost two years. Then the referral agencies who made this a whoring business said you won't take them for nothing then you don't get anybody. And that's what happened. We lost our referrals from Planned Parenthood and our referrals from Community Council.

"We've been trying to get men to come back in medicine and surgery. For example, we tried to get Jim Ruby back who used to keep a whole floor full with the noses that he fixed. Well, the mothers don't want their sixteen-year-old daughters going to this hospital to have their noses fixed because everybody is going to think they're here for an abortion. While they're getting their nose fixed, they're getting a quick job done below. It's also hard to bring a male patient into this hospital, although a lot of the patients like it when they see the young girls with their asses sticking out walking up and down the halls. But really, they shouldn't be on the same floor with abortion patients. It's not psychologically good. Say, for instance, a man with a stroke. On Sunday he gets moved up to the seventh floor, where they're all laboring with the saline, they're screaming. It ain't good for an old man with a stroke, but that's what happens if you come in on Sunday. . . .

"Basically every gynecologist doesn't like women, otherwise he couldn't work with them. He enjoys the position of mastery over them. The fact that he is the god, king, they do what he tells them, which is what he would always want women to do, because every man wants his women to be subservient to him. The patients are subservient to us, and when they rebel it's very simple: 'Go to somebody else. Don't come back to me, if you're not going to take my advice.' What better relationship can a man have with a woman? Besides if you fuck thirty women a day with your fingers, and in a way you do, this is a form of sexual violation. If you really want to be technical, it does interfere in many respects. . . .

"I don't do any saline. Why? Because it goes against me. I say if a girl can't make up her mind by the time she's four, four and a half months, and that baby is moving inside, she don't deserve to have an abortion. That's my feeling. My feeling is that, that it's a little baby. It's really a baby. I'm not saying that you shouldn't get it, or that I wouldn't recommend it, it's just that I don't want to get involved in it myself. It bothers me. Once the baby is moving I start to think maybe I am killing babies and yet I will do a hysterotomy on an eighteen- or nineteen-weeker. A surgical procedure. It's not the same as making them go into labor. At the beginning I did some salines. I would watch these girls. They're in pain and they're having labor pains and the labor is inefficient and they're making noises and I say, 'What the hell is this for?' I really feel that if a girl can't make up her mind to do it early she really doesn't want it.

"I have nothing to do with salines. No logic to it. It's all emotion. There's no question about it, the abortion is the same. The same result is there. There will be no child born. Whether I abort her at six weeks or somebody else salts her out at twenty weeks. It's just that, I don't want anything to do with it. It's just emotional. Also I don't like the procedure. It is much more dangerous. Ninety percent of the deaths come from the saline. I remember I had one young lady in my office. She was about twenty-eight, twenty-nine weeks pregnant. Nice, upper-middle-class family from out in New Jersey. Her mother said 'How could she do this to me?' I finally lost my cool and said, 'What do you mean? How could you do this to her?' I said, 'Where have you been the last three months? Her belly is out to here. She wears tight jeans. When did you last look at your daughter?' There's only one answer for it. Care!

"Marriage-American-style has lost its validity. Anglo-Saxon Judeo-Christian marriage was primarily for the protection of women and children. Because the women ain't helpless anymore, and children don't need protection anymore because they stink. Nowadays children are an economic liability rather than an economic asset. They must be nurtured, they must be supported, and they no longer provide for you in your old age. You're lucky if they'll talk to you in your old age.

"My wife was a very great asset in my younger days, in my practice. She was a good entertainer. But, overall, her function ceased by the time she became forty. For the last ten years she has done nothing except aggravate me. There's not much talking to her. The problem in our marriage has been that there is nothing that I need her for, there's nothing I want her for. Sex is just a chore, and I think she feels the same way about it that I do, you do it once in a while because it's expected. I am not burnt out. Elsewhere, I am not bragging, I think I'm pretty good. I don't have any fun with her anymore, we don't like the same things. That's why I say marriage, when it loses its identity based around the children, it has no other function. I mean two people can have a good relationship for a long period of time as long as they enjoy being with each other. The marriage contract I think gets in between that.

"My wife is overwhelmingly attractive to other men, just not to me. I don't see what they see in her, but I know it. They call her up, I answer the telephone, they hang up. She's attractive, she's charming, she's witty, she's very good with strangers, to me she's an absolute bore. But so am I to her. She thinks I'm the most boring person in the world. I've talked to you for an hour, right? I can't talk to her for five minutes. Once we separated. I enjoyed it; she was unhappy, very miserable. She cried to me. She said, 'After thirty years you owe me something.' And I do, I do owe her. I owe her companionship. Even a no-good husband is better than no husband, because a woman alone is a threat. It's rough on a woman. It isn't as easy as they think. Like I said, my wife is constantly being propositioned. I admit it, she flirts, so they proposition her. They think she's available, why the hell not? But the minute she ain't married no more, ain't nobody going to call. They're only calling because she's safely married. Then they run."

# Moshe Berkowitz, M.D., Age 51
## *Anesthesiologist*

*Dr. Berkowitz is a short, aging man with furtive myopic eyes behind thick lenses. His hair is gray, his face is ashen, he bites his fingernails. The tips of his fingers are cracked and appear painfully raw. When not in OR greens, he wears an ancient suit of indeterminate color. He likes to talk, but his message, like a fixed alternating current, switches only from resentment to envy and back again.*

*Dr. Berkowitz is a wreck, and by his own report he was never anything else. Being with him is an almost unbearably painful experience. I am flooded by disbelief, pity, disgust, rage, pity. And the haunting, horrifying thought that the man who regards wife, children, profession, and life itself as "a headache" holds in his hands daily the lives of others.*

"God only knows why I chose anesthesiology. I always did some anesthesia, from the time I was in medical school. I never really cared for it too much. I went into general practice originally. There were aspects of general practice I didn't care for either. My practice was interrupted when I went into the service. Korean war. When I came out, I went into anesthesia because you don't have to build a practice like in other specialties. I never really loved it, I still don't. I do it to make a living.

"I was an anesthesiologist with a group dominated by a chief, as most groups are. And, of course, they take off the cream and they give everybody else in the group less. I mean this is a great game that goes on all over. I blame the hospital administration for that. They give everything to the chief: 'Here it's all yours, this plum, divide it up the way you like. You're totally responsible for good anesthesia service, we don't care how we get it, we don't care how you milk it, just give it to us.' So he dominates it. Then anybody that works for him works under his terms, and he's real greedy, a real *chazer*, as they say, and then he keeps an awful lot of it for himself. Then that broke up, and I got affiliated with another hospital.

"When I came here, in 150 hours I made $11,000. I never saw so much money in my whole life, and at that time you didn't have to do so many cases to make that money, so it didn't wear you out.

"Volume built up tremendously. Over a hundred cases a day. You'd have so many people running back and forth between the recovery and the operating rooms, they could barely avoid stepping on each other. There were times it ran to two or three in the morning. We started at eight A.M. They were very good businessmen, but they were cutting corners here and there, they weren't strictly kosher, so to speak.

"We took over from them the idea of using Brevital, and the extent to which they used the Brevital we never did originally. In fact, when Davis first saw this, he heckled and said, 'This is terrible.' He wouldn't dare do it that way. We were much more cautious. We'd use Pentathol and less Brevital. This method is really very depressant to the patient. You noticed that when we get the patient too depressed and he [*sic*] gets a little cyanotic we oxygenate him [*sic*]. We're forced to, you can't stand there looking at a patient that's cyanotic very long. They're going to start losing some brain cells, as you said too.

"After a while they were very adept at doing abortions and they did them very quickly, so the whole time factor was compressed to a very short interval so you could get away with this depressant. At a certain point a lot of the patients are completely anoxic. They are not breathing on their own at all. You've knocked out their respiration completely, and they get cyanotic and you have to push oxygen into them until they begin to recover. If you had a nonhealthy patient, or if you had an older patient, and they had any real cardiac difficulty or respiratory difficulty, you could get into trouble with this kind of anesthesia. But these patients are pregnant and that in itself is a test of their ability to withstand all sorts of trauma. I mean pregnancy seems to be a very stressful condition in the female. You couldn't give any old patients, for instance, a fraction of what you could give these patients. They won't tolerate it, you'd have trouble. If you could take your time and did a case more leisurely, the best method would be to induce them with a smaller amount over a more gradual period of time. Then you don't get them into that badly depressed state. . . .

"Many of the girls and women that are having abortions have the attitude that they're completely free in getting pregnant. It's so simple: 'Oh we'll get pregnant, we'll get aborted, and then we go ahead and we'll do the same thing all over again. So what!' I think that's wrong. I don't think women should have that attitude, that they can engage in completely free sexual congress, get pregnant and get aborted, and that's a simple solution. I think they should have more of a sense of responsibility. They should be more concerned about not getting pregnant. I don't think they should be as promiscuous as they are, because they think they have a solution for everything. The girls are chasing around, sleeping around any way they like, with whoever they like, as often as they like. And one of the deterrents they had before to doing this is being totally removed.

"Not that I think they should be punished by pregnancy out of wedlock, it isn't that. It's just the idea that what they think are simple solutions are not as simple as they think. They can die, they can become sterile, and they can have many other complications. That unfortunately is the biggest evil of abortions. You'd have to educate women and young girls to a more sensible way of life, more sensible behavior, better contraception. I don't think complete sexual freedom is logical and sensible. I think it's destructive. They may not think so when they are engaged in it. They're not intelligent enough to realize it. They'll just develop all sorts of problems later on in life, not knowing why. . . .

"I don't think you'd define my marriage as good. I mean what some people want out of marriage, I don't suppose they would find mine as a good marriage. I came to the conclusion that I've probably made a big mistake getting married altogether. I'm not that type of person. Personality-wise I'm pretty much of a loner. I don't care to be involved too much with people, all the time.

"I think divorce is a very complicated legal affair, financially it can be a disaster. I think there are more headaches in divorce than two people just getting along together and making the best of things, so to speak. I'm not interested in having any mistresses, they just represent a headache to me, no more.

"We only wanted two children. I don't regret it. I'm more likely to regret having had any. I think they're not worth the headache. I had never felt that I enjoyed children that much, that it was worth all the trouble having children, and raising them. Everything is very moderate with me. I'd like to be financially secure, so I wouldn't have to work if I didn't want to."

———

Aside from the doctors, the personnel on this unit are young and black. The supervising nurse and the technicians are all tall fellows with sardonic eyes and street-wise, white-wary smiles.

When I first arrive on the floor they treat me with impenetrable courtesy. "Joe, get out of the lady's way," one calls to the other as I walk down the hallway. Joe takes a stylized ceremonial step to the side. The trouble is there is enough room to pass and everybody knows it. But I recognize the game. I am an experienced intruder, a well-practiced alien. Being a honky is no news to me. With changing years and progressive locations I have been many things: Das Judin, l'Etranger, la Polaca, the Greenhorn. Still, as I pass, my heart misses the same beat as it did decades ago in various echoing school corridors, and my back tenses and crawls with the same sudden defiant grief.

For weeks, I bear in silence their covert irony and formal antagonism. It can't be helped. Those are the rules. Gradually the men thaw. From "lady" I become "Doctor," then "Doc." We eat lunch together and talk. Themes emerge.

It is bad to be black. Possibilities narrow, hurts fester. It is hard to be a man. One has to be gentle and fierce, fair and self-assertive. The point of balance proves elusive. Work is important insofar as it generates money. Otherwise: "I never discuss my work after work. It's not something you carry around with you," says Mr. Smith, capturing the general sentiment. Abortions, well, abortions, it is difficult to be consistent in relation to them. They are lucrative. They are necessary. They make for a bad conscience.

As with all human visions of an overpowering downward spiral, the men construct arbitrary limits below which they say they will not descend, regardless of cost. Those who are endangered need such covenants. The prostitute will service but not respond, the captive will acquiesce but not assent, the apostate will officiate but not worship. *No*, illusory as it may be, is often the crux of salvation.

234

"If it's very large or if its heart is beating it makes you feel a little funny inside. But to work on the saline floor, where it comes out whole and in one piece, when it's able to live, then I wouldn't work there. I'd rather quit."

Maybe, says the Displaced Person in me, maybe. I have known some to sink below their set limits.

# Thomas Smith, R.N., Age 27

## *OR Nursing Supervisor*

*Mr. Smith is the only person in the hospital, other than doctors, who is consistently referred to by title. He regards it a point of honor.*
*Mr. Smith has the face of a poet, the body of a dancer, and the consciousness of a small burgher with pretentions. He thinks of himself as efficient, intellectual, and exemplary. "I am the best scrub nurse they have," he says without arrogance or shyness. "It was hard coming up, but I made it. And I will go further." That is impressive talk. And yet for all his appeal Mr. Smith is inauthentic, and his truths are separate from the struggles of his heart.*
*In time, I get to know intimately his blond white girl friend.*

"My duties is multiple. I basically work with the staff and help them in any way that's necessary. When I came here I made like plenty of money. Over $1,000 every two weeks. They paid me extra to work weekends. If I worked three weekends a month they paid me $25 a week extra every week. . . .

"It hasn't had any effect on me at all. Really. I don't look on an abortion in any strange way. I don't know if it's because I'm a male, but when I leave here I don't feel worried, as if I've done something wrong. It's like any other type of surgery, I just consider it a job. I once did say to myself, 'Gee, suppose I'd one day have a dream and see thousands of fetuses running after me.' I just think it's because we were talking about abortions and how it's in the dark, you know. People still sometimes feel kind of funny about it. They don't want to openly speak about it. . . .

"Our surgeons have a technique, even though I shouldn't really say this, where they don't really scrub between cases. They'll scrub once and they'll do a case and they'll go next door to the next room and put on a new gown and gloves. Without scrubbing in between. The surgery is only three to five minutes long. It could be shorter time than that for a smaller case. A person who is eight weeks in term only needs two minutes worth of surgery from a good doctor. . . .

"I wouldn't work on the saline floor where they do saline inductions because then I would really feel bad. During a D & C the fetal parts come out in pieces, it can't live in that state. If the patient would have a miscarriage at that point the fetus wouldn't live. Some of the saline abortions are done when the patient is as high as seven months, I was told. Sometimes the patients have delivered live fetuses that have lived for a little while, a few hours. I've told the nursing supervisor, before I would work on the saline floor I would quit the hospital. That I really feel bad about. First of all I don't think there is any need for a patient to come to the hospital so far in term. I think it should have been stopped earlier. When it gets too far in term and the fetus is able to live, and it's moving sometimes, I am completely against it. I feel funny sometimes taking out a fetus by D & C even, when you can see the heart beating. Even with D & C's you get these feelings that you're doing something wrong. Especially when you see arms and legs coming out. It comes out in so many pieces. We had nurses that couldn't adjust to this type of work. Many of them quit.

"I think what a lot of blacks need is some kind of inward feeling that black is good.

"When I started in the operating room everyone there was white and you really feel out of place. You feel as if there is no one you can communicate with, because there's always that kind of suspicion. Like you're not really wanted. There are more blacks up here now than whites. So every now and then we say to a white person, 'How does it feel to be a minority?'

"Occasionally we get a patient who will make a funny remark. I've heard a patient from the South tell me, 'I didn't know they had black people working here. This hospital used to be a very elite hospital, high-class, before it was taken over by the abortion owners.' Some patients are reluctant to talk to blacks. I'm prejudiced myself. I won't deny it. . . .

"I think people confuse marriage with the person they marry. Marriage is horrible they say, I wouldn't recommend it. Now when I say marriage is fine, I'm not even mentioning the fact that it might be my wife I'd be married to. I could be married to anybody, but I would like to be married."

——

The striated nature of reality is nowhere on earth more evident than on this OR floor. The pride of purpose, the vanity of achievement, the greed for money, the sense of doom, the smell of blood, the monotony of habit, the terror of death combine to form a microcosm of contingency where each is tested and each is demanded from.

People ply their trades and character. They gather and disperse, they breathe, weep, hate, laugh, quarrel, compete, become unconscious, find hope—all in the pivotal shadow of one decision, made over and over again, that this life, this heartbeat, this unique combination of unpredictable possibilities for good or evil, for glory or for shame, will not be allowed to become.

No one is untouched. No one is untorn. Each, propelled by who he is, builds his own mythical world where this is all right, that is wrong, one thing is just, another a crime. Morality is a fluid notion. Decisions are made in the forgotten histories of people. And there vulnerable innocence clamors for the preservation of growing things. Those who would ignore that are enemies.

And yet, the enemies of these growing things are also often innocent, and they are invariably vulnerable. Which one to choose then, whom to affirm, becomes a crushing burden. The saints, were they to occupy themselves with such mundane matters, might decide with ease, and well. The staff, being ordinary folk, are very uneasy. The patients mourn.

But let me speak more broadly. The impact of the OR floor is not confined to the shocking death of fetuses. There are other revelations nearly as disturbing. Sensibility is blunted through exposure. After weeks of trailing Holtzman from OR One to OR Two and back again, my sense of meaning dulls. I begin to see "cases," "cervical apertures," "fetal tissue." I am arrested by the brilliance of technical solutions. I worry about snags in tempo during operations, but no differently from the way I worry about an unfamiliar noise in the motor of my car.

One time a circulating nurse loses her wedding ring during surgery. She discovers the loss at the end of the operation as the orderly is about to fold the bloodied sheets on the floor. She takes the filled plastic bag from the wastebasket and empties it into the middle of the sheets. Both kneel and with their bare hands rummage frantically in the pile of placental tissue and blood and chopped-up fetal body parts. "It has to be here," she says nearly in tears. "We'll find it," he reassures her. I am all for them. It is frightful to lose one's wedding ring. The event is completely divested of its larger context. Hours later when the scene reasserts itself in my mind, I do not recognize myself. Is inhumanity a habit? Is indifference the result of the attrition of meaning? If so, one must watch the self like an enemy.

Then again, character also persists, and on this unit that is as bewildering as is its reverse. Hospital personnel are not superior beings, and the quality of the care they provide (even within the narrowed context or perhaps precisely because of the narrowed context) varies greatly with who they are as persons. Rosie of the recovery room, for instance, slaps gently, wets towels to suck, and sings to sleeping patients. I have seen others slap hard and delight in the helplessness of their charges. Berkowitz puts the oxygen mask on patients with the utmost reluctance and only at points of sharp distress. Dr. Ling, another anesthesiologist, keeps patients oxygenated throughout the operation. The flesh under the fingernails of those women remains pink, and they are not wracked by howling hiccups. Holtzman makes quick incisive decisions, some other doctors fumble and are at a loss.

Once the entire floor buzzes with alarm because the OR doors do not swing open for forty-five minutes, during which an attending aborts a single case. The first nurse to come through the doors is asked, "Did he perforate?" She shakes her head: "I don't think so. He just tarried. He just didn't seem to know what to do."

Renown is no guarantee of skill. Skill is no safeguard against cruelty. Patients are utterly vulnerable to the mental health of their helpers. The helpers should, therefore, be watched like potential enemies.

Whatever they say on this floor, it is not true at all that a fetus extracted through dilation and curettage, with its heart still beating, is in any way different from another fetus expelled in pain two floors below.

Nor is it tenable that abortions are justified in the wake of failed contraception. That is propaganda. Nor is it true that abortions are objectionable because they encourage female promiscuity. That is prejudice.

To say that of all things in this world the seeds are most worthy of preservation is a sentimental falsehood. The greatest of our men have died unreproduced or with progeny alien to their greatness. To say that the lives of those living are of larger import than the lives of those to come is the hubris of degeneration.

Abortions reside in the realm of individual struggle, personal defeat, private hell. The enemy is embedded in being human.

# Epilogue

Abortions have become legal in the Midwest, draining off a large source of business. D & C clinics have opened up all over the city, and each take a chunk of the pie. Abortions are more accepted and more advertised. Fewer women wait to become salines.

The hospital, therefore, gradually falls apart. Referrals taper off, work becomes scarce, morale declines. Three of six patient floors stand empty, the ground-floor waiting room develops an echo, it becomes possible to make an outside phone call without waiting for a line.

Fear, a commodity that until now was monopolized by patients, spreads to the staff. Rumors, like worms, riddle the social structure. One day it is said the hospital will close, another day that a major campaign has been mounted to recruit more work.

The normal tones of urbane speech cease. People shout at one another in irritation or else whisper secrets.

The nurses dread being fired and threaten to quit at the slightest cause. The doctors look glum but hold the fort with the courage of mortgage-desperation. No one anymore bothers to call Rachel "Ms."

The situation is attributed to political shifts, to geographic changes, and altered economics.

All of that is fact, and all of it is mere reality. The truth, I think, is that the hospital falls apart under the weight of its purpose. It disintegrates through a cumulative sense of horror.

Death is no easy companion. Not even in the veiled and necessary shape abortions lend it. Under pressure, the conspiracy of its denial cracks. In an astonishing turnabout I am sought out by the staff to be told by each what a hell of a business this has been. I am sought out to be told that one has to make a living but otherwise—otherwise, who *would* such burdens bear?

As the likelihood of collapse increases, the tyranny of profit ends. The hospital is pervaded by a sense of dread and rage, directed at abortions and not at the loss of work.

Even Rachel, strident, intrusive, opinionated upholder of the Rights of Women, loses her balloon assurance.

"I have never been pregnant," she confides in me with suppressed infinite sorrow. "I don't know why. I guess I am not that fertile." Her words lacerate my heart and highlight the irreconcilable paradox of this place, where what is done must be done, and yet what is done surely injures a higher order.

Altogether, Rachel is a lesson in humility, an exercise in decline. A parable in the ways of the world where the mighty fall and the downtrodden remain that way.

At the height of her powers I watch a pitiless Rachel command the lives of others, and the lives of their issue. She decides, she demands, she orders, countermands, reproves, sanctions, smiles, makes rules, judges, puts her thumb up or down at whim, making someone else's world turn this way or that. None of which she knows. She thinks she is doing her job without prejudice. Everybody hates her. When she gets fired she undergoes a major alteration. Her certainties pale, her convictions falter. In fact, she becomes a much nicer person. Yet spending time with her is now very painful because her new-found mellowness is of defeat and not of choice. She bends by force, not vision.

I find it unbearable when (officially dismissed from her job that afternoon), she says at our last talk, leaning toward me across the dinner table, her voice lowered to a whisper: "I used to not get along with people until a few years ago." Oh dear Rachel. Oh dear Lord.

With each passing day, as closing becomes more certain, the

243

tangential realms of patients and staff gradually merge. Those endangered fear the privacy of status. They seek the comfort of diminished distance from person to person. "We are all, after all, in the same boat." "I only work here." "Some of my best friends have had abortions." "Can I help you?" "There but for the grace of God. . . ." and so on and on as impending loneliness dictates.

There are no more cliques, subgroups, factions, racial ties, religious affiliations, or clusters by degrees of training. This is now a world of all for all and therefore, catch as catch can. Such is the demise of systems and structures built on gain. But then again, such is the demise of systems and structures built on love as well. Or so it seems, as one observes the patients.

Next to the why of abortions, the most pressing question in my mind is, why do people speak to me? What prompts them to open their innards to a stranger? What need does my probing fulfill, what deprivation do I meet? Are we all, in fact, so inattentive and so unheard that any willing listener will fit the bill of our isolation? Is it true, then, that love is no assurance of being recognized? Is it true, then, that all of us alone, our mouths filled with pebbles, would speak to the wind?

We carry the ghost of our deaths, partial and final, in our hearts and eyes and on our shoulders. The terror of abortions is not abortion itself. It is our consciousness of death that makes any death, however imposed, an occasion of great importance whereby we measure the worth of the sum of our previous years. Each of us numbered, on such a small planet whirling in unfathomable space, subject to undiscovered rules —how can any of us decide with ease on matters of dying? And yet we do. Everyday. In all realms. Aided by make-believe, apathy, and alienation.

Still, we know that no human life on earth is superfluous except by pretense. Each life hints at incomparable textures of experience in private worlds. And each anonymous self, however paltry, is the imprisoned keeper of a besieged kingdom.

As opaque fetal eyes stare at the beholder with the immovable fixity of death, this beholder, full of sorrow, shifts her sights. Ultimately it is not these fetuses I mourn. I mourn their mothers, and not always with good reason. The issue is not one of sentiment, but that of the future, in fact and in the mind. Because, for the race, survival is still a matter of children. Hope is still a matter of children. Meaning is still a matter of children.

At the root of human responsibility lies the knowledge that the world must be handed over to a next generation. To the extent that this truth is denied we fall into the torpor of indifference toward all things, including the self. The affirmation of generativity is the essence of a world without end. It is the pulsebeat of secular conscience. It is the core of our morality. Without it, the future is lost. The present is endangered. The past has no meaning. If the world is to have no heirs, preserving its values becomes absurd.

I am not speaking here of laws, regulations, strictures, orders, coercive governmental measures, or political expediency. I am not speaking of bigoted vision, despotic religion, prejudice, or the right of anyone to order anyone to have a child.

I speak here of different matters. Of the tragedy of our age that renders us unable or unwilling to acknowledge tragedy. I speak of our propensity to deny that we hurt, at the awful cost of turning to stone. I speak here of the fact that abortion is an abomination unless it is experienced as a human event of great sorrow and terrible necessity.

Abortion is not a legal issue or a social convenience. It is a decision of dreadful daring, through which personal worlds are validated. It is a frontier of individual rights to private destinies, be that redemption or inconsolable remorse.

No one undergoes this ordeal for the sake of societal gain. No one is here to reduce population growth. A given fetus lives or dies as the mother's needs dictate. And so it should be. But not without awareness. Not without a lingering attitude of restitution that would make of the mother's spared life something better. Lend it a nobler course, a higher fate, a commitment to the enhancement of the quality of life.

That is the heart of this struggle. The quality of life pitted against life. Whichever we choose, we lose. And that, too, is part of being human. That too is the dilemma of abortions.

At other levels, concerns reduce themselves to horse-trading. Give a little, take a little, most of us make do. Everything is livable if one so chooses. The coin of exchange is comfort with one's self. Each person has a private measure as to how much comfort is enough. Trouble starts when one tampers with that measure. The staff here comes very close to trouble in that regard.

Toward the last days of the hospital's existence several of us sit in the cafeteria around a luncheon table, eating overdone, tasteless stew. "What do you think this is made of?" someone asks. "Venison," I say. "Pigeon," says Betsy. "Don't be silly," says one of the counselors. "There is a hell of a lot cheaper meat to be found around here." All of us laugh, guffaw, splutter, and slap each other on the arms. It is the funniest thing we have heard in years. Berta nearly chokes on her mouthful from uncontrollable mirth.

"I think I'll throw up," Edie says, and she looks as if she meant it. "Get a hold of yourselves, ladies," Rachel says. "This is unseemly." She is right, of course, but all of us laugh again.

"I think it's a Greek dish," says Teresa, laughing so hard that tears begin to roll down her face and we can barely understand her. "It's fetustu." There is no containing any of us now. "There is mince meat pie for dessert," someone shouts. "And that isn't tomato juice you're drinking," adds somebody else. Most of us are doubled over. The air fills with our shrieks, and gasps, and gurgles. My sides begin to ache.

Our laughter is like the giggling of children at times of mandatory silence. As when lights go out the first night in camp and fear and loneliness crouch in every darkened corner.

The number of patients continues to decline. The composition of their ranks remains constant. Themes of individual entrapments repeat themselves with sobering regularity.

I speak to a man, father of a saline patient aged fifteen. He is despairing of her fate, he is infuriated by her transgression. "Have you ever had an extramarital affair?" I ask. "Yes," he replies. "Yes. But only in the afternoons."

I speak to a small, blond, freckled girl, twelve years old, sister of a thirteen-year-old patient. She is the embodiment of disapproval. She is crushed with pain and envy. "Have you ever been in love?" I ask. "Only with stars." "How do you mean?" "Robert Redford."

I ask a weeping mother, flushed with shame, wringing her hands in the waiting room: "Were you a virgin when you married?" "I was pregnant." "Have you told your daughter?" "I'd rather die."

I ask the middle-aged driver of a cab I hail in front of the hospital, "Do you know about this place?" "Yep." "What do you think of it?" "Whores. A bunch of whores."

Ultimately this hospital is simply another place where the grief of consciousness unfolds and the drama of our limitations is made visible.

Abortions, secondary to nothing else here, are yet secondary to the struggle of becoming and remaining a unique self.

At the same time, the one claim to immortality all of us share is that of genus. To be prototypical is to survive forever as Symbol. Our age overlooks this paradox and thereby causes endless harm to life.

To be one of a class, typical of a group, representative of a series, resembled and resembling, is to be charged with the preservation of the species. Individualized we are dispensable, frail, born to trouble.

In either case, we are also sovereign rulers of invisible galaxies of grandeur and pettiness, sin, retribution, penance, greed, envy, kindness, valor, treachery, compassion, courage, fraternity, and more. In either case, we are, in fact, mortal and terminally compromised from the start.

Abortions are an instance of our exposure. They are heartrending, ambivalent events of absolute necessity.